The Chart Institute of

CIM Companion:
effective management for marketing

CIM Publishing

CIM Publishing

The Chartered Institute of Marketing
Moor Hall
Cookham
Berkshire
SL6 9QH

www.cim.co.uk

First published 2002
© CIM Publishing 2002

All rights reserved. No part of this publication may be reproduced in any material form (including photocopying or storing in any medium by electronic means and whether or not transiently or inadvertently to some other use of this publication) without the prior written permission of the copyright holder, except in provisions of the Copyright, Designs and Patents Act 1988 or under the terms of a licence issued by the Copyright Licensing Agency Ltd., 90 Tottenham Court Road, London, England, W1P 9HE.

This book may not be lent, resold, hired out or otherwise disposed of in any form of binding or cover other than that in which it is published.

Series Editors: John Ling and Mark Stuart.

Applications for the copyright holder's written permission to reproduce any part of this publication should be addressed to the Editors at the publisher's address.

It is the publisher's policy to use paper manufactured from sustainable forests.

British Library Cataloguing in Publication Data
A CIP catalogue record for this book can be obtained from the British Library.

ISBN 0 902130 91 9

Printed and bound by The Cromwell Press, Trowbridge, Wiltshire.
Cover design by Marie-Claire Bonhommet.

contents

		page
Study guide		1
Session 1	Changing nature of business	12
Session 2	Management today	32
Session 3	The effective marketing manager	46
Session 4	Personal effectiveness skills	70
Session 5	Interpersonal communication	93
Session 6	HRM for marketing	124
Session 7	Effective teams	148
Session 8	Managing motivation	175
Session 9	Managing employee performance	195
Session 10	Training and development	213
Session 11	Managing client relationships and customer care	237
Session 12	Managing change	258
Session 13	Managing knowledge	279
Session 14	Managing in a global context	294
Session 15	Managing across borders	310
Glossary		324
Appendix 1	Feedback to Case Studies	335
Appendix 2	Syllabus	351
Appendix 3	Examination paper	355
Appendix 4	Specimen answers	361
Appendix 5	Assessment guidance	369
Index		374

Study guide

This companion is written to complement the recommended core texts:

Boddy, (2002), *Management: An Introduction*, 2nd Edition, Prentice-Hall.

Torrington & Hall, (2002), *Human Resource Management*, 5th Edition, Prentice-Hall.

Whetton, Cameron & Woods, (2000), *Developing Management Skills for Europe*, 2nd Edition, Prentice-Hall.

It aims to offer you support as either an individual or group learner as you move along the road to becoming a competent and proficient marketer. This is a process of learning that has two important elements:

Understanding marketing concepts and their application

The text in the following Sessions has been deliberately written to highlight the concepts that you will need to grasp as you start to understand marketing management fundamentals, what effective management can achieve, and how it is implemented. The overall aim of this Companion is to provoke thought and stimulate application rather than provide a summarised management text.

The material is described briefly and concisely, to enable you to cover a range of key material at this second stage level. It does not attempt to be fully comprehensive, and you should read widely from other sources, including:

- The recommended course texts (readings are specified for each of the Sessions in this book and shown in Table 2).
- The marketing press and national newspapers, to develop your understanding of the concepts introduced here.

More comprehensive relevant management textbooks are detailed on the module reading list, and provide a wider context for the concepts explained in this Companion, and provide more case studies and examples to illustrate management in practice.

Developing the skills to implement management activity

Equally important in the journey towards management excellence is the acquisition, development and refining of a range of skills that are required on a daily basis by marketers across all industries and sectors. These transferable skills hold the key to the effective implementation of the management techniques explored in this Companion.

Through studying the Case Studies and by undertaking the practical activities and projects in this book, marketers should be able to further develop their skills in:

- Using ICT and the Internet.
- Using financial information and metrics.
- Presenting information.
- Working with others.
- Improving and developing own learning.
- Problem solving.
- Motivating and managing self, individuals and teams.
- Managing change.
- Planning training and development activities.
- Managing across borders.

Using the Companion

This Companion has been developed to complement other sources of study materials, such as your course notes and recommended texts. Table 2 indicates which chapters of the core texts provide background knowledge for each of the Sessions, whilst Table 3 gives references for some models that you may find useful.

Each Session contains a number of practical activities spread throughout the text and three projects at the end. Feedback on the activities is given at the end of each Session to help you evaluate your answers. In some cases this may be highly specific, but in others it guides you towards the correct line of thinking. There is no feedback given for the projects, as these tend to be longer-term activities designed to help you develop your own learning within your own specific area of work.

All of the Sessions include a Case Study, which will help illustrate the practical aspects of management for marketing. Some are applied to a marketing situation, but others are not so that you can concentrate on the issues before applying them to your own workplace. Feedback for these is provided in Appendix 1. Again, these are designed to help you check your thinking rather than provide full specimen answers.

Appendix 2 provides a copy of the syllabus for this subject. The Companion in the main follows this structure, except that some management activities (such as negotiations and handling discipline and grievance) are covered at an earlier stage when marketing skills are explored.

Appendices 3 and 4 carry a sample exam paper and outlines for answers respectively. When you have completed the exam paper check your answers against the outlines given, which indicate what the examiner is looking for. Guidelines for the assessment of Effective Management for Marketing are given in Appendix 5.

The approach taken by this Companion is one that is designed to get you thinking about how people should be managed in an organisation, a marketing function, a marketing team and as individuals, in order that they are able to "give of their best". You will already be aware that there is no "best way", so the text helps you explore the issues by posing questions and provoking thought. At times this may appear unstructured, but suspend judgement on this until you have worked through the Session. In addition, this Companion assumes that students have some knowledge of management today via the role they carry out in their organisation or through being managed in their role.

There are many practical examples provided in the core texts, but for up-to-the-minute examples students are invited to review what is happening within their own organisations, others that they know well, and media reports of business news.

Table 1 – Web sites

Please note – these web addresses were active at the time of going to print. The owners of the web sites may move specific pages, so you may need to visit the home page of the site, and search for specific information via an alternative route.

CIM	
www.cim.co.uk	The Chartered Institute of Marketing.
www.connectedinmarketing.com	Everything you need to know about e-marketing.
www.cimvirtualinstitute.com	Key learning tool for CIM students.
Marketing	
www.new-marketing.org	Research updates into new marketing issues, customer segmentation and repercussions for marketing practitioners.
www.wnim.com	What's New in Marketing.
www.dma.org.uk	Direct Marketing Association.
www.theidm.co.uk	Institute of Direct Marketing.
www.prsource.co.uk	PR and marketing information sources.
www.ipr.org.uk	Institute of Public Relations.
www.mrs.org.uk	The Market Research Society.
www.keynote.co.uk	Market research reports.
www.verdict.co.uk	Retail research reports.
www.datamonitor.com	Market analysis providing global data collection and in-depth analysis across any industry.
www.store.eiu.com	Economist Intelligence Unit, providing country-specific global business analysis.
www.mintel.com	Consumer market research.
www.royalmail.co.uk	General marketing advice and information.
www.ft.com	Financial Times online newspaper and archives.
www.afxpress.com	Business news plus industry trends.
www.caci.co.uk	ACORN classification of residential neighbourhoods.

www.isi.gov.uk	Information Society site with details of government projects, pending legislation etc.
www.worldmarketing.org	World Marketing Association.
www.statistics.gov.uk	Office for National Statistics (UK).
www.homeoffice.gov.uk	Research development statistics.
www.business.com	Business search engine.
www.mad.co.uk	Marketing Week online.
Management	
www.bbc.co.uk/edu	News online, Learning Zone, and much more.
www.timesonline.co.uk	The Times newspaper online.
www.open.gov.uk	Gateway to a wide range of UK Government information.
www.durlacher.com	Latest research on business use of the Internet.
www.cyberatlas.com	Regular updates on the latest Internet developments from a business perspective.
www.whatis.com	Directory of Internet terms.
www.ecommercetimes.com	Daily news on the latest ebusiness developments.
www.nikkeibp.asiabiztech.com	AsiaBizTech is a source of business and technology information focused upon Japan and the rest of Asia.
www.ecasa.org.za	The Electronic Commerce Association of South Africa promotes the use of electronic commerce to improve commercial, industrial and government business efficiency.
www.worldmarketing.org	World Marketing Association promotes best practice and exchanges of information among marketing associations from around the world.
www.asiasource.org	Provides information on events across Asia.
www.ec-europe.org	Electronic Commerce Europe co-ordinates and assists the development of electronic commerce in Europe.
www.ansi.org	American National Standards Institute – represents US business interests with respect to the Internet.
www.ama.org	American Marketing Association.

www.kpmg.co.uk www.eyuk.com www.anderson.com www.pwcglobal.com	Major consultancy company web sites with research reports.
www.emerald-library.com	Full text journal articles on a range of business topics – practical and theoretical.
www.anbar.co.uk	General management topics.
www.belbin.com	Team roles and team working.

Table 2 – Background reading

The following references are suggested background readings for each Session. It is suggested that you undertake this reading before studying the relevant Companion Session.

Session	Reading from Core Texts:
	Boddy, (2002), **Management: An Introduction**, 2nd Edition, Prentice-Hall. Torrington & Hall, (2002), **Human Resource Management**, 5th Edition, Prentice-Hall. Whetton, Cameron & Woods, (2000), **Developing Management Skills for Europe**, 2nd Edition, Prentice-Hall.
Session 1	**Management: An Introduction** Chapter 1: Management and Organisations. Chapter 8: Organisation Structure and Culture. **Human Resource Management** Chapter 6: Organisational Design.
Session 2	**Management: An Introduction** Chapter 1: Interpreting the Management Role. Chapter 2: Models of Management.
Session 3	**Management: An Introduction** Chapter 7: Managing Marketing. Chapter 12: Power, Influence and Management Style. **Developing Management Skills for Europe** Chapter 1: Developing Self-awareness.
Session 4	**Developing Management Skills for Europe** Chapter 3: Effective problem Solving. Chapter 7: Effective Empowerment and Delegation. Supplement A: Conducting Meetings.
Session 5	**Management: An Introduction** Chapter 14: Communication. **Human Resource Management** Chapter 7: Organisational Communication and Systems. Chapter 32: Grievance and Discipline.

Session	Reading from Core Texts:
	Boddy, (2002), ***Management: An Introduction***, 2nd Edition, Prentice-Hall.
	Torrington & Hall, (2002), ***Human Resource Management***, 5th Edition, Prentice-Hall.
	Whetton, Cameron & Woods, (2000), ***Developing Management Skills for Europe***, 2nd Edition, Prentice-Hall.
	Chapter 33: Interactive Skill – Grievance and disciplinary interviewing. Chapter 38: Interactive Skill – Negotiation. (You may also wish to look at Chapters 15 and 23 on selection and appraisal interviewing respectively.) **Developing Management Skills for Europe** Chapter 4: Constructive Communication. Chapter 6: Constructive Conflict Management. Supplement C: Interviewing.
Session 6	**Management: An Introduction** Chapter 9: Human Resource Management. **Human Resource Management** Chapter 5: Planning – Jobs and People. Chapter 9: Strategic Aspects of Resourcing. Chapter 11: Recruitment. Chapter 12: Selection Methods and Decisions.
Session 7	**Management: An Introduction** Chapter 8: How Teams Develop. **Human Resource Management** Chapter 19: Team performance. **Developing Management Skills for Europe** Chapter 8: Teams, Leaders and Managers.
Session 8	**Management: An Introduction** Chapter 13: Motivation. **Developing Management Skills for Europe** Chapter 5: Effective Motivation.
Session 9	**Human Resource Management** Chapter 16: Strategic Aspects of Performance. Chapter 18: Managing Individual Performance.

Session	Reading from Core Texts:
	Boddy, (2002), ***Management: An Introduction***, 2nd Edition, Prentice-Hall. Torrington & Hall, (2002), ***Human Resource Management***, 5th Edition, Prentice-Hall. Whetton, Cameron & Woods, (2000), ***Developing Management Skills for Europe***, 2nd Edition, Prentice-Hall.
Session 10	**Human Resource Management** Chapter 24: Strategic Aspects of Development. Chapter 27: Career Development. Chapter 28: Interactive Skill – Teaching.
Session 11	No additional specific reading.
Session 12	**Management: An Introduction** Chapter 11: Managing Change.
Session 13	**Management: An Introduction** Chapter 10: The Developing Organisation.
Session 14	**Management: An Introduction** Chapter 4: The International Context of Management.
Session 15	No additional specific reading.

Table 3 – Marketing models

The text in the Companion Sessions refers to appropriate management and business models and concepts, but do not reproduce these as they can be seen in the core textbooks. The references for these are supplied in the following table.

Session	Marketing model	Reference:
Session 1	■ Tall and flat structures. ■ Organisation structures.	■ Management: An Introduction p239. ■ Human Resource Management p82.
Session 2	■ Factors affecting organisation outputs. ■ Competing values framework. ■ Systems model.	■ Management: An Introduction p40. ■ Management: An Introduction p43. ■ Management: An Introduction p58.
Session 3	■ Managerial grid. ■ Alternative organisational orientations. ■ Benefits of marketing orientation. ■ Structure of a consumer-centred organisation. ■ Marketing management process. ■ Stakeholder mapping.	■ Management: An Introduction p368. ■ Management: An Introduction p198. ■ Management: An Introduction p201. ■ Management: An Introduction p205. ■ Management: An Introduction p204. ■ Management: An Introduction p93.
Session 4	■ Time management matrix. ■ Time management pitfalls. ■ Prioritising. ■ Rational problem solving constraints. ■ Rational and creative problem solving. ■ Delegation. ■ Controlling meetings.	■ Developing Management Skills p108. ■ Developing Management Skills p112. ■ Developing Management Skills p114. ■ Developing Management Skills p176. ■ Developing Management Skills p209. ■ Developing Management Skills p429. ■ Developing Management Skills p537/8.
Session 5	■ Communications model. ■ Communication process. ■ Barriers to effective communication. ■ Grievance procedure. ■ Disciplinary procedure. ■ Interviewing. ■ Negotiation process. ■ Constructive communication. ■ Supportive listening. ■ Interviewing.	■ Management: An Introduction p427. ■ Human Resource Management p99·. ■ Human Resource Management p105. ■ Human Resource Management p536. ■ Human Resource Management p538. ■ Human Resource Management p241. ■ Human Resource Management p628. ■ Developing Management Skills p241. ■ Developing Management Skills p252. ■ Developing Management Skills p580/81/82/84/86/8790/91/93.

Study guide

Session	Marketing model	Reference:
Session 6	- HRM planning. - Succession planning. - Recruitment methods. - Person specification.	- Human Resource Management p62. - Human Resource Management p77. - Human Resource Management p172. - Human Resource Management p192/93.
Session 7	- Group development stages. - Team performance curve. - Teamwork relationships. - Self-managed teams. - Action centred leadership. - Team development.	- Management: An Introduction p463. - Management: An Introduction p457. - Human Resource Management p316. - Developing Management Skills p468. - Developing Management Skills p477. - Developing Management Skills p477/83.
Session 8	- Integrative motivation programme. - Motivating jobs. - Model of motivation enhancement.	- Developing Management Skills p284. - Developing Management Skills p303. - Developing Management Skills p310.
Session 9	- Key aspects of performance. - Performance management system. - Improving behaviour. - Performance diagnosis. - Managing conflict.	- Human Resource Management p297/99. - Human Resource Management p309. - Developing Management Skills p299. - Developing Management Skills p321. - Developing Management Skills p342/45.
Session 10	- Employee development. - Learning cycle. - Learning cycle (KOLB).	- Human Resource Management p440. - Human Resource Management p424. - Developing Management Skills p54.
Session 11	No additional models.	
Session 12	- Context of change.	- Management: An Introduction p323.
Session 13	No additional models.	
Session 14	- Relevance of national culture.	- Management: An Introduction p111.
Session 15	No additional models.	

Session 1

Changing nature of business

Introduction
This first Session explores the changing nature of business and the impact this has on organisational culture and marketing practice. It introduces you to the concept of the organisation and how external factors influence internal marketing and management practice. Finally, the concept of the learning organisation is also discussed.

> **LEARNING OUTCOMES**
>
> At the end of this Session you will be able to:
>
> - Describe the changing nature of business and change initiatives such as re-engineering, downsizing and outsourcing.
> - Discuss the forces driving business change.
> - Describe different organisational cultures.
> - Explain how organisational culture impacts on marketing management practice.
> - Discuss the characteristics of a learning organisation.

Characteristics of an organisation

A stranger to an organisation can observe a number of different things about it: its physical environment, what it produces, how its work is organised, the technology and tools its people use to carry out their activities, how they behave, and the identity the organisation creates for itself through corporate literature, brands and logos.

Models of organisations define the different components that make up an organisation, so different organisations can be compared and contrasted. Models can provide a useful way of considering organisations, but need to be linked back to actual observations. You also need to determine what they leave out or simplify, as well as what they include.

Two concepts that can be used to consider the changing nature of organisations are:

- **Structure** – the jobs and relationships between them. Who is responsible for doing what? What authority do they have over resources and decisions?
- **Culture** – a description of "the way we all do things around here".

Organisational structure

Organisations such as public services tend to have more traditional hierarchical structures, with clear lines of authority. However, where the work is less routine, then some organisations use a more team-based structure, where people might be working with several different groups of people at any one time.

Figure 1.1 shows examples of general trends and suggests possible drivers for these. This does not mean that every organisation should be structured along similar lines. Appropriate organisational structure depends on many factors, such as:

- The type of work an organisation is set up to do.
- Whether the company is product, marketing, sales or production oriented.
- The current capabilities and skills of the organisation and its people.
- The particular issues an organisation faces.

Figure 1.1 Trends and their impact on structure

Factor	Trend	Possible drivers
Span of control.	Increased span of control for managers, so they take management responsibility for more people or teams.	■ Empowerment – individuals are given more responsibility and authority. ■ Work is made routine and rule driven e.g. with the introduction of technology, reduced need for human intervention. ■ Introduction of non-traditional structures e.g. project based.
Chain of command.	Reduced number of organisational levels.	■ Empowerment – individuals are given more responsibility and authority.

Factor	Trend	Possible drivers
		■ Introduction of non-traditional structures e.g. self-managing teams. ■ Decentralisation.
Centralisation versus decentralisation.	Varies within and between organisations.	■ Centralise e.g. when increased consistency will enhance organisational effectiveness. ■ Decentralise e.g. when local tailoring is important.
Team and project-based structures.	Increasingly being used to bring together the most appropriate set of knowledge and skills for the task.	■ Pace of change. Project or team-based organisations seen as more flexible and responsive to change in a fast moving environment.
Job specialisation.	Customer-focused organisations achieved by: ■ Service/product-based structure. ■ Matrix structure.	■ Increasingly sophisticated, better informed customers, and fast moving competitors, driving a need to be highly connected with, and responsive to, the marketplace.

Consider the changes that have taken place in your organisation over the past few years and try and identify why they happened. In what way has the customer benefited?

Organisational culture

The culture of an organisation determines how things are done and how people behave, and is often deep-rooted in tradition.

Hall (1995) suggests that the elements of organisational culture can be described as Artefacts, Behaviours and Core values and beliefs (the ABC of culture). Therefore, corporate culture can be identified by:

- Visible symbols; which include logos, corporate literature, corporate facilities, delivery vehicles, uniforms, appearance and superficial behaviour such as greetings (Artefacts).
- Patterns you can observe just by looking and listening; "the way we do and talk about things around here" (Behaviours).
- People's mental models; attitudes, knowledge, skills, values and beliefs, which drive their patterns of behaviour. For example, marketing knowledge will result in people using marketing language to talk about product positioning and customer care issues; a value of excellence may result in people talking about and implementing actions which increase product and service quality. These may or may not be explicit or even understood by the organisation (Core values, beliefs and attitudes).

An organisation's culture is influenced by its customers, its competitors and its people.

Some recent general trends in organisational culture are:

- Organisations moving away from sales and product orientation to become marketing oriented.
- Customer focus and Customer Relationship Marketing (CRM) have increased in importance, and can now be found within most organisations' value set.
- Values of self development, learning and individual responsibility for career management have come to the fore e.g. the learning organisation.
- Employer/employee loyalty and paternalistic care have decreased in importance in many Western companies.

An organisation that has a strong traditional approach to business will present itself in a very different way to one that is entrepreneurial and dynamic. Compare the visual symbols of McDonald's and IBM to identify how their prevailing culture is visualised.

Organisational culture is also briefly discussed later on in this Session.

> **Activity 1.1 Structure and culture**
>
> For your organisation, or one you know well, consider how the structure and culture have changed and developed over the last few years. Find some people in the organisation to talk to about this topic, e.g. someone from the marketing function, someone involved in HR, or frontline staff directly involved with customers.
>
> - How do the changes relate to the material in this section?
> - How has the way the organisation does business changed?
> - How do they relate to changes in the markets in which your organisation operates?
> - In what ways have these changes influenced the way marketing is perceived in the organisation?

Organisational change

Activity 1.1 asks you to consider the changes in an organisation, and what forces have driven those changes. Organisations cannot be considered in isolation. They are both affected by and affect their business environment. For example:

- By developing and marketing a new product, an organisation may open up new customer markets, which in turn will attract new competitors reacting to the opportunity.
- New technological developments may be seized upon by several organisations to improve their product quality and customer care. This sets a new standard in the marketplace, which in turn is then expected as the basic level of service by customers.
- Consumer legislation may force organisations to increase the costs and quality of their delivery, while being unable to increase prices beyond their current levels. Such organisations may react to this by looking for cost savings from suppliers or possibly from job losses.

For any one organisation, different forces will be critical at different times.

Effective Management for Marketing

Figure 1.2 Examples of forces inside and outside an organisational boundary

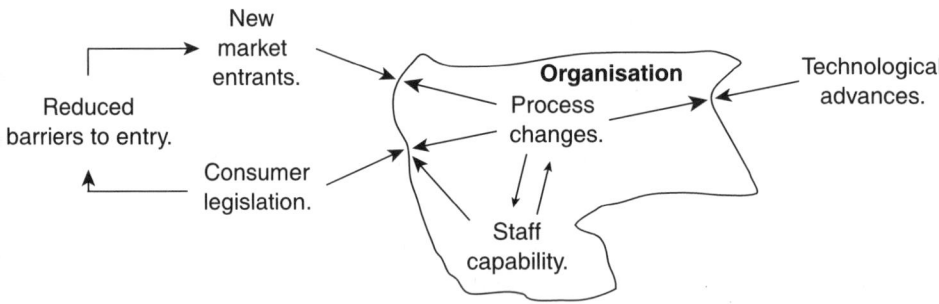

Organisations exist in a web of supplier/customer relationships, as well as national and global environmental forces. In addition, they are affected by internal forces such as their objectives, their culture and structure, their skills and capabilities, their pay and reward structures, and their processes and technology.

External forces

Identifying external forces is often done via an environmental analysis using the SLEPT factors – Social, Legal, Economic, Political, Technical.

Significant external forces for many organisations include:

- Globalisation – where national organisational relationships become less important than the international relationships. For example, this can mean dealing with people from many different cultures. Account must be taken of the needs of different national markets, the mental models of suppliers from different countries, and managing staff of different nationalities. Also methods have to be found for dealing around the clock in different time zones.
- Communications technologies now allow businesses and their staff to be in contact and to do business 24/7.
- The Internet has brought an additional channel for acquiring and servicing customers and suppliers.
- Consumer and employment legislation and attitudes. These differ from country to country.
- Increasing consumer power and pressure groups.

Internal forces

The way people within an organisation think about it (e.g. its mission, objectives, values, what is and isn't done), can be a powerful driver both for and against change.

Other significant internal forces include:

- Organisational structure. For example, the trend towards flatter structures and more devolved responsibility and authority tends to increase the speed of decision making.
- Reward structures. Rewards heavily driven by customer sales will drive change differently from rewards driven by customer service standards.
- Information and communication systems. An organisation with timely customer information will have the opportunity to respond quicker than one where the information is either hard to find, or always a month or two behind what is happening.
- Intellectual capital and capabilities. An organisation that is excellent at producing new products quickly will drive change in response to market conditions.

Activity 1.2 Change is ongoing!

Activity 1.1 asked you to consider organisational change retrospectively.

Considering the future:

1. Carry out an internal and external force analysis of your organisation. Which forces are the most important? Does your answer alter if you consider the short or the long term?

2. Discuss your findings with someone else in your organisation. How does their analysis differ from yours?

3. What would you notice if you were a customer of your organisation? Will their experience improve, remain the same, or otherwise be impacted? What about other **stakeholder** groups e.g. staff, shareholders, suppliers?

Change initiatives

In order to respond to the forces driving change, organisations develop change initiatives such as:

- **Business Process Improvement (BPI)**, sometimes called redesign, which might for instance look at your letter writing process, and identify improvements in either effectiveness or efficiency. For example, typed memos are more effective than handwritten memos, as the receiver can read them more easily. Using slightly poorer quality notepaper makes no difference to effectiveness but makes the process more efficient (as it is cheaper). In order to gain competitive advantage, many organisations attempt to innovate their processes (methodology) to be faster, more responsive to individual customer needs, or perhaps more consistent than their rivals. The business process view concentrates on putting customer requirements at the heart of all processes, so their needs are fundamental to the design of the process. Therefore, the need for speed of response and reliability demands that waste is eliminated between systems, functions, departments and teams. Marketing orientated companies such as McDonald's and Fedex embrace BPI to enable them to provide more customer-focused products and services than their rivals.

- **Business Process Re-engineering (BPR)**, which takes the more radical stance of completely rethinking the organisation. Using the example above, you may decide to use an email or a phone call instead of writing a letter: you are in the communications business not the letter writing business. Examples include cross channel ferry services (such as Brittany Ferries) which operate between England and France. They are no longer simply transporting passengers, they are in the entertainment business providing a variety of leisure facilities for customers. This rethinking has been partly driven by the need to compete with the speed of Eurotunnel services, which provide a fast rail link service between England and France via the Channel Tunnel.

  The introduction of new technology often goes hand in hand with BPI and/or BPR, however it is not necessary (and certainly not sufficient) for process change initiatives.

- **Outsourcing** – some organisations need to concentrate on their core capabilities and skills and not get distracted by running their own IT department or logistics department for example. Outsourcing involves finding a supplier who can run the relevant function more effectively and efficiently than you can, perhaps by exploiting economies of scale or using the latest technology.

  BPR may be a precursor to outsourcing. Organisations have found that it is usually far more effective to improve the workings of an area and to define its measures of success before making any radical decisions about sourcing externally.

> **Activity 1.3 Change drivers**
>
> Go to the site http://www.statistics.gov.uk/. This site contains a lot of information about economic and social data in the UK, relevant to different industries and organisations. Find the Transport Statistics section and then look at papers covering attitudes towards transport.
>
> If you were the organisation charged with improving the UK population's experience of, and attitudes to, congestion, what change drivers can you identify that are particularly important? How might you influence these? What are the shortcomings of this source of information?

What is an appropriate organisation culture?

As previously mentioned, the prevailing culture in an organisation is deep-rooted in tradition and the beginnings of the company. Similar to the culture of a country, the culture of an organisation can be observed in peoples' behaviour, rituals, traditions and "the way things are done".

You may have your own judgements as to what is an appropriate organisation culture, based upon your own background and national culture. However, in terms of performance it depends on what the organisation is setting out to achieve as to what culture is appropriate. Acting innovatively is very useful in an R&D environment, yet potentially disastrous in the nuclear industry!

Charles Handy developed a model of four different types of culture, each particularly suited to different organisations in different stages of development and environmental conditions.

- Power culture is found in small entrepreneurial organisations where power and authority radiate out from a central source.
- Role culture is typified by a highly structured bureaucratic organisation, with rules and procedures that are rigidly adhered to.
- Task culture is where people work in project teams, so they may be working with more than one group of people at any one time.

- Person culture is unusual because the structure exists to service the one person – consultancy firms may have this type of culture.

An appropriate culture is one that fits the environment and facilitates the way the organisation needs to operate. Hence structure, culture and people management must be congruent if organisations are to operate efficiently and effectively. Project teams cannot operate in rigid structures where people do not communicate and share information.

Organisational performance and change

Organisational culture can be difficult to change, as it involves identifying and changing people's behaviours – not just intervening at the observable level. Problems arise where there is an unhelpful interaction between the culture (and hence internal driving forces) and the organisation's environment. If the organisation cannot adapt fast enough then it may go out of business. For example:

- Customers demand a tailored service, and competitors adapt. A culture that honours repeatable procedures, honed over many years, may find this change difficult to take on board and therefore lose custom.

- An organisation that believes it is the best could get complacent, and its staff cease to innovate or pay attention to customer trends. Competitors then sense a weakness, and by the time the organisation realises it is in trouble it is nearly too late.

- The experience customers have of an organisation is at complete variance with how the organisation markets itself (i.e. its public image is completely different to its actions and words). The customers and staff attracted to the organisation's products and services value safety, security and stability, however what they experience is change, risk and unpredictability. Other people who might value the organisation are completely put off by its image.

A "learning organisation" adapts to feedback from its environment and hence its mental models keep in line with external changes. This is discussed more fully in Session 10.

Activity 1.4 Recognising culture

1. Apply the following models of culture to your organisation:

    - Hall (ABC model).
    - Handy (different types of culture).

    How well do they fit with the forces of change you have already considered in Activities 1.1 and 1.2?

2. Apply the same models from the perspective of a customer. It may help to walk through the buying process mentally, or observe customer interactions with your organisation. Now do the same for two competitors. Look at their Internet presence. Any customer letters? Advertising? What insights do you have?

3. Write up your findings as a short note (as if to your Director), making observations and recommendations about potential changes to your organisation.

Impact of business change on marketing management

Throughout this Companion you will be able to identify examples of how the changing nature of business impacts on marketing management. Some of the more obvious are:

- Outsourcing.
- Working in partnership with external agencies to increase specialist skill base.
- Working in teams to increase flexibility and creativity.
- Managing across borders.
- Working in cross-cultural teams.
- Encouraging people to learn from experience.
- Developing cultures that support improvements in customer service.
- Delivering stakeholder value (see Case Study at the end of this Session).

What is a learning organisation?

The learning organisation concept was popularised in Peter Senge's 1990 book *The Fifth Discipline*. The essence of a learning organisation is that it maximises its ability to learn quickly from, and act on, the results it achieves in line with its purpose. In order to do this, Senge believes there are five disciplines essential to embed throughout the organisation.

Note the word "embed". This means that these skills and disciplines are part of the culture ("the way we do things around here"), rather than an add-on to be indulged in when there is time and money.

Figure 1.3 The five disciplines of a learning organisation

Discipline	Brief description
Personal mastery	Ensuring lifelong learning is practised and focused on achieving the results we want: - In ourselves. - In others.
Mental models	Recognising that the way we perceive and hence act in the world is based on a set of internal assumptions or mental models, and then actively seek to explore and change these to improve results: - Refers to individual as well as shared (team, organisational) models.
Shared vision	Sharing a common mental representation of the future and how this future will be realised: - "How" refers to values and principles rather than processes and tasks. - Can operate at different levels i.e. organisational and team.
Team learning	Enabling the whole to be greater than the sum of its parts, by developing effective team learning and thinking skills.

Discipline	Brief description
Systems thinking	Recognising how different parts of an organisation, its customers, and the wider world, act and react with each other: - They produce different results than if they were acting in isolation. - Change needs to take account of the wider system.

Why bother?

The section above discusses some of the changes that organisations and individuals are subject to, and alludes to the increasing pace of change. Industries that have previously remained relatively static for decades (such as banking, telecommunications and retail) have changed and continue to change as never before.

- Merely keeping up with the competition requires continual environmental analysis and increased response times.
- Surviving and thriving requires an organisation to learn faster than its rivals to keep ahead.

Whilst in the past, organisations could get better results merely by continuously refining and improving their tasks and procedures (for example, by doing tasks and procedures with fewer errors and at less cost), this is no longer sufficient as a response to the changing environment. The same goes for individuals. Your ability to identify, learn from, and adapt to change is critical. As marketers you are in the front line as far as changes demanded by customers are concerned. You will have noticed that throughout this and the earlier sections the emphasis has been on the need to focus learning and development on achieving specific results rather than leaving it at a process and task level.

Learning organisations and customer focus

The way in which customers respond to an organisation is a very direct measure of results, reflecting the impact the organisation has on the world. Most organisations will have at least some aspect of their stated purpose and results related to customers. Some of the questions a learning organisation might be asking are:

- What is our shared vision of how we relate to our customers? What will they and we see, hear and feel as they do business with us? How do we know when we have achieved what we want? Where are we at the moment in relation to our vision?

- What mental models are driving us? What model do we have of the customer? Equal partner? Gullible? Loyal? What mental model do we have of the products and services we offer? Of ourselves as an organisation? Of our competitors? How are these assisting and inhibiting us? What happens if they are incorrect?

- What systems are in operation? What are the full consequences to the system of making changes? What are appropriate measures of results? Qualitative? Quantitative?

Learning organisations use information gained from internal and external sources to transform themselves into more competitive and profitable organisations.

Activity 1.5 Mental models and attitudes

Search the Internet to find four sites offering Internet customer services.

1. What can you infer about the mental model these companies may have of their customers and themselves? How do they differ? How are they similar?

2. After completing 1., what mental models are you filtering through as you look at these sites? How might this have affected your conclusions?

Case Study – Delivering stakeholder value and managing change

For decades companies have narrowly defined return on investment as the sole means of delivering shareholder value. As companies struggled through the 1990s, trying to maintain a competitive advantage and stay profitable, there has been a need to change approaches to the way work is done. Increasingly, senior executives have come to realise that there is also a need for a change in attitude.

An article that appeared in *People Management* (1998) highlights this change in attitude of business executives towards creating shareholder value.

'The Centre for Tomorrow's Company is an organisation set up to encourage employers to take a broader view of how to achieve business success. It has welcomed the results of a survey showing that company directors no longer concentrate all their efforts on pleasing shareholders. Nearly three quarters of the "captains of industry" questioned thought a business best serves its shareholders by considering the needs of its employees, customers, suppliers and the wider community.

These findings represent a significant shift in attitude from that of a few years ago, when pleasing shareholders was seen as the only purpose of the business. It is now accepted that to create value for shareholders, the interests of other stakeholders must be taken into account, crucially knowing what customers need and want, and managing employees in a way that meets those needs both efficiently and effectively.

After years of downsizing and reorganising, employers now face problems of skills shortages and meeting the demands of increasingly sophisticated customers. Efficiency drives have not delivered expected rewards, and adding value and being effective is the challenge that now faces companies.'

Source: *Effective Management for Marketing* Examination paper, December, 1999.

Questions

Having read the brief extract from the article that originally appeared in *People Management*, as a Marketing Manager:

1. Use your imagination to suggest ways in which the structure of tomorrow's organisations might change.

2. Use your imagination to suggest ways in which the prevailing culture of tomorrow's organisations might change.

SUMMARY OF KEY POINTS
- Organisations are affected by their internal and external environment.
- Organisations develop change initiatives to respond to these changes.
- The culture of an organisation is made up of visual symbols, behaviours, and values and beliefs that may enhance or hinder change.
- The changing nature of business impacts on marketing management in many ways, and successful organisations are able to adapt appropriately.
- Learning organisations use information gained from internal and external sources to transform themselves into more competitive and profitable organisations.

Improving and developing own learning

The following projects are designed to help you develop your knowledge and skills further, by carrying out some research yourself. Feedback is not provided for this type of learning because there are no "answers" to be found, but you may wish to discuss your findings with colleagues and fellow students.

Project A

Identify change initiatives that are operating within your organisation, or one you know well. What forces drove these changes? How appropriate are these change initiatives?

Project B

Identify the prevailing culture within your organisation, a club you belong to, or the department within which you work. How appropriate is it? How does the structure support the culture? How has it changed over the past few years? How do you expect it to change in the future? If the organisation is not customer focused, what are the consequences of this?

Changing nature of business

> **Project C**
>
> Talk to your Marketing Manager about how change has impacted on the management of people and activities in your organisation (this information will be useful when you study the next two Sessions, which look at management today and the role and function of the marketing manager).
>
> Would you describe your organisation as a learning organisation?

Feedback to activities

Activity 1.1 Structure and culture

Areas you might have considered are:

- Technology.
- Legislation.
- Customer awareness.
- Senior personnel. Changes at board level can have far reaching effects.
- Economy. Upturn or downturn in your organisation's markets.
- Globalisation.
- Structural changes. Have these made any practical differences to the way your organisation operates? (Sometimes informal structures are not particularly affected by changes in formal structures).
- Changes in people's mental models. Has the customer increased in importance? What has contributed to this? Falling sales? Consumer groups? Has there been a reorganisation along product and service lines?

Activity 1.2 Change is ongoing!

You may have used models such as SLEPT or the McKinsey 7S to help structure your answer. As a marketer the SLEPT factors should be familiar to you. The McKinsey 7S framework is a model of an organisation and can be used in a similar way to help you with your analysis. The 7Ss are Strategy, Systems, Structure, Skills, Staff, Style and Shared values. This model can also be used to compare different organisations.

Organisational change can impact in many ways on different stakeholder groups, and this needs to be factored into any plans. For example, an organisation with a monopoly position has very different concerns to one operating in an overcrowded marketplace.

Activity 1.3 Change drivers

As with many drivers of change, the issues are complex. Some solutions you may have considered are marketing related (e.g. how to change perceptions, how to market unpalatable solutions).

One of the issues with this information is that it is based on what people say they will think and do in certain circumstances, not what they will actually think and do. This is a common problem with marketing research information. Would the people who said that charges for driving through town centres would reduce their driving activity, actually reduce it in practice? Cultural attitudes to car usage are very important in considering how to tackle the issue of congestion. The UK government is no longer just looking at influencing the internal drivers of change, it is also looking at:

- Building more roads.
- Improving the quality of train services via the introduction of private finance and business practice.
- Producing statistics on transport efficiency.
- Influencing public opinion towards a more favourable view of public transport.

Activity 1.4 Recognising culture

You may have considered your organisation to be more or less adapted to its environment. Look at things from the customer's perspective. Many people find this easier to do with a competitor organisation than as a customer of their own, but it is an important skill for marketers to learn.

When writing your recommendations, to what extent did you consider how these could be framed to take account of the existing organisational culture? People tend to be more open to change when it is suggested in a way that positively supports their values. Did you find out what form notes to your Director usually take, or what type of note is most successful? This is also a cultural pattern.

Activity 1.5 Mental models and attitudes

1. You may have come up with a number of ideas based on the design of the site and how easy it is for customers to access information and services. For example:

- Jargon statements about what browser to use and what screen resolution to use. Mental model? The customer is IT literate (or the customer will put up with anything!).
- Customer guarantees and customer service contact details given high profile. Mental attitude? Customers are important people.
- Difficult to find what you want on the site. Mental attitude? Customers will put up with us whatever we do.

2. If you know the industry well then you may have missed some messages that others might have identified. For example, the use of industry jargon might have been interpreted as 'Customers are willing to speak to us in our own language' by someone unfamiliar with the industry, yet you may not even have noticed!

Session 2

Management today

Introduction

This Session concentrates on the development of management, and highlights some milestones such as scientific management and human relations. It is a theory Session rather than a practical one, so look for examples in the different organisations that you are familiar with – including your own. The role and function of a manager is also explored, which leads onto the next Session on the activities and responsibilities of the marketing manager.

> **LEARNING OUTCOMES**
>
> At the end of this Session you will be able to:
>
> - Discuss the views of relevant management theorists on the role of management.
> - Explain the role of the manager.
> - Describe the function of the manager.

Role of management

There are many different definitions of management. Our ideas of what it is are influenced by what we read, what people say, and how we perceive managers acting. It is a socially constructed term, so this means that if you were to ask different people for their definitions it would result in many different answers. Managers achieve their results or objectives through others, so they need to be able to manage people, information, resources and activities as appropriate.

As organisations have increased in complexity, so management theorists have looked for ways to help managers perform their roles more effectively and efficiently. In many cases, models are generalised and simplified versions of what actually happens, and are heavily influenced by the experience and attitudes of their developers. To apply a model effectively to a real situation requires an appreciation of its underlying assumptions and limitations with respect to the particular context. Applying Taylor's scientific approach (see overleaf) to a highly unstable environment is probably inappropriate.

The manager as a natural scientist

By the early part of the twentieth century, science had made a great impact on technological developments. In addition, the industrial revolution had led to managers' co-ordinating the work of large numbers of people in the new factories. This meant there was far greater control over which tasks were completed by which person, by when, and how the workers were paid for their labour.

Frederick Taylor, an American engineer, popularised an approach to management based on a logical scientific approach. He and his associates (the Gilbreths) showed that by analysing and changing work procedures, and then matching these to individual skills, productivity improvements could be made.

The ideas of Weber and Fayol also stressed the importance of managers taking a scientific approach to designing, standardising, and allocating tasks to workers. These approaches are linked to the modern business improvement and quality initiatives discussed in the first Session.

Modern "hard" operational research can also be traced back to the idea that management issues can be analysed and quantified using a scientific approach. This branch of operational research is used for issues such as:

- Ensuring customers receive products, whilst minimising the costs (logistics planning, stock control systems).
- Modelling queuing times at checkouts or at call centres, using different staff numbers, skills and shift patterns.
- Modelling the impact of changes to a production line. How do costs, materials and staff requirements change if we introduce the ability for customers to customise certain aspects of our products?

The manager as a social scientist

In parallel with the growth of the natural sciences approach, attention also turned to the human side of management, with psychological and sociological perspectives. Taylor's idea that money was the sole motivator was challenged.

- Follett advocated the idea of an organisation run as a democracy.
- Mayo stressed the role of human relationships. His work led him to believe that people's productivity is affected more by good interpersonal relationships than by money, and that informal work groups are more influential than management in setting working norms.

Organisational psychology is an important influence on modern approaches to management, underpinning many of the approaches discussed throughout this text. More recently, attention has moved to cognitive processes – how people perceive and process information from the outside world. This will be a familiar subject to marketers designing and marketing products and services.

Moving beyond?

As with so many models and approaches, effective managers use a combination of tools to handle different circumstances. For example, most effective change management approaches use hard, quantitatively based analysis and project tools alongside psychological theories of motivation and change. Neglecting one perspective altogether is unwise.

One approach that incorporates the natural sciences perspective and the social sciences perspective is that of systems. This approach:

- Recognises the interactions between an organisation and the outside world, and also those within the organisation.
- Recognises the importance of people and their mental and social processes, as well as procedures and technology.

Several management theorists have taken a systems perspective, such as Peters and Waterman in their literature on excellence in organisations. This approach is also adopted by learning organisations. Modern "soft" operational research uses a systems approach to model organisations, and uses a practitioner working with the organisation to develop a tailored model. This helps identify how organisations can create environments where people are able to give of their best, as well as assessing the more quantifiable aspects of the organisation.

> **Activity 2.1 Management perspectives**
>
> You have been getting complaints from customers that your products are of poor quality, and that your deliveries are erratic. What approaches might you take to analysing the situation from:
>
> - The natural sciences perspective?
> - The social sciences perspective?
> - A systems perspective?

The activity of management

The traditional view of a manager is of someone whose job it is to direct and organise resources in order to meet organisational goals. There are a number of implications in this description.

- The manager makes all the decisions about how work should be done.
- The manager does not do any of the work they direct and organise themselves.
- The manager has several resources at his/her disposal (other than themselves) over which they have complete control e.g. other people, capital resources.

This view dates from the time when the role of a manager was clearly delineated from that of other jobs. This is not the case today.

Instead, if management today is described as any intervention intended to enhance the effectiveness and efficiency of an organisation, then all these are management activities.

- Developing goals and objectives.
- Monitoring how effectively and efficiently goals and objectives are being reached, as a framework from which to make changes.
- Managing yourself and your own activity – making changes to how you do things.
- Making changes to the way other people do things, e.g. by directing, influencing, training, and giving feedback. This could include suppliers, people you report to or who report to you, or even customers.
- Making decisions about how to allocate non-human resources, such as money, equipment, etc.

Management skills and knowledge

The subject of management skills has produced many different theories and practices. While some of the activities articulated above are universal and most people carry them out at some point, different managers in an organisation will have different demands placed on them, and therefore require different levels of skill and knowledge. For example, a manager in a senior position will make decisions on far more complex and taxing situations than someone in their first supervisory role. In addition, some managers require specialised skills in some roles:

- A product manager will require an in-depth knowledge of marketing.
- A project manager requires project planning, work allocation, project risk management and benefits management skills.
- The marketing director of a multinational organisation requires different skills to the marketing director in a small to medium-sized organisation who might have more than one functional responsibility.

> **Activity 2.2 General management qualities and skills**
> Draw up a list of the qualities and skills you think managers might need in today's business environment.

Management in relation to other people

In today's organisations, making a significant management intervention almost always requires the commitment and action of people over whom the manager has no direct authority.

- Renegotiating the conditions of a supplier or customer contract.
- Resolving conflicts between different parts of the organisation.
- Managing change.

Even when a manager does have organisational authority, they will be most effective if they seek to motivate, inspire and develop people, rather than merely direct them.

Managing yourself

If you are unable to inspire, motivate, develop and lead yourself then how can you assist others? Management, like many activities, begins with yourself. The next two Sessions introduce some of the key skills you will need to develop and use to be an effective marketing manager.

Moving times

Session 1 looked at the changes taking place in organisational structure and culture. These have had, and continue to have, far-reaching consequences for today's managers and leaders of teams and organisations. The following briefly explores how management is changing and developing.

Managing ambiguity

The role of a manager used to be far more clearly defined, in terms of:

- What activities you and others were expected to perform.
- Clear authority and responsibility over the resources affecting your job.
- Career paths that allowed you to map out a structured progression up through the organisational structure.
- Firm reporting lines.

Today, in many organisations, most roles require a great deal more flexibility from both the job holder and those they report to. For example:

- In matrix organisations, an individual may have more than one reporting line.
- Project and team-based working can mean being in one team working on a brand launch one day, and in another team developing new products the next.
- Adapting to performing different activities and roles over time, according to the needs of the team, e.g. in self managing teams there may be no "official" leader.
- Career paths are no longer fixed. People take responsibility for their own development, and in today's flatter structures, individuals may need to move sideways to expand their skill base.
- People are often given a great deal of responsibility and autonomy over how they perform their roles.
- Getting things done requires working with and influencing many different people, rather than simply directing them.

Managing change

In addition to adapting to more flexible working practices within an organisation as part of their day-to-day changes, managers also have to adapt to environmental changes. In a stable environment, individuals could hone and perfect their skills without having to respond to and manage major changes. Today's managers are called upon to promote, embrace, and manage change as part of their skill set. For many people this is a highly stressful experience and one that requires careful management.

The growth of ideas about the learning organisation and transformational leadership are helping to address this aspect of organisational life. In addition to strong people skills, effective project management skills are also critical to success for today's managers. These ideas will be explored in the next Session and others.

Managing complexity

Change is not the only factor making the manager's role complex. Systems thinking asserts that only by understanding the interrelationships between the different parts of the organisational system and its environment can managers design and implement effective interventions.

Managing diversity

Globalisation and policies to encourage diversity in employment mean that today's managers are often involved with employees, suppliers and customers who come from many different cultures and backgrounds. They need not only to understand such differences, but also make the most of having such diverse points of view available to them. In addition, mergers, acquisitions and joint ventures can throw into sharp relief the differences between organisational cultures, which are usually far greater than the diversity within an organisation.

Activity 2.3 Statistics

Go to the site http://www.sbs.gov.uk/statistics/ and download the information on Small and Medium Enterprise Statistics for the UK. Note that this contains statistics on the number of businesses, employment and turnover for different sizes of business in the UK. Use a spreadsheet to analyse the information.

Calculate the numbers, employment levels, and turnover for each category of business. Use the sorting function on your spreadsheet to answer the following questions.

Which industry has the greatest number of large businesses? Which has the smallest?

Which industry employs the greatest number of people in small businesses? Which employs the largest number of people? What about large businesses?

What implications do these statistics have in relation to marketing? What are the implications for management?

Effective Management for Marketing

Case Study – Multi-unit managers in the hospitality industry

Multi-unit managers have become key figures in the hospitality industry. The industry is experiencing change with the rapid rise and expansion of the hospitality brand. Multi-unit hospitality businesses such as Forte Posthouse Hotels, Travelodge, Whitbread UK, Marriott Hotels, Pizza Express, Café Rouge and TFI Friday's have won large slices of the market as a result of their emphasis on consistent standards of service delivery. This market is considered a growth area, with a number of hotel and catering firms planning further expansion and entry.

Playing a pivotal role between unit managers of individual pubs, restaurants or hotels, and managers at senior executive level, are the multi-unit managers. Their jobs have changed from managing different brands within a region (they were known as area or regional managers) to managing a group of operations within their brand area. A main cause of stress for these managers is the time spent on the road travelling between sites.

Another problem for these managers is that many of the hospitality units now being developed are fairly big businesses in their own right. A multi-unit manager within Posthouse Hotels for example, may cover only three to six properties, but 150 bedroom hotels are much more complex than most pubs and restaurants. These managers have a crucial influence as the main interface between the strategic planning levels of management and the front line. They have a key role in implementing and maintaining the company's strategies and ensuring the integrity of the brand. The job holder must be an ambassador, a disseminator, and a facilitator, as well as having input into brand and concept development. They must ensure excellent business performance through managing and developing teams and through "tight but loose" control.

The change in structure has resulted in problems for the hospitality industry. A major element of the multi-unit manager's role is the focus on employee motivation, general management skills, and now marketing skills. This has impacted on the recruitment, selection and training of multi-unit managers. Knowledge and experience of managing unit operations is no longer enough. A broader range of skills is required and marketing experience is seen as crucial.

As a result, an extended period of induction and familiarisation is necessary, and most HR directors believe that newcomers to the industry will need up to six months development, including structured training and on the job experience with the brand. The intake of managers from other industries forms a small but growing proportion of the labour pool from which multi-unit managers are selected. But with a need for 34,000 additional people every year (according to forecasts by the Henley Centre), the industry must come up with recruitment and training strategies to support continued growth.

Source: *Effective Management for Marketing* examination paper, June 2000 (Adapted from an article in *People Management*, 1999).

Questions

1. What skills and experiences are required by multi-unit managers?

2. What special attributes would you include and why?

SUMMARY OF KEY POINTS

- Management today is a complex task that requires a combination of a "hard" and a "soft" approach.
- The approaches used today are built on those developed in the past, such as scientific management, the human relations school, and systems thinking.
- Mangers require a wide-ranging set of skills to carry out their management activities, in addition to the technical skills related to their job.
- Effective managers are good organisers of their own work and that of others, skilled in planning and control, monitoring and review.
- Effective managers can manage people through change, deal with complexity, and manage a diverse team.
- Management structures and control systems will differ according to the size of an organisation and the type of work it is carrying out.

Improving and developing own learning

The following projects are designed to help you develop your knowledge and skills further, by carrying out some research yourself. Feedback is not provided for this type of learning because there are no "answers" to be found, though you may wish to discuss your findings with colleagues and fellow students.

Effective Management for Marketing

> **Project A**
>
> Make a list of all the activities you do as a manager, or if you are not in that role, that your line manager undertakes. How has the management of people, information, activities and resources changed within your organisation over the past ten years? What were the driving forces for these changes?

> **Project B**
>
> Review the management activities you identified in Project A, and note down the skills and experiences managers require to carry these out effectively.

> **Project C**
>
> People have a tendency to believe that the way they are familiar with doing things is either the only way or the right way to do it. They also tend to have a high resistance to change. How are managers encouraged to manage people through change in your organisation? Consider different types of change, such as planned and unplanned. What suggestions for improvement can you make?

Feedback to activities

Activity 2.1 Management perspectives

1. In considering the natural sciences perspective you might:

    Observe how your products are produced, and map the processes used and the skills of those operating them. Interventions you might suggest include:

    - Reorganising the work, specifying what procedures staff need to follow.
    - Train the staff doing the work.
    - Provide the staff with new tools.

    Map the delivery process, perhaps using computer-modelling techniques to analyse its effectiveness. Interventions you might suggest include:

    - Changing delivery routes and times, perhaps to avoid black spots and so shorten the total travelling time.

- Changing the number of vans and drivers you have available throughout the day, perhaps by re-allocating vans to different times of day, or changing shift patterns.

2. In considering the social sciences perspective you might:

   Consider how the design of people's jobs and their reward structures support your objectives of a high-quality product. Your suggested interventions might include:

   - Changing job descriptions to increase staff interest and motivation.
   - Creating teams so that people can rotate around different jobs.
   - Changing the way people are rewarded to emphasise product quality and delivery on time.
   - Include the staff actually doing the job in resolving customer issues, and allow them to take responsibility for improving things.

3. In considering the systems perspective, you might facilitate communication between staff and managers to map out together the interactions between the many different factors. For example:

   - What is the interaction between information on product quality and delivery and our behaviour? Are we listening to our customers? What mental models are we using to process the information?
   - How do customer orders affect our production line effectiveness and delivery quality? Do increases in orders result in an increase in our production rate, which causes mistakes and lower quality? Are our delivery schedules under capacity?
   - How is a customer's perception of delivery time and product quality affected by changes in the marketplace? What competitor activity is there? Is our marketing creating expectations we can't meet?
   - How might these factors feed through to the organisation's profitability?

   Interventions depend on the interaction between all the factors. Rather than directly addressing the symptoms you may decide that changing the way you are marketing the product would be an appropriate intervention. Perhaps you are currently attracting customers who would rather pay far more for a higher-quality product.

A word of warning. Systems theory is very attractive because of the way it takes into account the many factors. This same feature also means that it suffers from the "garbage in, garbage out" syndrome. It is possible to create misleading models, particularly when these have been produced with the aid of a computer and have therefore gained a spurious authority. Systems thinking is a very useful tool and can give many insights. However, as with all tools, a little knowledge can be a dangerous thing.

Activity 2.2 General management qualities and skills

Your list may contain some or all of these.

Qualities	Skills
Honest.	Objective setting.
Trustworthy.	Information gathering.
Flexible.	Communication – questioning, listening, giving feedback, report writing, etc.
Unbiased.	
Diplomatic.	
Disciplined.	Observation.
Fair.	Appraisal.
Consistent.	Delegation.
Reliable.	Problem solving.
Imaginative.	Decision making.
Enthusiastic.	Influencing.
Energetic.	Negotiation.
Determined.	Planning.
Confident.	Controlling.
Self-motivated.	Monitoring.
Approachable.	Reviewing.
Respectful.	Time management.
Sociable.	Assertiveness.
Organised.	Analytical.
Cheerful.	Team building.
	Training and development.
	Presentation.
	Briefing.
	Conflict handling.
	Discipline and grievance handling.

Activity 2.3 Statistics

Depending on when you download the information (we have the version for 2000) the calculations required may vary.

The first thing you need to do is to multiply the totals in the first column of each table (number, size and turnover) by the percentages in each of the other columns. You then need to use the sorting function to rank the businesses by different columns.

Note the limitations of the data and hence the approximate nature of the calculations. This means that your answers are subject to error and potential misinterpretation. Understanding the data sources and the methodologies used for analysis and collection is essential before relying on any data for decision making.

From a marketing perspective, there is now a lot of free data on the Internet, even before you start paying for customised reports and data. You may have some particular observations on this data, specific to your own organisation's products and services.

From a management perspective, almost 45% of UK employees (in 2000) are in companies of 250 or more employees. These organisations are having to deal with management activity in complex internal situations, as well as complex supplier and customer markets.

Session 3

The effective marketing manager

Introduction

The marketing manager is involved in a wide range of activities, particularly in small organisations where the person undertaking the role may need to be multi-functional. In larger organisations there will be a greater number of specialist posts, such as the PR manager or events manager, who concentrate on more specific activities, with a team of marketing assistants in support.

This Session explores the role of management in marketing, and also reviews effective leadership styles, as managers today need to have leadership skills. Team leadership is also discussed in Session 7 on team building. Finally, you will learn how to carry out a personal skills audit and put together a meaningful personal development plan.

> **LEARNING OUTCOMES**
>
> At the end of this Session you will be able to:
>
> - Discuss the responsibilities and activities of the marketing manager.
> - Describe different leadership styles.
> - Carry out a personal skills audit.

Key marketing roles and tasks

A summary of some of the main marketing roles and associated tasks is shown below. These may be the responsibility of a marketing team or of just one individual. The marketing function can be organised in a number of ways. In smaller companies several of the tasks may be carried out by just one person or by a small team. The marketing function may also buy-in from external suppliers the skills and expertise needed to meet their marketing needs. In large companies marketers often specialise in just one of the various tasks.

Market analysis

Gather and provide information on the company's current and potential future markets, including analysis of the main forces affecting current and future demand and satisfaction, competitor positioning and supplier issues.

Marketing strategy

Determine the company's approach to its markets. For example its customer segmentation and targeting, market positioning, approach to company strengths and weaknesses, maintaining/building competitive advantage, underlying assumptions and confidence level, implementation of plans/business case, allocation of resources, marketing mix.

Brand management

Design and enhance the brand image to support marketing strategy and plans. Ensures internal and external marketing activity supports the brand.

Product management

For a given product or service, or family of products and services, plan and co-ordinate all supporting activity to ensure maximum value for the company. This will include operational delivery, all promotional activity, and profitability management.

Public Relations (PR)

Provide advice on PR traps and opportunities. For example briefing the CEO prior to a press interview. Ensure all PR activity is monitored and assessed for effectiveness, and that any adverse PR is managed. Archive media coverage, press cuttings etc. on your company and your major competitors. Monitor the consistency of company communications.

Advertising

Plan and manage media advertising campaigns. Brief and manage advertising agencies. Also project and monitor advertising effectiveness, often in conjunction with market research specialists.

Direct marketing

Plan and co-ordinate direct customer contact marketing activity, e.g. direct mail, phone, email. Also co-ordinate any company customer relationship management activity, such as loyalty cards and schemes. Responsible for integrity and legality of customer databases, which in the UK for example means ensuring compliance with the Data Protection Act, 1998.

New product development

Develop and redesign new products and services in line with strategy. Suggest new product and service ideas and research new technological developments.

Market research

Provide customer information to support marketing decisions, for example new product design, promotional activity. Market research is usually commissioned from external suppliers, as it requires specialist statistical and psychological knowledge. A badly designed market research survey is at best worthless and at worst misleading.

You will see from the above that marketing encompasses a wide range of knowledge and skills, from strategic planning through to project management and supplier management. Some organisations combine the roles of marketing and sales management at director level. The role of sales management is not considered here as sales is a separate function to marketing, although their efforts are interrelated.

Activity 3.1 Marketing skills

Using the Internet, collect some information on marketing careers and jobs. What are the main marketing skills being requested? What generic management skills seem to be important?

What is effective marketing management?

Management involves ensuring that the company's resources are co-ordinated in order to produce the desired outcome. Effectiveness and efficiency as a manager includes achieving this in a way that maximises value and minimises cost. While specialist marketing skills and knowledge are necessary, they are insufficient to ensure the effectiveness of the marketing function. Marketers require management skills to be effective.

Figure 3.1 Marketing activities with associated management skills

Marketing activity	Associated management skills
Ensuring that all the members of their team work together to deliver a product launch event, addressing and resolving any problems as they occur.	■ Communication. ■ Project management. ■ Team leadership. ■ Delegation. ■ Time management.
Developing joint action plans with suppliers and/or other functional areas to improve delivery to the customer.	■ Working across organisational boundaries. ■ Negotiation and conflict resolution. ■ Project planning.
Dealing with customer complaints.	■ Listening and questioning. ■ Influencing. ■ Conflict resolution.
Influencing senior management to agree to a new marketing strategy.	■ Influencing. ■ Communication.
Managing the performance of their staff.	■ Performance management. ■ Coaching. ■ Counselling. ■ Discipline and grievance interviews.

Personal barriers to effective marketing management

As you work your way through this course, you will have the opportunity to apply management tools in your working life. As you consider doing this now, you may identify some of your own barriers to being an effective manager. These will be different for each individual, and will change as your experience grows. Some examples of common barriers are listed opposite:

- Believing that you don't have anything more to learn.
- Thinking that because you are the boss:
    - You must be right.
    - You must know everything.
    - People should obey you without question.
- Not being clear about what your marketing team is there to do, and how this fits with the organisation's business goals and objectives.
- Blaming everyone or everything whenever anything goes wrong, instead of learning from the situation.
- Doing everything yourself, because that way you are sure it will be right.
- Attempting to make yourself likeable to everyone, all the time.
- Making hasty assumptions about people and/or situations without checking the facts.

From the above, you will appreciate that although you work in marketing, management is a generic activity and the principles associated with good and bad practice applies equally well to many organisational functions.

Activity 3.2 Barriers to effective management

Talk to managers in your organisation, preferably those in marketing (although this is not essential). Interview them about the challenges they face in managing effectively, and the management skills they use to overcome these challenges. In addition, share with them the "Barriers to effective management", and ask them (tactfully!) if they would like to add to the list.

Using the information from your discussions together with your own experience, identify:

- The personal barriers you need to overcome.
- The personal skills that will enable you to manage effectively.

This is a useful activity to carry out when conducting a skills audit, prior to preparing a personal development plan.

Management and marketing

As outlined previously, major marketing tasks require a variety of management skills in addition to marketing expertise. Examples of responsibilities that the marketing manager may be given include:

Project planning and management

Virtually any marketing task will require some aspect of project planning and management skills. You might be called upon to:

- Manage a market research study, co-ordinating activities between your organisation and that of an outside agency.
- Plan and implement an improved customer contact strategy.

Effective project planning and management also requires you to:

- Know what the project will achieve, what the starting point is, and how the project's success will be measured.
- Plan intermediate steps.
- Allocate and confirm resources (e.g. time, money, people, capital) to each stage and activity in the project.
- Identify, monitor and mitigate risks to the project's success, via such techniques as contingency planning.
- Have in place control and monitoring systems that enable you to measure progress, and measure the planned benefits of the project.
- Solve problems and make decisions based on the status of the project.

As more and more organisations use the project format to carry out their activities, project management is becoming increasingly important. In order to manage projects effectively you need to be able to manage yourself – the next Session reviews the important element of time management.

Working with teams

Marketers are often called upon to work with team members from other parts of the organisation, as well as those outside the organisation, in addition to the people they have immediate contact with on a day-to-day basis. For example:

- Redesigning a product may bring together outside agencies and consultants,

operational staff, IT specialists, sales staff, customer input, and the finance department. Almost certainly they will not have worked together before.
- Sales managers may work with team members who are spread across the globe, and who rarely come together.

Teamworking and leadership skills are of vital importance if marketing initiatives are to be effective. Session 7 covers this area in more detail.

Performance, training and development

Marketing managers are required to ensure that the environment exists for their team to develop, so as to fulfil organisational objectives. Without developing these skills, marketers are risking the effective delivery of all their marketing tasks. Sessions 8, 9 and 10 cover these areas in detail.

While the comments above might suggest that responsibility lies with an individual's manager, we all need to take responsibility for our own careers and development. Part of a manager's responsibility is to enable and support their staff in this activity, and in addition, enable their teams to learn and develop. Session 13 reviews this from an organisational learning and knowledge management perspective.

Self and organisational development

Marketers need to recognise their own development needs and address them. Session 4 looks at this area. In addition, many of the activities ask you to incorporate findings into your personal development plan.

Customer interface management

For a marketing-led organisation, understanding and managing the customer interface is a central activity and concern. Of particular interest is understanding and enhancing the customer's experience of interacting with the organisation, with a view to gaining competitive advantage. Session 11 covers this area.

Responding to forces for change

Sessions 1 and 2 have already discussed this area from the perspective of changing management and organisations. Session 12 discusses the effective management of change. Sessions 14 and 15 extend this discussion to consider the international influences on management. Marketers must not only be able to work across and outside organisational boundaries within their own country, they must also be able to work across international boundaries.

Effective Management for Marketing

> **Activity 3.3 Marketing planning**
>
> As a marketing manager, imagine you have been asked how to prepare an outline marketing plan for a local theatre group or club you know well. Prepare an outline presentation of your main points, describing your approach to putting the plan together (as if presenting it to a meeting of the management committee).
>
> Consider what needs to be done and why, the benefits of planning, how to identify clear goals that are achievable, what activities need to take place in order to achieve the goals, and how to measure the effectiveness of the plan. (If you are not familiar with planning take a quick look at the answer to see how it is structured.)
>
> Present your answer as a series of headings to cover the main points, with bullet points on specific information that you wish to convey under each heading.
>
> What management skills would you require to follow the activity through?

Models of leadership

Different models of leadership are based on different ideas of what a leader is and the impact leaders are expected to have on those around them. For example:

- What is the main role of a leader? Is it to direct? Inspire? Facilitate?
- Are some people natural born leaders? (Trait models.) Can someone learn to change their approach, and if so to what extent? (If not, there is very little point in leadership training programmes.)
- Are there certain behaviours that, if exhibited, will assure excellent leadership? (Behavioural models.)
- Does the situation influence the effectiveness of a leader? To what extent can a leader influence the situation? (Contingency models.)

As you consider the models outlined in the core texts for this module, notice how these factors change from model to model. While these elements are still open to debate in many quarters, some assumptions can be made.

- A leader's role is to enable their followers to achieve the goals of the organisation as effectively and efficiently as possible. They may use direction,

facilitation, power and influence to achieve this goal.
- Different behaviours ("styles") are appropriate to different situations.
- While leaders may have a preferred style, they are able to learn to adopt different styles to adapt to different situations.
- Effective leaders understand and act, taking account of the attitudes, values and beliefs of their followers, as well as reacting to observable tasks and behaviours.

Session 7 examines John Adair's Action Centred Leadership model in relation to teams, which is a useful example of the application of leadership. Other styles include the "transactional" and "transformational" approaches to leadership (James Burns first coined these terms in 1978).

Transactional leadership

Transactional leadership assumes that followers follow because they get something out of it for their pre-existing goals. Leaders using this style may affect culture and individual behaviour through such actions as:

- Providing rewards for employees who exhibit certain behaviours. For example, if you only promote people who demonstrate through their actions a concern for customer service, it will encourage customer-centric behaviour.
- Coaching and mentoring employees to exhibit particular styles and behaviours. For example coaching someone in the use of marketing research techniques.
- Discovering what in particular motivates an individual; what their values, aspirations and goals are, and then seeking to link these to achieving organisational goals.

One of the features of transactional leadership is that it works well in stable situations. It is sometimes labelled "management" rather than "leadership", and can be a highly effective approach. Its basis is the power an individual has to exchange something in return for labour directed towards organisational goals. The more organisational power a leader has, the more influence they will have over the culture, and the more others will adopt their preferred ways of working.

Transformational leadership

Transformational leadership does not just seek to work with people's existing mental models and aspirations – it seeks to change them so that they align with and support the leader's vision and aspirations. Transformational leaders may emerge at any level in the organisation, and influence people regardless of their relative organisational authority. They are expert marketers and salespeople in getting commitment to goals and values, and thus changing the culture.

Organisations value this style of leadership, particularly in times of major organisational and environmental change, when people are required to adopt new vision, values and behaviours quickly. There are some issues that critics level at this style:

- To what extent should it be assumed reasonable for leaders to persuade followers to act against their best interests? There may be undesirable long-term implications, for example stress, breakdown of family life, resentment – a form of buyer's remorse.
- How can such leaders ensure their ideas are appropriately challenged? If their personal power is so great, people may be too uncertain or unwilling to raise legitimate concerns.
- How can an organisation ensure that those people with transformational leadership skills are using them in the best interests of the organisation?

Transformational and transactional leadership represent two ends of a spectrum. Most leaders use a combination of the two to achieve their goals. The most effective leaders are flexible and adaptable individuals who judge which approach is best in each situation and adopt the appropriate style.

Activity 3.4 Influencing customers

The ideas of transformational and transactional leadership can also apply to marketing products and services to customers. Get together with colleagues to discuss the following:

- What strategies does your organisation use with its customers to persuade them to buy your products? Are the strategies predominately transactional or transformational?
- Which products and services have been successfully launched which sought to change people's attitudes and perceptions so that they valued the offering? Which products and services have failed in this?

Personal effectiveness and development

This section helps you identify current strengths and weaknesses and consider what additional knowledge and skills you might need in the future.

As previously mentioned, individuals are increasingly taking greater responsibility for their own development. However, self-assessment can only be done usefully once you have identified where you want to be and when. For example, focus on one year from now.

- I want to succeed in my job and gain a promotion.
- I want to be better at my time management.
- I want to be a good communicator.

Most of the above targets will be judged by someone else rather than you, such as by your boss or your colleagues. If you cannot persuade yourself that you can reach the appropriate standards, it is highly unlikely you will convince anyone else. You need to find out what knowledge, skills and competencies you should be able to demonstrate, and what evidence you can provide for this. For example, "good communicator" is too vague an ambition. You need to know what specifically someone would see and hear you doing if you were demonstrating the required level of skill of a good communicator.

Your best source of information on what will define your achievement or otherwise is the organisation or individual you will be judged by.

Find out not only what the standards you are aiming for are, but also which are the most valued in relation to your outcome. In the language of job advertisements, some of these will be "essential", whilst others will "be an advantage or desirable".

Set yourself specific outcomes or objectives that are SMART – Specific, Measurable, Achievable, Relevant, Time-bound.

Identifying where you are: self-assessment

Now that you have something to assess yourself against, it is possible to carry out a self-assessment for each area. For some areas this may be easy, whilst for others you might find this hard: notice which areas you are confident in, and which you struggle to make a self-assessment in.

This is where having specific behavioural indicators for each area is essential. My "good" and your "good" may be very different. If you are assessing yourself against areas defined by your own organisation, you can use the assessment scale and forms they already have in place. Otherwise you may need to design your own simple form. Two examples are provided in Figures 3.2 and 3.3.

Figure 3.2 Example of self-assessment

Area	Level of skill required	Assessment
Knowledge – Marketing models and how to apply them.	Able to explain and apply models in CIM Advanced Certificate syllabus.	Excellent. Demonstrated through gaining the qualification and through use at work.
Questioning and listening skills.	Able to use a wide range of questions; open, closed, divergent and convergent. Able to elicit all required information from interviewee. Able to respond to information from the interviewee with appropriate questions. Able to put interviewee at ease.	Do not yet have sufficient range of questions. Sometimes miss important areas of questioning. Can miss what the interviewee is saying.

This method requires you to identify what skills you require, the level of application you need, and how that can be assessed in order to identify performance gaps and areas for improvement.

Figure 3.3 Skills analysis

Skills	Level of competence	Strengths	Weaknesses
Professional/ Technical skills Those you need to perform job tasks.			

Skills	Level of competence	Strengths	Weaknesses
Social and interpersonal skills For example, leadership, appraisal, conflict resolution.			
Communication skills For example, report writing, interviewing, presentation.			
Administration and organising skills For example, problem solving, decision making, planning.			
Personal skills For example, time management, delegation.			
Other			

This method asks you to assess your level of competence for each of the skills you require, in order to identify your strengths and weaknesses. The level of competence might be graded as follows:

Level 1: Competent in all areas of work.
Level 2: Occasionally requires guidance and support.
Level 3: Requires further development.
Level 4: Not competent.

By assessing your level of competence, priorities for training and development can be identified.

Most people underestimate or overestimate the ability they demonstrate to others, particularly if they are not used to considering themselves from another person's perspective. Whatever the reason, it is important to check. The best people to provide you with feedback are those who are with you most. Whilst peers, staff who report to you, and your manager are obvious choices, close friends and family are also likely to provide good information for you.

When asking others for feedback you should consider:

- It may feel as risky for them to offer information as it is for you to ask.
- Judgements are just sources of information. Ask people what they saw or heard you doing to lead them to form their judgement. Do this for "excellent" as well as "could do better".
- Find out what they would see or hear you doing differently if you were performing to a higher standard. Find out what you do at the moment that they want you to continue with.
- You don't need to agree or disagree there and then.
- Obtaining a number of different opinions from the people who work at your level, and those above and below you (360 degree feedback).

> **Activity 3.5 Self-assessment**
>
> Carry out an assessment of your skills, making use of the information in this section.

Personal development planning

Personal Development Plans (PDPs) can benefit you by:

- Clarifying your goals and how you will go about reaching them. This can include exploiting your strengths as well as tackling your development needs.
- Giving you a starting point from which to get others to help you achieve what you want (e.g. your manager, your peers, the staff who report to you, human resources department).
- Giving you an explicit framework to compare and monitor your achievements against.

- Providing one way of marketing yourself and your success to other people in your organisation e.g. to help you in your career.

Writing your PDP

Your PDP should include your long and short-term goals, together with your personal skills assessment. Your first aim is to set goals that will close the gap between where you are and where you want to be. In addition to using the SMART acronym, you will stand a far better chance of achieving your goals if you consider:

- Is this something that will benefit me? What will it do for me? (Doing it for someone else, or because you think you ought to, does not provide a very good incentive to achieving it).

- Are there any sub-goals that would be helpful? For example, breaking down a major goal like "improving interviewing skills" into sub-goals, such as preparing for recruitment interviews, questioning and listening skills etc.

- Is this a step to something else or an end in itself? Are there any circumstances where I don't want this?

- What losses and gains might this have, positive and negative, for myself and for others? What can I do to eliminate the losses and enhance the gains?

- Do I need other people's help? A mentor or facilitator perhaps. If so, what is in it for them?

- Am I really committed to this? Does it feel right? What is the first step I will take and when? What is my plan for achieving it? What contingency plans can I put in place?

As a rough guideline, work on a maximum of three key goals per quarter. Too many and you will be overwhelmed. Once you have decided on your goals, one format you could use to record them is shown overleaf in Figure 3.4.

Figure 3.4 Example of a PDP

Goal	Measure	Supporting actions	Immediate next steps
To demonstrate my excellence in using marketing models. **By:** End Quarter 2 2003. **Assessment:** By line manager.	■ Explicitly reference my use of models in reports and meetings each time I use one. Target: twice a week. ■ Discuss my application of them with my line manager at bi-weekly review meetings.	■ Keep list of models on my desk as a reminder. ■ Keep record of models used and their application. ■ Discuss use of models with colleagues. ■ Run "refresher" skills course for department.	■ Pin list of models up by this Friday. ■ Start "Marketing Models" file by this Friday. ■ Put item on review meeting agenda.

Gaining buy-in to your PDP

Most people's PDPs are intended to support their career development, so getting support and buy-in from others, such as your line manager, is very important. You will need to persuade them and yourself that:

- The plan is realistic and will support business and personal objectives.
- Your priorities are appropriate.
- The measures you have in place are appropriate and assessable.
- You will be supported in achieving your goals, e.g. training courses, informal development opportunities.

Activity 3.6 PDP

Draw up your own PDP and review it with your line manager, and if appropriate your team.

Case Study – New work practices and implications for management

Teleworking, with a broader definition that includes other forms of working from home and hot-desking, can now be regarded as a mainstream form of employment in Europe. The initiative has been driven in part by the European Commission. A key issue was to bring more diverse employment opportunities into rural areas, to compensate for job losses caused by the reform of the Common Agricultural Policy. Teleworking is seen as a way of creating new jobs and increasing flexibility throughout the economy, and is a trend that is likely to continue. The European Commission developed a policy on teleworking with new regulations in 1999.

The trend is not confined to Europe. Teleworking is popular in the USA and many multinational companies have set up teleworking operations around the world; in fact 70% of large companies now recognise teleworking. It is also not confined to large businesses. Small and medium-sized businesses in particular can benefit from these new ways of working.

According to statistics from the British Government, one employee in 20 in the UK is now a teleworker. This figure has grown from just under a million people working from home in 1997. A new survey, using the broader definition of teleworking, puts the UK figure at more than 2 million. However, the UK is trailing other parts of the European Union, where the practice is growing much more rapidly. In some countries in Europe it may even be twice as high. In 2000 the estimated total in the EU was over 9 million.

Countries where teleworking is growing rapidly include the Netherlands, Finland and Italy. Active support by government varies. For example, in Sweden there are tax allowances for homeworkers, and employers in Denmark can buy personal computers for their employees to use from home without incurring tax. Examples of companies which are embracing the new form of working include a Danish insurance company, France Telecom, British Airways and Andersen Consulting (now Accenture). The public sector is also using teleworking, for example in Social Services and Leisure and Environment departments.

With the rapid advancement of technology, acceptance of new forms of working from home is set to become a key pattern of working in the future. Government support for, and legislation on, teleworking, helps encourage growth – but for the manager and employee adopting this new style of working it brings new and different problems. Practical problems such as health and safety, insurance, and less tangible problems such as isolation and motivation, are just a few of the challenges facing businesses that adopt teleworking.

Source: *Effective Management for Marketing* examination paper, June 2001.
(Adapted from an article in *People Management*.)

Questions

1. What are the likely problems of these new work practices for managers and employees?

2. What are the main implications for the business, such as the impact on business operations and the implications of setting up teleworking?

SUMMARY OF KEY POINTS

- In small organisations marketing managers may undertake many different roles and responsibilities, whereas in larger organisations the marketing function will contain specialists who undertake specific responsibilities relating to PR, advertising etc.
- Effective marketing managers develop skills relating to managing people, individuals, activities and resources, in addition to the professional skills required to undertake their marketing role.
- When carrying out a self-assessment to identify any performance gaps obtain feedback from others to help validate your assessment.
- Ensure learning objectives are SMART.
- When drawing up a PDP, include details on resources, time scales for completion and immediate action to get started.

Improving and developing own learning

The following projects are designed to help you develop your knowledge and skills further, by carrying out some research yourself. Feedback is not provided for this type of learning because there are no "answers" to be found, but you may wish to discuss your findings with colleagues and fellow students.

The effective marketing manager

> **Project A**
>
> For your job role, make a list of your responsibilities and the key activities you carry out. How does this compare to your job description? Are you able to identify what you should be spending your time on in order to achieve your objectives? These are important tasks, and you will need to be able to identify these before you move on to examine your personal effectiveness in the next Session.

> **Project B**
>
> Review your leadership skills and style. How adaptable are you? What prevents you from adopting an appropriate style? What support do you receive from your peers, mentor and organisation, to help you develop effective leadership skills?

> **Project C**
>
> Find ways to develop the skills you have identified as requiring some improvement. For example, if you want to improve your communication skills try chairing a meeting. You may need to enlist the help of your line manager or use a mentor.

Feedback to activities

Activity 3.1 Marketing skills

Depending on the search engine and key words you used, you will have come up with different information.

One good site to use is http://www.searchthingy.com/search.asp, as it allows you to search on several different engines at one time.

You may have found information from web sites advertising courses in marketing, company careers web sites, and job adverts. Some of the skills that may have come up are:

- Communication skills – including the ability to communicate across borders.

- Strategic analysis and planning.
- Project management.
- Planning – taking a proactive approach.
- Group problem solving and decision-making skills, as a significant amount of a marketing manager's work takes place in team situations.
- Ability to take a global marketing perspective.

Specialist marketing skills and knowledge are not enough!

You may also wish to look at Figure 3.1 to increase your list of specific skills.

Activity 3.2 Barriers to effective management

Depending on your organisation and your experience, the results of this activity will be different for different individuals. As you reflected on the interviews, you may have realised that you could have managed them more effectively. For example:

- Did you make the outcome and agenda clear to each interviewee prior to the interview?
- Were you able to manage the time so that you covered everything you wanted to?
- Were you able to put the interviewee at ease, and use appropriate questioning and listening skills to gather the information you wanted?
- Did you consider how the interviewee could get value from the interview, and build this in to the process? For example, you could have offered interviewees a compilation of the interviews, written to protect anonymity, if this was of interest to them.

You may have discovered some common themes running through your interviews. What connections, if any, do these themes have with:

- The culture of your organisation?
- The structure of the organisation?
- The way people are managed?
- Your own development needs?

Activity 3.3 Marketing planning

One approach you might take for a theatre group is as follows:

Why do we need to market effectively? - Numbers of members are falling. - Ticket sales are down year on year. - Grants have reduced. **If the trend continues we will have to close.**
Benefits of putting a plan in place: - Ensure we spend effort on the best return. - Co-ordinate our activity. **We may be able to turn the situation around.**

Putting the plan together: where we are now?
- Analyse current profiles of:
   – Members.
   – Theatre goers.
- Examine current performance offerings.
- Examine current promotional activity and its impact.
- Identify competitors and offerings.
- Analyse potential customer base.
- Undertake a SWOT analysis.

Putting the plan together: where do we want to be? - Define target markets. - Define customer needs. - Define our brand and offering. - Plan promotional activity – cost/benefit. **Clear outcomes/objectives in place.**
Putting the plan together: activities. - Identify tasks. - Prioritise tasks.

> - Resources required.
> - Schedule for completion.
>
> **Realising what can be achieved.**
>
> **Putting the plan together: implementation.**
> - Roles.
> - Responsibilities.
> - Timescales.
> - Barriers to achievement.
> - Monitoring and review.
>
> **Summarise achievement of objectives.**

Many of the management skills discussed in this Session are required to prepare and implement this particular plan. You have probably thought of gathering valid and reliable information (research), analysing information, problem solving and decision making, communication skills, presentation skills and planning skills.

Activity 3.4 Influencing customers

Most organisations seek to meet and anticipate customer needs based on people's existing goals and values. This is most in common with transactional leadership.

One example of transformational leadership of customers is Sir Clive Sinclair's success with the home computer. He fared less well with subsequent products, such as the Sinclair C5 electric car.

Activity 3.5 Self-assessment

You may have come across some surprises if you are not used to carrying out this type of activity. If so, you may want to ask for support from people (either inside or outside your organisation), to assist you with understanding and accepting your strengths and development needs. You may also want to review where you want to be and when as a result of this activity.

Activity 3.6 PDP

This activity follows on from the last one. As you work your way through the rest of this Companion, you will have plenty of opportunities to revise and update your PDP. In any case, it is good practice to do this on a quarterly basis.

Session 4

Personal effectiveness skills

Introduction

This Session discusses some specific skills that are relevant to a marketing manager's daily tasks, starting with organising self! Different tools and techniques are discussed to help you improve your time management skills, delegation skills, and your ability to plan, prepare and control meetings. We will also explore problem solving and decision making.

When you have studied this module, you should review your own effectiveness in these areas and identify what you would like to improve. Add these to your PDP.

> **LEARNING OUTCOMES**
>
> At the end of this Session you will be able to:
>
> - Recognise how to improve your time management.
> - Delegate tasks to members of your team.
> - Manage meetings to achieve objectives.
> - Describe the stages of effective problem solving and decision making.

The importance of being a good time manager

Time is a valuable and limited resource. Everything that you do has a value associated with it, to the organisation, your team, and yourself. The impact of poor time management can make itself felt in many ways:

- Missed deadlines.
- Poor quality work on key projects.
- Lack of attention to team and individual performance issues.
- Stress related illness.
- Deteriorating personal life/work balance.

Highly effective time managers can be far more successful than colleagues with better marketing skills yet poorer time management skills.

Allocating priorities

Knowing your objectives, their relative priority, and being able to reassess them as your priorities change, is at the heart of effective time management. In addition, you need to communicate these so that:

- They are in line with your manager's priorities.
- Your team's priorities are in line with yours.

A plan of what you intend to achieve over a period can then be put in place, and used to guide your time management over a period.

Planning time management

When planning to use time more effectively it is important to know what you currently do with it. A simple time log, like the one shown in Figure 4.1, can help you identify the amount of time you spend on the right type of activities, compared to that spent less fruitfully. Review your job description, or the list you made in response to Project A at the close of Session 3, to see which are the right type of activities for you.

Log a "typical" week, including all breaks and interruptions. To determine your effectiveness, compare what you did with what you should have achieved. It is advisable to complete the log during the day, not at the end of the day, so that you remember to record all the interruptions and unplanned events.

Worthwhile activities are those that:

- Help you achieve your objectives.
- Support core activities.

Activities that are not worthwhile are those that are superfluous; they are not part of your core job, or supportive to it, and may be someone else's task. It may be possible to delegate these.

Personal effectiveness skills

Figure 4.1 Time log

Time (½ hour intervals)	Activity	Worthwhile or not worthwhile (W/NW)	Planned or unplanned (P/U)

Lack of time is one of the most common excuses for not meeting deadlines, but it may also be due to an inability to prioritise completion of tasks. In order to improve effectiveness, managers need to plan their time to complete important tasks by the due dates (see Figure 4.2).

Important tasks are generally those that help you achieve your objectives, and are therefore important! Tasks can be urgent because they have a close deadline, but may not be important. Important and urgent tasks should be done first, followed by the urgent, not important one's, followed then by the not important, but urgent tasks, and finally those that are neither urgent nor important.

Figure 4.2 Categorising tasks

	URGENT	NOT URGENT
IMPORTANT	**Important and urgent** Do these tasks first, taking sufficient time to get the job right first time! Plan time to achieve this.	**Important, but can wait** Do these when you are at your best! Is your concentration highest in the morning or afternoon?
NOT IMPORTANT	**Urgent, deadline approaching** Do quickly to the right standard, but spend as little time as possible on these.	**Not important or urgent** Leave until last. Delegate if possible.

Ideally, managers will schedule their time over a period, so that important tasks are completed over a manageable period, as opposed to being left to the last minute. Be very aware of your ability to put hard or less glamourous tasks off. Being busy doing not urgent/not important tasks is a great way to miss achieving your objectives! Also, if you are always heroically completing important tasks just before the deadline, you are leaving no room to reallocate your time if something urgent and unplanned suddenly needs your attention.

Activity 4.1 Important versus urgent

Using a grid similar to the one shown in Figure 4.2, prioritise the following tasks to distinguish between the urgent and the important.

- Reply to an administrator's email re a hotel booking for a meeting you are to attend next week.
- Draft next year's marketing plan.
- Order new chair.
- Agree presentation for tomorrow's briefing.
- Ring customer X to resolve pricing issue.
- Arrange meeting with team to set objectives for next year.
- Review subordinate's draft paper on the future of product Z to give them feedback.
- Complain to canteen about food.

Using a "To Do" list

Many effective time managers use a "To Do" list to help them plan and prioritise task completion. Tasks are written down and assigned a priority code (A, B, C or similar – see Figure 4.3) according to importance, and are then given a deadline for completion. Work can then be planned so that the tasks are completed in the right order.

Lists should be updated as necessary and checked regularly – usually at the end of each day so the next day's work can be scheduled. Use a planner or diary system to help you plan your activities, so you know what spare time you have available for new tasks.

Figure 4.3 Assigning priority to task completion

A = High Priority

Important and urgent work that must be completed on time. Any delay must be avoided. Top priority for attention.

B = Medium Priority

Equally important work, but with a longer deadline. However, today's medium priority work can soon become next week's or next month's high priority.

C = Low Priority

Non-important work that can generally be deferred, scrapped, or delegated.

Controlling your time

You will find it virtually impossible to manage your own time if you always allow others to set your priorities for you. Some strategies for preventing this are:

- Saying "no" to people. Although sometimes it is appropriate to take on a task for a colleague, often it is not – for example, when it interferes with you achieving your objectives and has minimal value to the organisation.
- Challenging entries that appear in your diary. Do you really need to be there? Is it the best use of your time?
- Scheduling quiet times in your diary and letting it be known that you cannot be interrupted at those times. In open plan offices, some managers use notices on top of their workstations to indicate if they are open for discussion, whilst others shut the door if an "open door" policy is in place. Use these quiet times to complete important tasks.
- Keeping records of how you spend your time, and reviewing them regularly for ideas to improve things.
- Delegating appropriately – this is discussed in the next section.
- Planning to make telephone calls and answer emails at certain times, so they are not spread throughout the day.
- Controlling interruptions – identify a set time of day when your team can come to you for help with problems.

- If someone asks for five minutes of your time – give them five.
- Go to someone else's office for an informal meeting – it is easier to leave when the meeting is over.
- Plan and conduct meetings effectively, so they start and finish on time and achieve objectives.

Time management support tools

There isn't a "one size fits all" time management tool. The important thing is to find the tools that work for you and use them effectively. None of them work if they sit in your briefcase or as an icon on your computer! Time management tools include:

- Personal organisers, incorporating diary and contact management systems, as well as prioritised lists of goals, objectives and tasks. Electronic personal organiser systems can be used to manage across groups of people, not just individuals.
- Mind maps provide a highly visual way of displaying priorities and activities for both individual and team use. Start in the centre of the paper with your problem or issue and then draw lines to related issues (see Figure 4.4). Brainstorm each and keep going until you exhaust all your ideas.
- Gantt charts. Used for managing time on projects and with teams, some people find them equally effective for personal use.
- "To Do" lists as previously mentioned. However, there is a danger that you end up with numerous separate lists on different bits of paper, and it is hard to see your priorities at a glance. Keep all of your to do lists and other scheduling tools and diaries together.

Figure 4.4 Starting mind mapping

Activity 4.2 Getting more from your time!

How much more can you get out of your time?

a. Prepare a spreadsheet with the activities you do over a week. Include all your personal as well as work activities; for example sleep, time spent with family, exercise. Make sure you cover everything you do (within the bounds of taste and decency!).

b. On the spreadsheet, rate the activities you have listed from 1 to 4, according to what value they provide to you (1 = little or no value, 4 = high value). In determining value, take into account money factors (such as the impact on your job performance and hence your career), and non-financial factors (such as the enjoyment and satisfaction you derive). Then, using an additional column, rate "what value the activity provides for others", again using the scale from 1 to 4.

c. Work out how many hours there are in a week, and allocate your "ideal" week between all the activities.

d. Over the next week, keep a timesheet of how much time you actually spend on each activity, making sure that you cover the full 24 hours/ 7 days. Enter the results on your spreadsheet so that you can compare your "actuals" with the value you place on each activity, the value for others, and your allocation for the ideal week. What conclusions can you draw?

e. Identify the actions you can take to increase the time you spend on high value activities, to reduce the time you spend on low value activities, and to achieve a better balance between your personal time and work time. Incorporate your findings as appropriate into your personal development plan.

Delegation

Effective delegation is an extremely important time management technique. It allows you to devote your time to your important and urgent tasks, and also assists in staff development and motivation. To delegate, you need to be clear about:

- The specific tasks that need to be done, to what standard, and by when. These details must be unambiguous.

- Who has the capability and time to do it? Who may benefit?
- What accountability and authority will be needed to do the task?
- The risks associated with delegating the task, and whether and how these can be mitigated.

Delegation is not about abdicating or dumping unwanted jobs. The manager still has responsibility for the effective and efficient completion of the task. Delegation empowers the delegate, holding them responsible for carrying out a task to a pre-defined standard and within clear limits.

Checklists for effective delegation

Use the following checklists when delegating to ensure you brief the delegate comprehensively, and so that you both learn from the experience.

Delegation briefing and support

- Match the task to the right person.
- Set clear targets with realistic deadlines for completion.
- Make sure you are communicating effectively – always check your delegate's understanding.
- Give your delegate full information on organisational policy and procedure (if they relate to the task). Pay attention to the task details that may be "second nature" to you. It is easy to assume the delegate knows as much as you do – this is rarely the case.
- Make sure the delegate knows why the job is being done, and how it fits in with their other work.
- Define the limits of authority/responsibility and ensure that others know that the task has been delegated, so that they give the same support as they would to you.
- When the delegate is ready, allow him/her to go ahead without interference.
- If a mistake is made, help the delegate to put it right – do not rush in yourself.
- If the delegate comes to you with questions, help them to find the answers rather than simply providing them yourself.
- Set up a system of progress review points. Maintain the agreed level of control sensitively.

Delegation debriefing

Following the completion of the delegated task discuss the outcome with the delegate. This gives you the opportunity to praise a job well done and assess the development that has taken place. It also opens the door to the future.

- Has the task been completed as required?
- How proficiently has it been performed?
- What needs to be done to correct any revealed shortcomings?
- Was the initial briefing good enough?
- Was the right person chosen?
- Was the work correctly allocated?
- Did the work provide sufficient challenge?
- Was the work too difficult for the delegate? If so, why?
- What has the delegate contributed creatively on top of their requirement to perform proficiently?
- What lessons have been learned for the future?
- Can other tasks be delegated, leaving you more time to tackle more important work?

Effective meetings

Meetings may be called for a variety of purposes, such as:

- To formulate a marketing plan.
- To discuss and identify action points from last quarter's sales figures.
- To convey and take questions on a new marketing strategy.

Generally, meetings are used to exchange and disseminate information, solve problems and make decisions, generate ideas through discussion, debate issues, and use creative techniques such as brainstorming. Unfortunately, in some organisations meetings are held not because they are the most effective means of achieving a purpose, but because they are a cultural norm. Before arranging or attending any meeting ask yourself:

- Does the proposed meeting have a clear purpose?

- Can the purpose be met more cheaply and effectively, for example with an email?
- Does the benefit to the organisation justify the cost? Take preparation and travelling time into account in estimating costs. Remember this is a minimum cost, given that people could use the time elsewhere.

Asking such questions is the responsibility of everyone attending the meeting. If you are arranging the meeting, ensure you invite only those people who really need to attend in person.

Activity 4.3 Spending time in meetings

How much time do you spend in meetings, both personally and professionally? What benefit do you get from the meetings? After your next meeting record on a spreadsheet database:

- The purpose of the meeting.
- Its duration.
- Your role in being there.
- The estimated cost of your time in being there.
- The estimated cost of the whole meeting, including the cost of the others time.
- Whether the meeting achieved its purpose.
- The estimated benefit to you of the meeting.
- The estimated benefit to others e.g. the organisation.

Calculate the totals for the duration, the costs and the benefits. What actions can you personally take to increase the benefits and decrease the costs? Incorporate any actions in your personal development plan.

Planning a meeting

If a meeting is justified, good preparation is essential to maximise its benefit and reduce the meeting time. As a minimum you should consider:

Figure 4.5 Managing the meeting process

What to think about	Example
Purpose.	We will identify a list of actions following last quarter's drop in sales of product X.
Who needs to attend the meeting for it to achieve its purpose, and why (check with proposed attendees before finalising).	Product Manager – may require product changes. Sales Manager – will lead sales team actions. Salespeople (phone Sales Manager for advice on attendees) – first hand customer/product sales knowledge, need to buy-in to actions.
Agenda and timings. **Warning:** "Any Other Business" can be a time-wasting agenda item, just included from habit.	Recap/agree purpose and agenda (Product Manager: 10 minutes). Factors affecting last quarter's sales (all: 15 minutes, Product Manager to facilitate). What we could do (all: 20 minutes, Product Manager to facilitate). Agree action plan (led by Sales Manager: 30 minutes).
Pre-meeting briefing and preparation.	Sales Manager to provide detailed breakdown of sales figures two days before meeting: all to read. Require two flip charts, sticky notes, pens and meeting room booked – Product Manager to arrange.
Who will facilitate/chair?	Product Manager. Attendees' objectives are aligned, so a third party or facilitator is not required.
Should the meeting be held offsite?	No, all attendees will be briefed to ensure they are not interrupted. Meeting duration 1hour 15 minutes.
Record taking.	Managers will ensure actions are recorded on flip charts. Product Manager will arrange follow-up communications and monitoring.

Meetings can take a variety of forms, ranging from a presentation briefing plus questions, to a discussion and actions meeting such as the one outlined above. If you are called on to present to a meeting, or to provide information prior to a meeting, then you should consider:

- In the context of this meeting, what is the specific purpose of me providing this information, for myself and for each attendee? How is it relevant to them?
- What do they know already? What do I need to do to get everyone to the same understanding?
- How long do I have to present? How long is it reasonable to expect them to spend on pre-meeting reading material?
- What is the most effective way of conveying this information? Are communication aids necessary?

At the start of the meeting, the chairperson should get a formal agreement of the purpose and agenda, and ensure that all preparation work is complete. It is also useful to agree ground rules.

- One person speaks at a time.
- If anyone is unsure how a discussion contributes to the meeting's purpose or agenda item they must challenge the speaker.
- No parallel discussions.
- All mobile phones to be switched off.

With this framework in place, it is difficult for an attendee to hijack a meeting to discuss something other than the purpose of the meeting.

The chairperson requires good communication skills, together with an understanding of managing teams and groups, and this is covered in later Sessions.

Follow-up

This will vary from meeting to meeting. Examples of follow-up action might be:

- Checking the progress of agreed actions.
- Sending out meeting notes or minutes.
- Contacting attendees by phone to debrief.
- Providing a means for attendees to raise any questions that occur to them after the meeting.

As with preparation, follow-up action is essential to ensure that the meeting achieves its stated purpose.

> **Activity 4.4 Responsibilities of the chairperson**
>
> A colleague is chairing a formal meeting for the first time. Write a checklist of the responsibilities of a chairperson for the colleague to include in their planning for the meeting.

Decision making

The decisions made by marketing managers range over a wide spectrum. They have to make decisions on a variety of issues, such as:

- Which logo to use in a rebranding exercise.
- Which advertising agency to select.
- How to address a customer's complaint.
- What company strategy to follow.
- Whether X is ready for promotion.
- Whether blue or green is the best colour to use for the dot points on a slide.

In your day-to-day lives you might not necessarily be aware of the many reasons behind your decisions. Decisions are often made in a split second. However, taking business decisions requires the process to be far more explicit and structured, which has several advantages:

- The decision is easier to consider and challenge, as underlying assumptions and facts are laid open to scrutiny. This leads to more objectivity, or at least to explicit subjectivity.
- Individuals become more aware of their personal biases, prejudices and blind spots.
- All available options are considered.

The problem solving and decision-making process

"What shall we do about X?" and "What shall we do to achieve Y?", are just two sides of the same coin. The process that you go through to get to the answer can be called "problem solving", "solution finding", or "decision making".

When the process is broken down, it tends to include the stages outlined in Figure 4.6. Compared to novices, experienced problem solvers tend to spend a relatively long time defining the issue, or identifying the exact problem that needs to be solved. This is because the time spent identifying the exact problem actually saves time later on, as it is not wasted on attempting to solve the wrong issue.

Figure 4.6 Resolving problems and taking decisions

Stage	Example
Defining the issue:	
■ Where are we now? What will happen if we stay like this?	■ Our customer Mr G has threatened to leave us. We don't know why or how to prevent this.
■ Where do we want to be? How will we know when we have taken the appropriate action? What will happen if we achieve what we want?	■ We want Mr G satisfied, or to leave us contentedly if we cannot meet his needs profitably. We need to resolve this urgently.
■ Is this really the area we need to consider, or is there a wider issue?	■ We also need to improve our customer relationship management (we've been here before). Initiate a separate project to resolve wider issues.
Gathering and analysing information:	
■ What information do we need? ■ What can we conclude from it?	Details of all our interactions with Mr G, from our records and from interviewing our staff, show that our records are incomplete. We suspect Mr G was given incorrect information about our product. At an interview with Mr G he produced a letter with incorrect pricing details.

Personal effectiveness skills

Stage	Example
■ We need to consider: 　– Interviews. 　– Company data. 　– Outside sources, for example the Internet.	
Identifying options: ■ Generate as many ideas as possible. ■ Ensure everything is considered. ■ Narrow these down to a few options.	■ Give Mr G what was promised. ■ Apologise, explain the situation, and take it from there. ■ Ask Mr G what he wants. ■ Offer compensation as well. ■ Any of the above plus compensation.
Assessing options against criteria: ■ Compare criteria with issue definition. ■ Capture full consequences of options, both financial and non-financial. ■ Remember all stakeholders	■ Criteria are financial, plus impact on our reputation. ■ Offer compensation and an apology. ■ Need to gain agreement from Regional Office.
Implementing selected option.	Regional Office and Mr G accepted terms.

Stage	Example
Monitoring implementation: Ensure benefits are realised.	Relationship plan in place, includes phone call to Mr G after 3 and 6 months to check on customer satisfaction.

Required skills

Decision-making and problem solving skills need to be combined with **communication skills**. You will also need.

- **Analytical skills** – particularly for defining the issues, analysing the information, and option evaluation. The first is particularly important.
- **Creative and intuitive skills** – when coming up with options, and finding ways to collect data.
- **Information gathering skills** – questioning and listening, research.
- **Facilitation skills** – for planning and managing group problem solving and decision making.

The quality of your decision making, in particular for decisions you have little time to consider, also depends on the extent of your experience and knowledge of an area.

As a marketing manager you will be required to make decisions as an individual and contribute to group problem solving and decision making. Groups are able to deal with more complex problems than individuals due to the wider range of knowledge, skills and experience available. However, as you have probably discovered in meetings, not everyone participates equally, so the full potential of the knowledge, skills and experience present are frequently not used. In addition, people who tend to be unsure of themselves may allow others to dominate the debate, even though they have important knowledge to contribute.

Groups may use consensus decision making, whereby everyone listens to each other's views and opinions and then makes a group decision. Other means of reaching a group decision are by majority voting or by the person with the highest level of authority having the final say.

The Case Study outlines what is happening in one company where the culture tends to discourage participation and co-operation, both of which are vital elements in the development of sound group processes such as group decision making. Notice that in the Case Study people tended to act in isolation, concentrating on the issues that related to themselves rather than looking at the bigger organisational picture.

> **Activity 4.5 Holiday budget**
>
> Decide on an appropriate budget for your next holiday. Prepare a spreadsheet to assist you in comparing options, taking into account both the financial and non-financial aspects of the holiday. What is the relative importance of each criterion? Are there any "show stoppers"?
>
> Use the Internet to research your options, and then enter them into your spreadsheet. From the under/overspend on your budget and your non-financial criteria decide on your preferred option.

Case Study – No easy solution to problems at Royal Mail

There will be no quick fix to the dire state of industrial relations at the Royal Mail, a leading independent review academic has claimed.

Recommendations made in Lord Sawyer's independent review call for the Royal Mail and the Communication Workers Union (CWU) to agree an end to industrial strife and work in partnership. But this would be difficult to achieve quickly in the face of increased competition, according to Gregor Gall, a senior lecturer in industrial relations at Stirling University, who gave evidence to Sawyer's review.

'My analysis suggests change is going to be slow and very fractious,' Gall said. 'If it were simply a matter of sending out a memo, it would be done pretty quickly. It has been done in the past and it doesn't work.' He added: 'It is very hard to say how the situation could be turned around.'

The Sawyer review, which described the state of industrial relations between the Royal Mail and CWU as "dire" and "disastrous", was critical of both parties in equal measure. But calling for a period of no industrial action across Royal Mail risks overlooking the individual cases of poor management and conditions that led to industrial action in the first place, Gall warned.

In failing mail centres, the review found an authoritarian style of management with little concept of how to motivate people. Among its recommendations it suggested that the Royal Mail should review its management training methods and procedures, with emphasis on leadership skills, coaching and counselling employees and working in partnership.

The review also found that union representatives at failed centres did not attach any priority to the aims and values of the business, or recognise the need for change. They backed employee grievances, irrespective of their merit.

It was recommended that the union should exert its authority over officials who broke union rules and agreements, and that it should work in partnership, focusing on the needs of the business and customers.

Consignia, which runs the Royal Mail, and the CWU agreed that the report had been even-handed. 'We will meet the union to look at Lord Sawyer's recommendations and see how we can take them forward,' a company spokeswoman said.

Source: Article by Chris Taylor, published in *People Manager*, 9th August, 2001, and reproduced with kind permission.

Questions

As the marketing manager for a company that is facing similar problems to those referred to in the Case Study, you have become aware that your team are not solving problems well – they tend to jump to conclusions or spend too long looking for the best answer. Prepare some slides for a short training session on problem solving and decision making.

SUMMARY OF KEY POINTS

- Effective time managers are able to identify what is important, and prioritise their work to achieve these tasks in the time required.
- Successful delegators match the task to the person, and provide the support required by the delegate to ensure the work is completed to the standard required.

Personal effectiveness skills

- Effective meetings achieve their objectives within the time available.
- A strong chairperson that can control individual contributions to ensure that they stay relevant is essential if meetings are to start and finish on time.
- The first stage of effective problem solving is to correctly identify what problems need to be solved.
- Gathering information is an essential part of problem solving, to ensure all available options are considered.
- Making the right decision depends on comparing the options with the criteria. What best meets the needs of everyone involved or affected by the decision?

Improving and developing own learning

The following projects are designed to help you develop your knowledge and skills further, by carrying out some research yourself. Feedback is not provided for this type of learning because there are no "answers" to be found, but you may wish to discuss your findings with colleagues and fellow students.

Project A

Plan to delegate a selected task to an appropriate member of your team.

Identify:

a. The exact task to be undertaken and the deadline for completion.

b. The level of responsibility and authority to be delegated for the task, and how this will be communicated to the relevant personnel.

c. The profile of skills, knowledge, experience and attitudes required by the delegate.

d. The potential barriers to task completion.

e. The phases of the delegation process, with a brief description of each phase.

f. Examples of targets that could be set to monitor and measure the success of the task.

> **Project B**
>
> If you have not done so, arrange to chair a meeting and ask a colleague to give you feedback on your performance. Also, make notes after the next few meetings you attend on how effectively the group communicated. Were the meeting objectives achieved within the time allowed? How well controlled was the meeting? What would you have done differently?

> **Project C**
>
> Review the way problems are solved and decisions made in your organisation, or one you are connected with. What suggestions for improvements can you make? What tools and techniques are used to help managers make good decisions?

Feedback to activities

Activity 4.1 Important versus urgent

	Not important	Important
Urgent	■ Reply to Jim's email re hotel booking. ■ Review Jane's draft paper on the future of product Z.	■ Agree presentation for tomorrow's briefing. ■ Ring customer X to resolve pricing issue.
Not urgent	■ Order new chair. ■ Complain to canteen about food.	■ Arrange meeting with team to set objectives for next year. ■ Draft next year's marketing plan.

Activity 4.2 Getting more from your time!

When people carry out this task for the first time, it can often come as quite a shock to see how they spend their time in relation to the value they achieve.

Activity 4.3 Spending time in meetings

Most people when they carry out this activity are shocked by the way they have been spending meeting time – and remember, if you have used staff hourly costs as a basis then the cost to the organisation may be even higher. For the example given in the text, there would be the salary of the salespeople involved in the meeting, plus the cost of the sales they did not make by being in the meeting!

You may have found it difficult to estimate the cost of personal meetings. For example, the hour and a half you spent with that salesman who would not take no for an answer is often inappropriate to quantify. Set against the time you could have spent with your family or by yourself you may be very clear on the cost/benefit balance!

Activity 4.4 Responsibilities of the chairperson

The main responsibilities of the chairperson can be listed as below:

Pre-meeting
- Purpose of meeting – clarifying and informing.
- Setting and distributing agenda.
- Deciding who should attend.
- Arranging a convenient time and place.
- Format – type of meeting, refreshments etc.
- Arranging for minutes to be taken.
- Controlling confirmation of attendance and agenda amendments.

At the meeting
- Starting the meeting on time – welcome, opening statement.
- Controlling the agenda.
- Controlling the participants.
- Heading discussions opening out/bringing in/closing down.
- Explaining and summarising each stage.
- Maintaining the interest and involvement of participants.
- Overcoming personal agendas and attacks.
- Making sure appropriate decisions are made.
- Getting decisions/actions recorded.

- Closing the meeting and thanks.
- Confirming circulation list for minutes.

After the meeting
- Reviewing and evaluating meeting processes and procedures.
- Reviewing and evaluating meeting results.
- Checking minutes prior to circulation.

Activity 4.5 Holiday budget

Your spreadsheet will be personal to you. It might have included such issues as:

Financial calculations:
- Basic cost of holiday.
- Supplements.
- Other subsistence costs.
- Pet care.
- Child care.
- Travel insurance.
- Spending money.
- Change out of your budget.

Non-financial criteria:
- Hours of sunshine.
- Quality of accommodation.
- Likely snowfall (usually unwelcome on a beach holiday!).
- Average temperature.
- Activities.
- Location.
- Travelling time.
- Number of days.
- Suitability for children.

As a marketing specialist, you may also have some observations about the use of the Internet for this purpose. You may wish to bookmark the sites you found particularly easy and those you found difficult to navigate for comparisons on web site design.

Session 5

Interpersonal communication

Introduction

Following on from the previous Session, we continue the theme of personal effectiveness by exploring what is meant by effective communication and how marketers can achieve this in a number of situations. The Session starts by discussing the elements of effective communication before moving onto what might go wrong. The Session goes on to explore non-verbal communications and then moves on to specific skills such as questioning and listening, before reviewing two management situations where effectiveness is essential to the outcome – negotiating, and discipline and grievance interviewing.

Internal marketing is discussed in the final sections, which also includes information on planning internal communications. This is a lengthy Session, but experienced marketers will find that it builds on existing skills. If you are fairly new to a marketing role then take time to study each section and find opportunities to put your learning into practice.

LEARNING OUTCOMES

At the end of this Session you will be able to:

- Describe what is meant by effective communication.
- Recognise how to improve your questioning and listening skills.
- Communicate effectively in a variety of management situations.
- Explain the process of negotiation.
- Discuss how to conduct discipline and grievance interviews.
- Plan effective internal marketing communications.
- Prepare and deliver effective oral presentations.

Use of communication skills in marketing

Communication skills have always been, and continue to be, recognised as core skills in any marketing activity. For example, marketers are required to use:

Figure 5.1 Examples of communication skills in marketing

Communication skill	Example use
Presentation.	Briefings, meetings.
Questioning and listening.	Interviews, customer and staff meetings.
Writing.	Reports, external and internal marketing literature.
Negotiations and conflict resolution.	Customers, staff, team meetings, meetings with other departments.
Influencing.	Any interpersonal interaction, with customers, colleagues and suppliers.

The process of communicating

Communicating a message always involves at least two parties. At any one time there will be someone who has a message they want to encode and transmit, and someone who is receiving and decoding that message, making decisions about what it means and what they will do as a result. Without effective methods of communicating organisations would stop functioning. However, as shown below even simple messages can get scrambled.

Figure 5.2 Encoding and decoding information

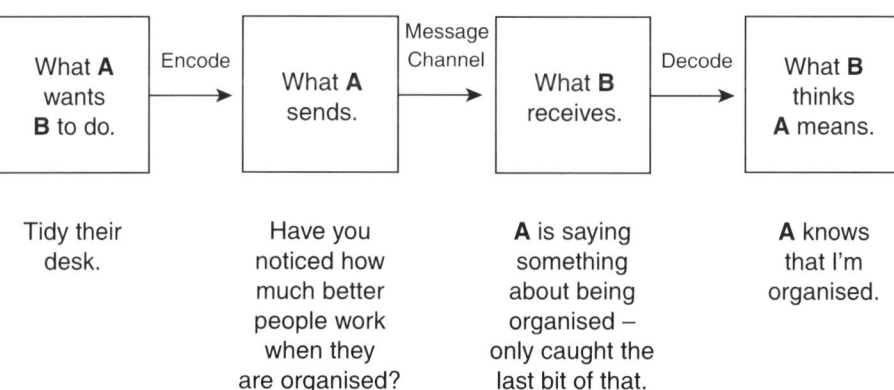

What **A** wants **B** to do.	Encode →	What **A** sends.	Message Channel →	What **B** receives.	Decode →	What **B** thinks **A** means.
Tidy their desk.		Have you noticed how much better people work when they are organised?		A is saying something about being organised – only caught the last bit of that.		A knows that I'm organised.

Sending and receiving messages

Sender

When sending a message to someone else:

- Have a purpose that requires other people to take action(s). The action(s) will vary between messages and receivers, for example:
    - **To follow instructions** – telling front line staff to use a new form when interviewing customers.
    - **To use information relevant to them** – Sales Manager gives salespeople an article on selling techniques.
    - **To give feedback** – Product Manager wants comments on the first draft of the yearly plan.
    - **To agree to a decision** – Brand Manager needs the Marketing Manager's sign-off for new literature.
    - **To motivate people** – customers to buy our products, our employer to promote us, the examiner to give us a good mark.
- Decide what specific information each receiver needs to have.
- Select an appropriate communication channel (email, post, meeting, phone call, briefing), considering the pros and cons of each.
- Prepare the communication. Encode the information into a message.
- Communicate it – send the message.
- Note the impact (is it what was intended?) and respond appropriately.

Only when feedback has been received, such as when the receiver takes the right action, does the sender know that the communication was effective.

Selecting a communications channel

The communication channel should be selected on the basis of its probable effectiveness in communicating the message and its cost. Options include:

- Written communications such as email, letter, fax.
- Telecommunications, for example video or phone conference, one-to-one phone calls.
- Training or other facilitated sessions.

Interpersonal communication

- Roadshow presentations and Q&A sessions.
- Newsletters.
- Articles in company magazines.
- Posters on staff notice boards.
- Intranet – for many companies this channel is increasingly important.

Receiver

The receiver also has responsibilities in the communication process. They:

- Decode the message.
- Check out anything unclear or ambiguous with the sender.
- Decide what action to take and initiate it.

Barriers to effective communication

When planning any communication, the potential barriers to communication and the ways to overcome them need to be considered carefully.

Figure 5.3 Examples of barriers to effective communication

Source of barrier	Example(s)	Possible impact
Sender is unclear on the purpose of the message.	Sending something "for information", just in case anyone is interested.	Receiver doesn't know what to do with the message.
	Replying to "all" on email when the message is only relevant to the sender.	Receiver gets overwhelmed with information, so important messages get overlooked.

Source of barrier	Example(s)	Possible impact
Sender codes the message in such a way that it does not meet the receiver's needs.	Giving a busy executive a fifty-page report, when a two-page summary is more appropriate. Unclear handwriting. Using obscure jargon. Poor language skills. Sending everyone the same message, regardless of individual needs.	Receiver considers the message (and possibly the sender) as irrelevant, incomprehensible and boring.
Sender uses a message channel that is unsuited to the message.	Sending a letter requiring urgent action to peripatetic sales staff.	Receiver does not act on the message in time.
Sender does not consider how they will get feedback.	Requesting an action on behalf of a customer but not following it up.	Sender has no idea of the message's impact.
Message channel does not transmit the message as intended.	Presenting in a noisy room. Using colour for presenting data, which will probably be photocopied by others in black and white.	Receiver doesn't get the same message as the sender intended.
Receiver decodes information that the sender is unaware of sending.	Sender acting in a way that is interpreted as aggressive.	Receiver places a meaning on the message that the sender did not intend.

Source of barrier	Example(s)	Possible impact
Receiver decodes the message in a completely different way to the intended meaning.	Sender asks for something urgently, meaning "I need it today". Receiver decodes urgently as "by the end of the month".	Receiver acts at variance with the sender's intentions.
Receiver does not clarify the sender's meaning.	Someone new to a company not wanting to ask questions.	Receiver acts at variance with the sender's intentions.

Barriers to effective communication are usually considered under the following headings:

Physical – includes physical barriers such as walls, distance, distracting noise, poor listening skills and temperature.

Physiological – includes emotions such as anger or excitement, prejudice and lack of interest.

Semantics – the language and words spoken, technical jargon etc.

Communicator – may have poor communication skills.

Consider what hinders effective communication between the sender and the receiver in your marketing team.

Hidden messages

Marketing managers need to be aware of the hidden messages they send out, and the assumptions they may be making about what they receive. We have already covered this briefly. Other examples are:

- Poorly written presentation. Spelling mistakes can reduce the perceived value of the content and devalue the sender. Equally, take care not to prejudge information provided to you on the basis of its presentation alone.
- Being silent may give out the impression that you have nothing to add. Managers should be aware that quiet people might surprise you with their insight if encouraged to speak.

- Folding your arms across your chest may look defensive. However, this is a natural, comfortable position for some (body language is discussed later on in this Session).

> **Activity 5.1 Communicating effectively**
>
> Collect some examples of communication messages (listed below) from a number of different sources, both within your organisation and outside it. You may even want to include some of your own communications.
>
> - Letters (including direct mail).
> - Web sites.
> - Advertisements.
> - Reports.
> - Presentations.
> - Meetings.
> - Emails.
> - Phone calls.
>
> For each one, consider:
>
> - What is the purpose of the communication? Is it clear?
> - What about the encoding of the message?
> - Is the channel appropriate?
> - What are the barriers to the communication? What did the sender do to overcome them?
> - What are the hidden messages to you? Do you think these will be the same for the other receivers? Were they intended in your view?
> - What could the sender have done differently to make the communication more effective?
>
> Start a file to collect communication examples that are:
>
> - Highly effective.
> - Highly ineffective.
>
> You can use this file as a reference source when you are communicating.

The purpose of questioning and listening

Both questioning and listening are information gathering skills. As we have seen already, communication is complex, and messages can easily become garbled between the sender's intended meaning and the meaning the receiver actually picks up. Good listening and questioning skills help ensure that this does not happen:

- Hearing what is actually said, as opposed to what you think should be said or your interpretation of what has been said.
- Encouraging the other person to talk, through showing an interest in what they have to say, as opposed to looking for opportunities to talk about your own views.
- Filling in gaps in the information by asking questions, as opposed to interpreting according to your own experience.

These skills will impact on your effectiveness as a marketing manager in many different situations:

- Understanding and responding to customer needs.
- Negotiating with suppliers.
- Meetings and interviews, such as appraisal and disciplinary.

Effective listening

For most people the most important factor in improving their listening skills is how much time they spend listening. If you are talking, you cannot be listening.

- Do you tend to "hold the floor" in conversations?
- Do you talk to yourself about what you are going to say next, or go inside to think your own thoughts when someone else is speaking?
- Do you hold what you want to say in mind, waiting for an opportunity to feed it into the conversation?
- Do you make up your mind about what the other person wants to communicate (and its value) before they have even finished speaking?

Any of these will stop you listening. In addition, the person who is attempting to communicate to you will get the impression you are not interested in what they have to say, which will also stop them communicating. Effective listening starts with being so focused on what the other person is saying that you are not aware of your own processing. It takes a lot of practise.

Being genuinely interested in what the other person has to say (as opposed to your response to it) will automatically elicit encouraging responses. Nodding and maintaining eye contact are useful ways to demonstrate your interest in what is being said. Using these while being disinterested is very irritating. You can probably think of situations where the other person seems "absent" (not listening), even though they are making all the right gestures.

As you bring more and more of your focus onto the other person (and less on yourself), you will also start to sense intuitively what they may not be saying, through being aware of their non-verbal signals. These hunches will be more accurate with practise and with people you know well. Remember they are hunches, not reality, and if you want to confirm them you need to use effective questioning. Effective listening is a skill all managers need to develop.

Effective questioning

Questioning is used in several ways; to obtain more information, to confirm the information we think we have received, or to show interest. It is all too easy to assume meaning, as our brains automatically bring our own experience to bear on what is being heard. In seeking to understand, we may want to:

- Obtain more information (open questions).
- Home in on specific information, including "yes/no" responses (closed questions).
- Confirm that we have understood correctly, for example by summarising or reflecting back and asking for corrections/confirmation.
- Clarify what has been said.

Silence and an encouraging expression also invite the speaker to say more. Its use can be extremely effective.

When asking a question, you need to be clear on the type of response you want, and choose your question accordingly. This may sound obvious, yet it requires you to have several question types in your toolbox, and to have a knowledge about their likely impact. There are also questions that are not useful when you genuinely want to know more information:

- Why? This tends to encourage defensiveness and excuses, although it can be used effectively if the tone of voice is soft and encouraging rather than hard and accusing.

- Leading questions favouring a specific answer. For example 'Surely you must accept that this option gives us the best chance of success?'
- Two questions asked at a time often produce a response to only one.
- Either/or questions, e.g. 'Do you want the red one, or the green one?' invite limited options.

The next activity is designed to help you use your questioning and listening skills in an interview situation.

Activity 5.2 Interviewing not interrogating

You will need to identify a friend or colleague for this activity. Each choose a topic about which you would genuinely like to know more. Example topics might be:

- A recent marketing project the other person has been involved in.
- Their role in the organisation.
- Developing community PR.

The interviewer is to use their listening and questioning skills to discover more about the topic, in a time agreed by the two parties (say twenty minutes). The interviewee is to notice and record the types of questions asked. Following the interview, review the experience together to discover:

- Which questions were the most effective? Answer from both the interviewees and interviewers point of view.
- How many different styles of question were asked?
- What important information about the topic was not discovered?
- What would have made the interview even more effective?
- Did the interviewee really feel listened to?

Incorporate any learning into your personal development plan.

Non-verbal communication

It's not what you say...

Messages are conveyed partly by their content (around 7%), partly by the tone of voice (around 38%), but mostly by non-verbal cues (around 55%). Therefore, if the speaker's body language contradicts what is being said it will cause confusion.

The real message is conveyed through the combination of posture, gaze, the way the head is held, and what is done with hands, arms, legs and other non-verbal signals.

Eye to eye

In order to establish a good rapport with someone you need to meet their gaze for around 70% of the conversation – this shows interest and sincerity.

A person who makes eye contact for less than 30% of the time can appear dishonest. Avoid wearing dark glasses when negotiating because this doesn't make you look cool (unless of course you actually are a film star or gangster), it blocks eye contact and makes it look like you have something to hide. Prolonged blinking also arouses suspicion. Staring without blinking can also (unsurprisingly) be interpreted as aggressive.

Where you direct your gaze is also important. In a business discussion do not drop your gaze much below the other person's eyes or bridge of their nose. Looking within the triangle between the eyes and the mouth leads to the development of a more social atmosphere.

Head gestures

Holding your head straight is neutral, whilst tilting your head to one side makes you appear thoughtful and interested. However, you signal your disapproval when your head is down. Putting your hands behind your head can demonstrate superiority and a "know it all" attitude, especially if you look down on the other person.

Hand to face gestures

Stoking or holding the chin is one of the signs a salesman looks for because it means the person is considering what has been said and may be coming to a decision.

However, rubbing your nose or placing your hand over your mouth can indicate you have something to hide. If the other person does this to you while you are speaking it may mean they think you are lying or being deceitful!

Arm and leg barriers

Folding your arms and crossing your legs is just like putting up barriers, and shows a negative or defensive attitude.

Clenched fists with crossed arms indicates hostility, but gripping your arms however demonstrates a firm attitude. Crossing your arms with your thumbs up indicates superiority.

When communicating, use positive, open body language to create confidence in your sincerity and integrity. Positive body language is important in presentations, negotiations and other interview situations.

The next section explores oral presentations where both verbal and non-verbal communication is important. You will deliver very confusing messages if your body language is not consistent with the verbal communications you are delivering.

Effective oral presentations

When planning communications, such as presentations, PASS is a useful "word" to remember! It stands for:

Purpose
- What is the overall purpose of the presentation?
- What are the specific points that help you achieve this purpose?

Audience
- Who are they?
- What do they need to know?

Structure
- How should the content be organised?

Style
- What is the best way of delivering the message?
- What language is appropriate?

You can see that there are some fundamental elements to consider when planning and preparing a presentation – purpose, audience, venue and how long. The following checklist will help you plan and prepare presentations that engage the audience and ensure the presentation is focused and relevant. Notice which element of PASS each fits into.

- What is the general purpose of this presentation?
- Why have I been asked to do this – am I the right person?
- Do I need to inform, persuade, influence…?
- Who are the people making up the audience? What do they need to know?
- How well informed is the audience already?
- What is "normal" language for this audience?
- What level of technical language and jargon will the audience appreciate?
- How long have I got?
- When and where?
- How will the audience be seated? What room layout is best?
- What do I already know about the topic?
- What else do I need to find out about the subject I am presenting?
- What method of delivery is best?
- What visual aids and handouts do I need?
- Do I need to give a demonstration?
- What other support do I, as the presenter, require – music, props?
- How do I need to dress?
- What additional resources do I need?
- Who else will be speaking? What subjects will they be covering?

Effective speaking

When giving presentations you should ensure that your delivery is clear, concise and relevant, using your voice to reinforce the message. Consider:

Volume

Don't shout, but project your voice to promote a strong image. The size of the room and level of background noise will also affect the volume required.

Diction

Pronounce words accurately and clearly so you can be easily heard and understood.

Punctuation

Stress the importance of a point by slowing down, and pause to let it sink in. Lower your volume to convey importance, confidentiality or concern, but raise the volume slightly if you wish to convey enthusiasm.

Pitch

If you are tense or nervous your voice can become squeaky because your vocal chords are stretched tight. Use deep breathing exercises to relax your throat muscles – it is impossible to breathe out and keep the muscles tight at the same time.

Speed

Be careful of speaking too quickly if you are nervous.

Tone

People "switch off" or stop listening if a speech is delivered in a monotone. Varying the tone adds interest and emotion. The meaning of a word is changed according to the tone used.

Using your voice effectively can help sustain audience interest in the same way as using interesting visual aids and demonstrations can. Other ways to engage an audience's interest include using relevant facts, figures, stories, anecdotes and analogies.

The final sections of this Session look at specific situations where effective communications are essential if a successful outcome is to be achieved – negotiations, grievance and disciplinary interviews, and internal marketing.

What is negotiation?

For many people, the word negotiation conjures up the idea of conflict, e.g. protracted discussions between employers and employees over pay and conditions. This is not necessarily the case. The process of negotiation is simply one that enables parties with different interests to agree to a course of action. Typical situations might involve:

- Finalising a contract with an advertiser.
- Bidding for a limited amount of financial and other resources.
- Agreeing product specifications, prices and delivery arrangements with customers.

Individual models of negotiation

The word "model" is used here to represent the (often) unspoken assumptions, beliefs and values which an individual, organisation or country may have about the process of negotiation. For example, many holidaymakers find their first experience of purchasing a carpet in a market disconcerting. They are used to paying a fixed price and do not expect to negotiate the price displayed, whereas the vendor fully expects a bargaining session.

Other examples of negotiation assumptions that differ across cultures are:

- Extent of adherence to a strict timetable.
- Expectations of size and role definitions of negotiation teams.
- Assumptions about the strategies that are appropriate (see next subsection).
- When and how to raise and discuss contentious issues.
- Signals, e.g. those which indicate an agreement has been finalised.
- Duties of each party to the relationship.

Understanding and taking such differences into account when planning and taking part in a negotiation is critical. Note that some of your assumptions may be so "obvious" to you, so "normal", that you may not at first realise that there is a difference – like with the holidaymakers referred to above.

Negotiation strategies

A clear idea of what you want to achieve and why is critical to selecting a negotiation strategy, whatever the content of the negotiation. As a negotiator you need to know:

- What specifically you want to happen, and by when.
- What benefits your proposal brings for you.
- What is not negotiable, for example an ethical principle.

Interpersonal communication

- What specifically will happen if you do not achieve your outcome (e.g. for each month's delay in Project X, the product launch delay will lead to opportunity costs of £300,000).
- How important and urgent is the issue.
- Other stakeholders' positions on the above, and how they relate to you.
- Information which led to your conclusions.

A crucial distinction to make between negotiation strategies is between a "win-win" (also called integrative or collaborative) approach and a "win-lose" or "lose-lose" (also called distributive or adversarial) approach. This is shown diagrammatically below for a marketing professional negotiating with an advertising agency.

Figure 5.4 Negotiation strategies

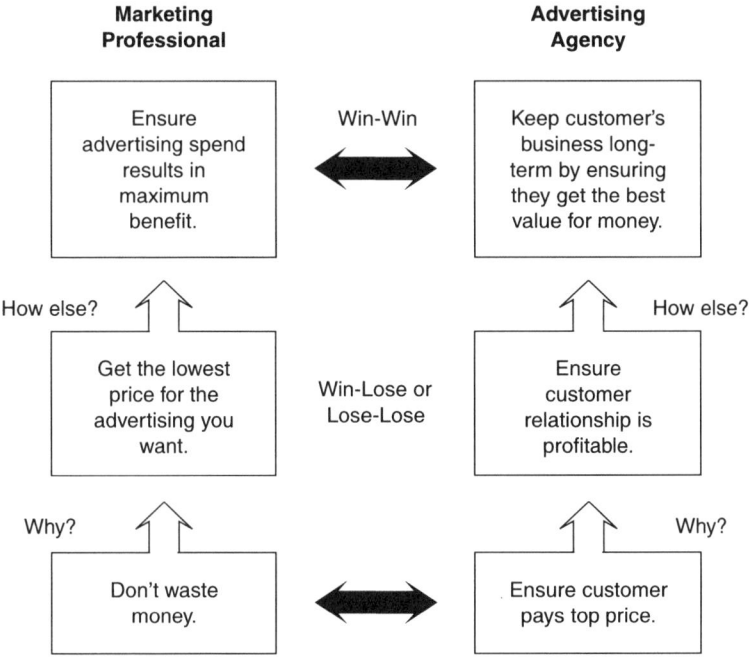

Win-win situations can also arise when each party agrees to a concession of little value to them yet of great value to the other party.

Managing the process of negotiation

A skilled negotiator employs effective communication and problem-solving strategies. They need to be as knowledgeable about the other party's position as their own, in order to respond flexibly to new information (including emotional cues).

A typical negotiation process includes the following stages:

Figure 5.5 The negotiation process

Stage	Objectives	Activity
Pre-negotiation.	To agree the how, when, where and why of the negotiations.	Agreement to the way in which the negotiations will be conducted (roles, timetable etc.). Preparation of case.
Understanding each other's position.	To identify and communicate all the relevant factors for the negotiations, from all points of view. To establish common ground.	Statement of outcomes and rationale from each party to the negotiations. This stage is one of exploration and understanding, and if it is collaborative it will include establishing mutual goals.
Proposals.	To establish points of agreement. To resolve issues (where possible) to the benefit of all parties.	Proposals put forward by each party, on their own or jointly. This may take the form of bid/counterbid and joint problem solving, depending on the approach adopted.
Agreement.	To get signed an agreement and commitment to a proposal.	Formal agreement to a proposal.

Stage	Objectives	Activity
Implementation planning.	To agree a timetable of activities, responsibilities and accountabilities.	Commitment and agreement to an implementation plan.
Follow-up and fine-tuneing.	To monitor, and if necessary, take further action to ensure success.	Follow-up to ensure commitments are met and "iron out" any issues. This step is crucial and often neglected.

In some cases an independent mediator may be used to manage the process, or to challenge and unstick a foundering negotiation. This is particularly valuable if one or both parties have difficulty in seeing the issue from the other's side.

> **Activity 5.3 Negotiations**
>
> Identify an outstanding or emerging situation that you consider is appropriate to resolve by collaborative ("win-win") negotiation. Ideally this will be a work situation, such as problems between your department and an internal customer or supplier, or perhaps negotiations with a customer. You can choose a personal issue, such as resolving a consumer complaint, or agreeing on where to go on holiday next year, but remember to select a situation that is relevant to marketing.
>
> Get agreement from all the parties for you to take on the role of mediator or negotiator to resolve the issue for the purposes of this activity. Write up your planned approach, including the rationale, and then implement it.
>
> After the negotiation, if appropriate, solicit feedback from the parties involved (including yourself) on:
>
> - Their emotional reaction to the process. Enjoyable? Frustrating?
> - Their opinion on the effectiveness of the solution.
> - What went well.
> - What they would like to see done differently next time.
>
> Incorporate your findings into your personal development plan.

Disciplinary interviewing

A disciplinary interview is held when an employee's behaviour has fallen well short of organisational expectations and previously agreed standards. For example:

- Consistent lateness without explanation.
- Consistent under performance, despite assistance.
- Actions which go directly against procedure or instructions.

For a performance issue to reach a disciplinary interview, a manager must be assured that matters cannot be dealt with through day-to-day performance management. The manager must ensure that they are completely familiar with their organisation's disciplinary procedures. Different organisations have different guidelines; some require managers to undergo training before conducting such interviews. Failure to correctly follow the procedures could result in expensive litigation.

When dealing with poor performance a manager may initiate:

- Informal interviews/warnings, keeping the matter within the department. If the matter is still not resolved, then this can be escalated to…
- Formal interviews/warnings, involving a human resources specialist, which could result in eventual dismissal.

Disciplinary interview preparation

Careful preparation is essential. In addition to ensuring you know the correct procedures:

- Discover facts, **NOT** opinions.
- Provide examples of the unacceptable behaviour, with dates, times and names of witnesses.
- Provide evidence of unacceptability – specifically how it breaches a code of conduct, company procedure, written performance criteria, etc.
- Consider any mitigating circumstances, such as poor training, no previous feedback given, unclear instructions or excessive workload.
- See if any action has been taken to rectify the situation. If the behaviour has not been challenged, the employee may be unaware that there is a problem.
- Find out if you need to invoke the organisation's formal procedures

immediately e.g. summary dismissal. If so, immediately contact your line manager and human resources specialist.
- Establish a possible acceptable resolution. Be very specific.
- Prepare short, objective, fact based and unequivocal statements on:
  - What you will initially say to the employee about what the problem is, your evidence for it, and the consequences of it.
  - What the employee must do, given what you know.
- Consult your line manager about your proposed course of action, and decide with them how human resources should be involved.

Conducting the interview

For the interview, ensure there is plenty of time and that you can not be overheard or interrupted. This, and a formal meeting layout, help underline the seriousness of the situation.

Take care at the start to ensure that the employee is in an appropriate state of mind for the interview, then come to the point very quickly. Asking leading questions in the style of a TV detective in the hope that the employee will spontaneously admit their failing is unacceptable. The agenda should be as follows:

- State your understanding of the problem (see preparation above). Do not propose a solution at this stage.
- Listen to the employee's perspective, questioning carefully. You may adjourn to consider new information.
- Propose actions and gain agreement. Ensure that the actions are timed, realistic, and objectively and observably assessable (nothing open to interpretation). If actions cannot be agreed, explain the consequences (such as formal disciplinary procedures).
- Agree the next review date.
- Ask the employee to sign the meeting notes.

Formal interviews follow a similar structure, but the employee may be represented and human resources specialists may be used to conduct the meeting.

Follow-up

It is essential to follow up any agreed actions and to record them formally, or else the process can be undermined. If the required improvement in behaviour does not take place then a process of informal and then formal warnings may lead to eventual dismissal. The employee may take legal action, so again, following procedure is essential.

Grievance interviews

These may be initiated by an employee as a result of a disciplinary interview, or from other causes, such as unwanted changes in working hours or because of bullying. Again, failure to deal appropriately with such grievances may result in legal action later on.

As with disciplinary cases, the manager must follow organisational procedures to the letter. The basic preparation and structure of the interview follow that of the disciplinary interview, but in these circumstances it is the employee that states the problem at the outset. Following careful questioning, the manager may postpone the remainder of the interview until they have gathered additional facts, particularly if it was not possible to gather sufficient facts before the interview. You must remain impartial until you are sure of the facts: some grievances may result in disciplinary action. Again, the involvement of human resources specialists and line management may be required if the grievance cannot be settled immediately.

Activity 5.4 Staying within the law

Using the Internet, research relevant employment law and best practice on grievance and discipline where your organisation operates. You may wish to supplement your research by using your local library, or by talking to your human resources specialist.

What is internal marketing?

As well as marketing their products and services to their external customers, a company will also market within itself. A company can use internal marketing for:

- Conveying the benefits of its products so that staff can sell them more effectively to customers.
- Enthusing staff about the company's products, results and future plans, so that they act to support these plans. This may be an ongoing programme.

Interpersonal communication

- Marketing a department's services to internal customers.
- Supporting the implementation of a change management programme, such as process redesign, rebranding, or organisational changes.
- Encouraging staff to value and use remuneration package benefits.

Marketing models and tools are as applicable to these internal communications scenarios as they are to external customers. A marketing professional must pay particularly close attention to their own communications, as any errors will cast doubt on their ability to communicate well with customers.

Planning internal communications

Just as a marketing campaign carried out with no regard to the operational impact might overload a call centre, internal marketing needs to be integrated into related plans and activities. Basic questions to ask are shown in Figure 5.6.

Figure 5.6 Communications checklist

Question	Example
■ What activities will the communication support?	New process to be implemented to speed up delivery of Product X by 06/2003, prior to any communication with customers.
■ What is the overall purpose, benefit and timetable?	Expected to protect revenue of £500,000 per year.
■ Who is to be communicated to and about what?	Staff who need to go through the new process, require the procedures one week in advance. Managers need to be advised two weeks before.
■ Are there different segments to be satisfied e.g. salespeople, Head Office managers?	Salespeople need to be told not to advise customers until the implementation is complete.
■ Is the information flow two-way?	The implementation team require feedback.

Question	Example
▪ What are you promoting to each segment?	Staff will go through the new procedures. Managers will monitor and report problems.
▪ What do you want them to do or think about differently as a result of it and by when e.g. sell more, carry out different procedures? (If the answer is "nothing", why do it!)	Salespeople will only inform customers once the project is successful, and need to be aware of the project and the implications for future sales. Implementation team will identify and resolve any problems.
▪ What other communications are these people receiving?	Main communication is by phone and email. A new procedure communicated recently by this method was not implemented.
▪ In what form?	Local manager/staff meetings once per week, are considered more effective.
▪ When? ▪ Where? ▪ From whom? ▪ How effective are these channels?	The sales team tend to ignore communications, except those from their regional sales managers. There already is a channel for providing feedback on problems; it is virtually unused.
▪ Is separate branding appropriate?	Decision made to use brand designed for all process change initiatives.

From the information gathered, a high-level communications plan can then be formulated, together with a draft business case for the work.

It is important that control mechanisms enable plans and budgets to be integrated with other activities, together with benefits monitoring. In the above example, training sessions might be provided for staff as part of the local managerial staff meetings, on the basis that email is ineffective in this instance. This is a more costly option, so it would be best to run a pilot session to test that the approach will work. It might also be a good idea to stop some of the email communications, reducing background noise.

A final point on internal marketing is that many of the tools used for external marketing are valid in this situation. Communication must be two way, so customers' needs are identified and satisfied and continue to be satisfied. Again feedback tools are the same as in external marketing, such as surveys (face-to-face, email or by telephone) and focus groups.

Activity 5.5 Internal marketing

1. Identify a recent or planned change in your department or organisation with which you are associated.

2. Produce a high-level communications plan for the change. If the change has already been made, compare this with what you know happened in practice. From this, identify two different segments that need to be informed of the changes (for example the sales and operational staff).

3. Select and justify a communication channel for each of the two segments, and write the corresponding targeted communication. If possible, contrast and compare this with what was delivered in practice. In addition, identify two individuals who are either highly representative of your target audience or else very familiar with their needs, and get them to give you feedback on the material you produced.

4. Now draw up a "best practice" list to refer to when writing or reviewing communications and plans. Incorporate any actions as appropriate into your personal development plan.

Case Study – Brands fail Olympic recall test

A survey conducted by CIM in the year 2000 suggested that despite the vast sums of money currently being poured into sports sponsorship deals, audience recognition levels of certain brands are disproportionately low.

The survey of over 1,000 adults revealed that public recognition of the official sponsors of the 2000 Sydney Olympic Games, the biggest sporting event in the world, did not always justify the large chunks of budgets needed to secure sponsorship deals.

The minimum spend for sponsorship of the Sydney Olympics was a cool $40 million, a figure that helped the International Olympic Committee (IOC) generate $315 million in sponsorship revenues, which according to IOC marketing chief Michael Payne, is 50% more than its original target.

Yet brands such as Visa, Panasonic, Samsung, Sports Illustrated, Fuji, Xerox and UPS, all scored less than 5% recognition as a brand or product associated with the Olympics. Bigger names such as Coca-Cola, Adidas, Nike, McDonald's and Reebok fared relatively better, although none of the brands included in the survey achieved more than 25% recognition.

33% of consumers identified either Adidas or Reebok as brands most associated with the Games, although neither of these brands is actually an "Official Team Millennium Olympic Partner"!

Survey responses also revealed differences in brand recognition levels based on age and gender. For example, 19% of women and 22% of men were able to name Coca-Cola as a brand associated with the 2000 Olympic Games. Of the 19% of consumers who associated Adidas with the event, 26% were aged between 19 and 24, compared with only 13% of over 55s.

CIM Director of Marketing, Ray Perry, cites the clutter of messages as the fundamental problem encountered by sponsors of major sporting events, and is the reason why the impact of branding is often compromised. 'An increasing number of brand names are associated with events,' notes Perry. 'Official event or competition sponsors are supplemented by team and individual sponsors, equipment sponsors, broadcast sponsors and even sponsors of the stopwatch. Add to this the presence of advertising in broadcast media in the intervals, and it is little wonder that the message just isn't getting through to the consumer.

Another common marketing tactic that can diminish the impact of official sponsors of sporting events is the interference from competitor's brands engaged in ambush marketing, whereby an event is used to sell a product without paying a sponsorship fee.

There are various examples of ambush marketing strategies in practice. Broadcast sponsorship of an event for example, creates a brand association that ultimately reaches a far larger audience than the on-site audience. Advertising around relays of the event is another example, although this may become more difficult in the future with those responsible for granting television rights to sporting events working more closely with sponsorship agencies. This means TV rights could eventually be sold with stipulations as to who can advertise or buy broadcast sponsorship.

Interpersonal communication

Creating non-sponsorship promotions that coincide with large sporting events is another way of diverting attention from official sponsors, although this strategy can backfire. Duracell recently landed itself in trouble with the IOC after offering consumers free tickets to the 2000 Sydney Olympic Games as the main prize in an on-pack competition. As the brand was not an official sponsor and had not sought permission from the IOC prior to running the promotion it had to be pulled.

Sponsorship experts insist that the key steps to ensuring a worthwhile return on sponsorship investment is thorough research beforehand, benchmarking, and setting clear objectives followed by measurement of brand recognition and association. Sponsorship deals should also be backed up by a truly integrated marketing campaign.

'By keeping up a sponsorship over a period of time, and integrating the sponsorship with other activities, marketers can minimise the chances of their brand becoming less visible,' says Perry. 'Ensuring that the brand values of the company match up to the brand values of the event in the first place is also vital. Sponsors who fail to meet any of these criteria are potentially wasting their money.'

Source: *Marketing Business*, October 2000.

Questions

1. What does the Case Study suggest are the main barriers to effective communication with consumers at large sporting events such as the Olympic Games?

2. As a marketing consultant, what advice would you give to an organisation sponsoring a large sporting event, to help them ensure their communications are more effective than those suggested in the Case Study?

SUMMARY OF KEY POINTS

- Effective communication means that the receiver decodes the sender's message correctly and initiates the action required.
- Successful communicators and interviewers have good questioning and listening skills.
- Use PASS to plan effective communications.
- When negotiating, know what is negotiable and what isn't.
- Plan negotiations carefully, and employ appropriate strategies by taking account of what you want and what the other party wants as a minimum.
- Before implementing disciplinary or grievance procedures, ensure you understand and follow company policy.
- Prepare well for disciplinary or grievance interviews by collecting facts, interviewing witnesses, and using specialist support when necessary.
- Use the same tools and techniques for internal marketing as you would for external marketing.

Improving and developing own learning

The following projects are designed to help you develop your knowledge and skills further, by carrying out some research yourself. Feedback is not provided for this type of learning because there are no "answers" to be found, but you may wish to discuss your findings with colleagues and fellow students.

Project A

Read a book on non-verbal communication – you will find suitable books in the CIM library, your local library or on amazon.com.

Project B

Evaluate your own presentation skills and ask a colleague to also give you feedback. Identify areas for improvement and plan to develop the required skills. Listen to other people's presentations and learn from what they do well and what they don't!

Interpersonal communication

> **Project C**
>
> Review your organisation's (or one you are connected with) disciplinary and grievance process. How easy is it to understand? Where do you believe your organisation could strengthen its policy? Why might an organisation adopt best practice beyond that required by local employment law? Are managers supported effectively if they have to implement it?

Feedback to activities

Activity 5.1 Communicating effectively

Depending on what you have collected, you will have different results from this activity. Check that you have considered each aspect of the communications process when coming up with your answers:

- Purpose.
- Choice of channel.
- Receiver segmentation.
- Encoding.
- Operation of channel.
- Decoding.
- Feedback and follow-up.

Activity 5.2 Interviewing not interrogating

This activity should have helped you recognise where you are in the development of your questioning and listening skills. It should encourage you to practise your listening skills and to extend your vocabulary of questions. Observing others as well as yourself will also enable you to extend your skills.

Activity 5.3 Negotiations

Using the collaborative approach successfully is a key skill for an effective manager. To what extent were you able to:

- Select an issue that lends itself to such an approach?

- Assess correctly the assumptions and values each party would bring to the negotiation?
- Ensure both parties had clear outcomes for the negotiation, and appropriate information to back them up? To what extent was this achieved by active listening and questioning during the negotiation process?
- Establish clear roles and responsibilities for the negotiations? Were the right people present? Could the negotiator agree on behalf of their department?
- Manage to establish common ground at the outset of the negotiation?
- Come to a win-win conclusion? If not, why not?

Activity 5.4 Staying within the law

Government and trade union sites are often good sources of information. Do not assume that what is appropriate best practice in one country will apply in another. US law tends to provide employees with fewer rights than in UK law for example. Some organisations may choose to adopt more employee-friendly procedures than local legislation demands, recognising the role such procedures have in supporting employee morale, or perhaps recognising the need to align such procedures with the company ethos.

Activity 5.5 Internal marketing

Some common criticisms of communications may have surfaced during your research for questions 2 and 3 of this activity. Here are some points that may have come up:

- Apparently worthless information – recipient completely uninterested.
- Inappropriate channel chosen.
- Communication missing important information, with no way to find out more.
- Communication takes no account of what is known to be important to the recipient, and seems to have been written for someone else.
- Use of jargon unknown to the recipient.
- Unclear what action is expected from the recipient. Key actions are hidden away, left to the imagination, not timed, or are unspecific.
- Actions are completely unrealistic.
- No indication of what happens next.

- No indication of the timing of events that would be important to the recipient.
- Communication badly presented, e.g. unstructured, poor spelling and grammar.

Ensure that these and other criticisms are addressed by using the "best practice" list you produced for question 4 of this activity. For example, the first point opposite, "apparently worthless information", would be addressed by a best practice item "ensure every statement in the communication has a purpose for the recipient, and that the purpose is clear".

Session 6

HRM for marketing

Introduction

This Session considers the importance of Human Resource Management (HRM) in planning to get the right person in the right job at the right time! It explores the practical aspects of recruitment and selection, in addition to identifying the strategic importance of HRM alongside marketing.

> **LEARNING OUTCOMES**
>
> At the end of this Session you will be able to:
>
> - Understand the importance of HRM planning.
> - Explain the importance of conducting a job analysis.
> - Discuss the different stages of recruitment and selection.
> - Complete a person specification.
> - Write a job description.

The role of Human Resource Management (HRM)

Traditionally the personnel department tended to focus on areas such as pay, selection and recruitment, training, resolution of disciplinary and grievance issues, human resource demand and supply, and succession planning. Often these activities were carried out in isolation from the main business – sometimes this can still be the case. However, line managers (such as marketing managers) are increasingly being asked to take on many of these tasks, with the support of specialists.

The more strategic view of HRM recognises that people are of crucial importance to the performance of any business. From a marketing perspective, each time an employee makes contact with a customer there is the opportunity to either promote or undermine the brand. In addition, without the right skills, knowledge, and competencies, marketing strategies and plans cannot be formulated or implemented effectively. Strategic HRM seeks to make the link between people strategies and organisational strategies explicit and coherent, through:

Organisational design

A bureaucratic, multi-layered organisation will find it difficult to develop a culture of innovation and informality. HR initiatives can be employed to align the required structure and culture to assist people to be more customer focused and responsive to change.

Pay

Pay based only on meeting sales targets does not easily support a company marketing itself on high levels of customer service. Strategic HR works with the other functions of the organisation to develop a reward system that does.

Performance management and development

For example, what systems need to be put in place to ensure that employees understand, buy-in to, and exhibit the behaviours needed to support the company brand?

Marketing and HRM

The implementation of a marketing plan is dependent on many different functions within an organisation. Without a knowledge and understanding of these functions a marketer will be unable to:

- Decide when to ask for specialist help.
- Know how to specify their needs in terms the specialists can understand and work with.

Examples of how HRM might be required to support marketing are given in Figure 6.1.

Figure 6.1 HRM in support of marketing

Marketing	Issues	HRM activities
New product line P will appeal to segment S. It will replace the current product line.	P requires more highly skilled staff to sell and deliver it than we have at present. What is the impact on costs?	■ Resourcing options; such as training, recruitment of different staff. ■ Job analysis and new job descriptions.

Marketing	Issues	HRM activities
		■ Costs and timescales for delivery. ■ HRM planning of demand and supply.
Launch of a new brand planned following a strategic review.	Our culture is out of line with the new brand.	■ Gap analysis (for example, culture, procedures, and performance management). ■ Change programme planning and management.
Economic value of delivering the service at less than production costs.	Operations say a cut-down service can be delivered at a lower cost.	■ Plan and manage any job losses and reduced human resource demand. For example, new job descriptions and grades, new human resources plan. ■ Involve staff bodies/unions. ■ Consider legal aspects.
Forecasts show a changing product profile over the next 2-5 years.	■ Need to ensure that costs fall in line with product volumes. ■ Skills profile of staff is different.	■ Feed new assumptions into the human resources plans. ■ Change recruitment and selection plans in line with the new requirements.
Sales have suddenly increased 20% more than expected.	■ Service standards have fallen. Need to increase service standards fast.	■ Recruit short-term contract and temporary staff. ■ Identify staff for secondment to problem areas. ■ If it is a long-term trend, action increased recruitment of staff to cope with the demand.

> **Activity 6.1 HRM and marketing**
>
> Think of some companies you are a customer of. Find their sites on the Internet and explore them. From these:
>
> - What messages do you receive about their brand?
> - If you wanted to recruit people aligned with the brand, what characteristics would you expect their staff to have? In your experience is this the case?
> - What else can you deduce about their possible HRM policies and procedures, if these were aligned with their brand?
>
> Do the same for your own organisation.

Involvement in recruitment and selection

Most, if not all, managers are now heavily involved in the recruitment and selection of their people. Getting the right person for the job is not only important for the success of the business, it is also critical for your needs and those of the person you are recruiting. Many performance management problems can be traced back to inappropriate recruitment and selection decisions, which resulted in inappropriate candidates being selected and appointed.

An outline of the main tasks is shown in Figure 6.2.

Figure 6.2 Outline of the main tasks in recruiting and selecting a candidate

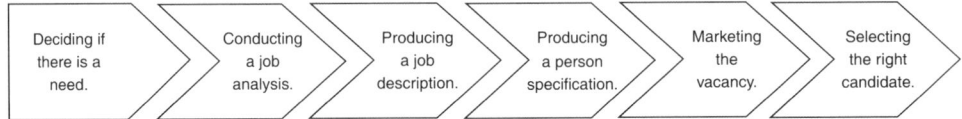

The management process does not just stop once the candidate has been selected. Appointment, induction, and relevant training are also required if the person is to fill the vacancy successfully.

The main tasks outlined in Figure 6.2 are now discussed in detail.

Deciding if there is a need to recruit

Recruiting is one option when the demand on human resources outstrips supply. This may arise because:

- Someone has resigned.
- Demand is increasing.
- A skills gap is identified.
- A reorganisation has taken place and a new structure has been created.

Before deciding on recruitment, managers need to consider other options carefully:

- Using an external supplier to do the work.
- Reorganising workload.
- Cutting activities.

For many roles internal recruitment may be desirable and appropriate. For others there may be a need to look outside the organisation. As shown in Figure 6.2 this process follows several stages, and in any case it is not sufficient to replace like with like.

Job analysis

Its purpose for recruitment is to describe the role in sufficient detail so that a job description can be filled out and the job evaluated.

A job analysis is designed to identify the:

- Objectives it has to meet.
- Performance standards.
- Relationships with other parts of the organisation, such as reporting and control mechanisms.
- Products and services it provides, such as information and projects.
- Resources it uses.
- Resources it controls.
- Levels of authority, accountability and responsibility.

- Processes, activities and tasks it carries out in order to meet the above requirements and their related performance standards.
- Core knowledge, skills and competencies required to deliver the above.

This is as true for an individual as it is for a team. A job analysis will lead to a record of all these elements. When conducting a job analysis remember to get the job holder's input (if any).

There are various reasons for conducting a job analysis, some of which may overlap or need to be co-ordinated. A job analysis might be carried out:

- As part of an organisational design. If you were asked to review or design the structure of your team, you would need to:
  - Agree the overall description of the team, using the checklist above.
  - Analyse the current jobs being done in support of the team's objectives.
  - Determine any changes in activities. What gaps are there to be filled? What overlaps are there?
  - Decide how best to organise the team to carry out the team's activities and meet its objectives.
  - Produce new job analyses for all team members.
- As a precursor to recruitment. You may need to produce a job analysis or amend/use an existing one. Job analyses are sometimes used to provide a vital input into producing job descriptions.
- For job evaluation. This may be required if jobs are being re-graded, perhaps as part of a new remuneration structure, or if a job has undergone substantial changes since it was last evaluated. It is also used for new jobs.
- For performance management. Job analysis can assist in identifying the key performance measures for an individual.

As indicated above, a job analysis is not an end in itself. You therefore need to consider what its purpose is, and how to conduct it in order to meet that purpose. For example:

- There is little point in aiming for an independent assessment of all the tasks, down to 1% of the role, if its purpose is to feed into job evaluation and performance management systems that are mainly competency based, and which require far less detailed activity descriptions.

- An analysis produced for the purpose of a job evaluation is likely to provide insufficient input into a process redesign project, where a detailed breakdown of the activities to task level is what is really required.

Suppose you were asked to come up with a job analysis for a proposed new role in your marketing department, that of competitor analysis. Up until now this task has been carried out by individual product teams, and it is felt that dedicating one person to the role will result in less duplication, improved quality, and more time for the product teams to carry out their other duties. You might approach this by:

- Contacting your HR specialist, or someone with previous experience of this type of activity, to get advice and to determine what specific information you will require for job evaluation and recruitment.
- Holding a meeting with product team representatives to determine the objectives, nature and demand for services, and the performance standards for the proposed role.
- Sending round a questionnaire to determine what competitor tasks are being done by the product teams at present, how long they spend on them, and to gather some sample tasks.
- Writing a draft job analysis, based on the information you have gathered, and then agree it with the product teams and your line manager as appropriate.
- Meeting with your job evaluation and recruitment specialists to ensure that the job analysis you have produced will result in the role you require being filled, and get an estimated cost.

Activity 6.2 What do I do?

Analyse your own job. If possible, compare it with the most recent job analysis for your role, or failing that your job description. Does it differ markedly from the one written? Discuss the results with your line manager or HR specialist, or alternatively with a colleague. Are there differences in their perspective?

Job description

The process here is described in detail later on in this Session. The job description is completed following the job analysis and forms the basis of what the employee needs to do to perform the job successfully.

Person specification

This is the stage of the process where you decide exactly what sort of person you want to target with your recruitment campaign, using the job description as input. A person specification details the essential attitudes, skills and capabilities required by the job holder. This is again covered in more detail later on in this Session.

> **Activity 6.3 Recruiting marketing managers**
>
> Explore the Internet to discover what knowledge, skills and experience are required at the different levels in marketing by those organisations advertising for marketing personnel. What skills are mentioned? What trends do you notice for the more senior roles?

Marketing the vacancy

This is where your marketing experience comes into its own. You want to target as closely as possible those individuals who will be able to do the job **AND** those who really want to do the job. Don't be tempted to overstate the benefits when advertising or selling the job during selection. If there is a mismatch it will lead to demotivation and underperformance. The purpose of the advertisement is to attract suitable applicants, so it must contain sufficient information for potential candidates to identify if they are the right person to apply. Include details on the position, salary (if applicable), the organisation, contact details and what the applicant needs to do in order to apply.

There are many different methods that can be used to attract appropriate applicants, apart from advertising, including:

- Internal staff recommendations.
- Recruitment roadshows.
- Recruitment agencies.
- Headhunting.

Remember to work closely with your organisation's HR specialists. You have a lot of experience to offer, and so do they, so make sure you get the best out of both of you. For example, you will be able to advise on appropriate media for advertisements.

In addition, be aware of the legal requirements when advertising job vacancies (e.g. in the UK you must act in accordance with the Equal Opportunities legislation).

The recruitment and selection experience, from advertising to appointment letters, is all part of marketing the vacancy.

Selecting the candidate

Candidates need to be compared against the person specification and job description/specification. Matching the two is very important.

- If you want someone with excellent telephone skills, then interviewing them face to face is insufficient, you must test their telephone skills.
- If specialist knowledge is critical for the job, you must ensure that they are assessed by a qualified person.

Candidates need to be assessed against each aspect of the person specification as objectively as possible, with everything recorded in writing at the time of the selection process. This is both for practical and legal reasons. Some organisations require specialist training for selectors.

Selection can be expensive, as can poor selection decisions. Various tools are available to help reduce the risks of a costly mistake:

- Pre-interview screening via application forms, CVs, telephone interviews.
- Face-to-face interviews. Some organisations use competency based interviewing, where the candidate is asked for specific examples of how they have used the required skills.
- Demonstrations or tests of skills, such as presentation, telephone or IT skills.
- Assessment centres. These are designed for candidates to demonstrate their application of skills, not just their ability to talk about their skills.
- Psychometric tests. These can provide useful information for candidates and interviewers, but need to be used by a qualified person and should never be used on their own.

The techniques used depend on the cost/benefit for the specific vacancy. For example, recruiting a senior executive may involve most of the above techniques, whilst for a junior role an application form and face-to-face interview will usually be sufficient.

Finally, the preferred candidate is contacted, qualifications and references checked, and terms negotiated.

Some of the process may be contracted out to a recruitment agency. If this is done it is crucial to provide a very precise person specification, and some organisations may shadow the recruiter for a period to ensure that their requirements are fully acted upon.

Activity 6.4 Recruiting sales staff

You have been asked to review the recruitment process for the sales staff. At the moment, the process consists of:

- Advertising in local papers.
- Sifting through the applications.
- Face-to-face interviews with the candidates, and selection on that basis. This involves two selectors interviewing ten candidates per day between them.

You have been provided with the following information: the average of the last four recruitment campaigns.

No. replies	No. interviewed	No. employed	No. still in role after 1 year
400	100	20	10
Cost of advertising		£1000	
Cost of interviewing		£5000	

It costs £1000 to train a salesperson. A novice salesperson is 50% as effective as someone who has been in role for one year. After a year a salesperson makes the company £100,000 per year.

Outline your investigations and some of the conclusions you might draw from the data given.

Purpose and contents of a job description

A well-considered job description is useful in providing both employer and employee with a common understanding of what is expected from the job holder. It is important in job evaluation, and also as a step in the recruitment process.

The precise contents of a job description vary from organisation to organisation. It should be based on a job analysis, and contents usually include:

- Job title and grade.
- Working hours and arrangements.
- Reporting lines.
- Responsibilities and underlying tasks. These may be broken down by the percentage of time the job holder is expected to spend on each part of the job.
- Authority – what levels of decision can they take without reference to someone else? What resources do they have control over?
- Accountability – what the job holder will be held accountable for, including how performance in the role will be evaluated.
- Knowledge, skills and competencies (or Attitudes, Skills and Knowledge – ASK) required from the job holder. This aspect is sometimes called the job specification.

Interpreting a job description

Most people have at least heard of individuals who insist on performing no more than the duties of their job, perhaps with the words "it's not in my job description". In addition, jobs are often changeable, particularly in project and team roles. For this reason, job descriptions are changing their focus towards accountability for results-based performance measures and competency assessment, and away from the traditional lists of very specific job duties.

This change in focus brings its own challenges. Listing tasks is easier for many people than defining key competencies and performance measures. However, not clearly defining key competencies and performance measures can lead to serious misunderstandings.

- 'Requires good marketing knowledge and skills'. This could mean a GCSE to one person and an Advanced Certificate in Marketing to another!

Effective Management for Marketing

- 'Accountable for substantially improving sales performance year on year'. How do you define substantially? How are you measuring performance?
- 'Requires excellent communication skills'. According to what definition and standards? How would you know?

A good test is if two people can independently assess an individual's suitability for a role, based on the job description, and still come up with the same answer. Existing job holders should also be given an input into and agree their job descriptions.

Writing a job description

A sample job description is given in Figure 6.3.

Figure 6.3 Sample job description

Job title	Grade 2 Administrative Assistant.
Hours	35 hour basic week. Must be prepared to work flexible hours between 8am and 6pm as directed.
Reporting lines	Reports to Grade 4 Customer Advisor. No direct reports.

Responsibilities	■ Making appointments for Customer Advisor (50%):
	   – From prospect list.
	   – As directed by Customer Advisor.
	■ Taking direction from Customer Advisor for follow-up actions after customer interviews (20%). Example tasks:
	   – Arranging product delivery.
	   – Following up potential customer orders.
	   – Requesting payment.
	■ Dealing with phone calls from customers (20%). This is likely to include:
	   – Complaint handling.

	- Making appointments. - Dealing with queries, including redirecting them as appropriate. ■ Completing sales returns (10%). ■ As required by Regional Office, including keeping records and collating sales figures.
Authority	■ Diary management. ■ Customer compensation up to Level A, may have further authority up to Level B if delegated by Customer Advisor.
Accountability	■ Completing sales returns on time and to standard set by Regional Office. ■ Taking actions to time and standard set by Customer Advisor. ■ Meeting telephone answering standards set by Regional Office. ■ Meeting customer satisfaction and mystery shopper targets set by Regional Office. ■ Making on average seven customer appointments per day for Customer Advisor, including follow-up and customer requested appointments.
Essential skills and knowledge	■ Telephone skills – Grade A standard on "Telephone skills" course (including complaint handling). ■ Company product knowledge – pass "our products" CBT course. ■ Numerical ability – GCSE Mathematics Grade A-C or equivalent. Language skills – GCSE English Grade A-C or equivalent. ■ Office skills – at least six months of general office duties in a regional or local office.

Essential competencies/ attitudes (Maximum 4)	■ Prioritisation Level 2 (able to work to changing priorities set by manager, and can demonstrate and explain rationale for work priorities). ■ Customer Focus Level 3 (can explain the importance of meeting customer needs, respond to urgent customer requirements, make judgements on customer compensation – in line with company policy). ■ Customer Relationship Building Level 3 (actively seek information on customers, proactively suggest products to customers, able to brief salesperson on basis of customer knowledge, and achieve good or excellent standards on customer satisfaction reports). ■ Accuracy Level 4 (demonstrate a concern for accuracy, learn from errors, seek to put new procedures in place, and work consistently – meeting or exceeding company standards).

Activity 6.5 Job descriptions

Find several job descriptions from your organisation, including your own, and preferably covering several different marketing jobs. If you have a team, make sure you include their job descriptions in this activity. To what extent do you believe:

- The information to be up-to-date and accurate.

- A recruitment consultant or other person outside the company could accurately interpret the description without resorting to making assumptions.

If you have any questions about your job and/or those of your team as a result of this exercise, you may want to discuss these with your line manager or HR representative. If you have no job description, you may want to write one and check it with the relevant people in your organisation.

Purpose of a person specification

A person specification is usually completed so that someone can be recruited into a role. It acts as a:

- Basis for your recruitment strategy, e.g. marketing and selection techniques.
- Template against which candidates are assessed during selection.
- Basis for planning the induction of a newly appointed job holder.

A person specification is different from the job analysis and job description in that:

- It is unlikely that you will find an exact match between the job requirements and the job candidates. Anyone who fulfils the job requirements will probably want a more demanding role. Anyone who exceeds them will usually be bored.
- It may be more cost effective to train up someone internally than recruit someone new.
- Some of the requirements may be organisation specific (e.g. knowledge of internal systems) and an external recruit may not have them.

Occasionally a person specification for existing job holders may be completed, as an input into a job description. For example, you may research the attitudes or competencies, skills or knowledge critical to success in your top salespeople, as an input into job analysis and job description.

Contents of a person specification

The contents of a person specification should be based on the attitudes or competencies, skills and knowledge of the job description.

Consider:

Assessment Standards for each aspect of the job requirement:

- These are the standards against which your candidates will be compared.
- They must be independently assessable and based purely on the requirements of the job.
- Often a scale with written assessment criteria for achieving each standard is used, e.g. scale of 1-5, person specification is Level 3.

Essentials (must haves):

- If the person does not meet the standards, then they will definitely be unsuitable for the role. If a job requires someone to speak to customers in both French and English from day one, then if they are not bi-lingual they are not suitable.
- These are the grounds for rejecting candidates. Make certain that judgements are not based on poorly founded assumptions. As an extreme example, it used to be assumed that married women could not be committed to both a job and their marriage. An underlying requirement might be flexibility of working hours – nothing to do with being female or married.

Desirables (nice to haves):

- All "must haves" being met, these may be used to further decide between shortlisted candidates.
- Examples could be knowledge of a particular industry which might be useful to the organisation (outside of the direct job requirement), or extensive activity in the local community, something that might assist in building networks.
- Take care that such considerations are objective, based on organisational requirements, and are non-discriminatory.

Before finalising the person specification, an excellent question to ask is 'Does the target market for this person description exist in sufficient numbers?' For example:

- Is the specification too stringent? Do candidates for a product manager role really require a degree in marketing, over ten years of international blue-chip experience, fluency in four languages, and a qualification in Advanced Statistics?
- Are some of the requirements contradictory and unlikely to exist in one person? How many strategic, big-picture thinkers will want a job that requires them to follow stringent processes methodically, with a high attention to detail?
- Imagine you are the person specified, with all the characteristics you have detailed. Would you want the job? What concerns would you have?

Induction of new staff

Once a new job holder is appointed, you will need to have an induction programme in place to:

- Help them settle in and feel welcome (meet the rest of their colleagues, get to know the organisation etc.).
- Assist them to understand the requirements of their job (go through their job description so that they know exactly what is expected of them).
- Deal with any queries they have.
- Provide them with the development they need to perform their role effectively.

It is essential to have this planned well before they turn up for their first day at work. Their introduction to the organisation and/or their new job will have a big impact on their motivation to perform and their understanding of their work.

Who to induct?

Many companies do not put part-time staff or temporary workers through an induction programme. This is done in the misguided belief that they will not have the same commitment or interest in the organisation. Employers rarely consider that by not putting them through such a programme they are actually contributing to the overall apathy and lack of interest.

All staff should participate in an appropriate induction programme.

What to include in an induction programme

A formal or structured approach is desirable. A lack of systemisation usually leads to confusion and mistakes, leaving the new recruit disappointed with their new post, and so demotivated that they perform poorly.

Good induction programmes should include a follow-up element, and should be reviewed regularly to ensure that the needs of the individual, organisation and management are met.

The following are usually included in an induction programme, which may take place over one day, or perhaps be spread over a number of days, usually during the first month of employment.

- Terms and conditions of employment.
- Structure of the reward system, including wages and benefits, expenses claims.

- Housekeeping and security issues, such as catering facilities and data protection.
- Health and safety regulations.
- Company policies, such as disciplinary and grievance procedures, equal opportunities.
- Training and development opportunities.
- Company profile and its markets; such as its mission statement, history, product markets, communications.
- Job performance issues, such as job description, standards, reporting structure, appraisal and role within the department.

Case Study – How UEA is smartening up it's act

No fewer than 77 pay grades coexist at the University of East Anglia (UEA) – the result of years of piecemeal revisions to terms and conditions. But that will change as the university conducts an institution-wide drive to 'do HR better than ever before'.

Consultants are now helping UEA's Personnel Department to rationalise its current sets of terms and conditions and to incorporate new legal requirements, such as the legislation on parental leave. The Hera job evaluation scheme is central to this process.

The university is currently categorising each member of staff into generic job groups. But this approach is potentially explosive, according to David Baker, vice chancellor of HR and academic infrastructure, who is also a member of the task force set up for "single-table" discussions of role analysis.

'Role analysis by job category is a sensitive issue, because you can find that people are being simultaneously underpaid and overpaid,' he says. 'I expect to see most anomalies in terms of "equal pay for work of equal value" in the academic-related and clerical/secretarial categories. The next difficult issue is the cost of rebalancing grades and pay levels.'

One of the driving forces behind the university's new approach to HR is the need to break down barriers between different groups of staff. For example, the work of senior secretaries sometimes overlaps with that of academic-related staff, but they are often on different pay grades. By removing these artificial distinctions, the university hopes to create greater flexibility and give people more scope to develop.

UEA is also developing a more systematic approach to succession planning, with a view to reducing its reliance on short-term contracts. Under the new system, an employee who has been in a job for six years must be offered an indefinite contract or an alternative strategy must be agreed.

'You hear of people being on a succession of short-term contracts for 20 plus years, but this is a way of not making a commitment to them,' says Baker. 'It's not just about funding – if you can get funding for 20 years you must be committed to the project, if not the person.'

The university is also moving towards mandatory, role-related training for all its staff. Until now, attendance has been largely a matter of individual choice. UEA does not want to lose this voluntary culture entirely, but wants to ensure that those people with significant supervisory or management responsibility receive training in the critical areas of recruitment and selection, health and safety, bullying and harassment awareness, and equal opportunities.

Baker explains: 'We've introduced mandatory equal opportunities training for chairs of selection committees, because sexism can still occur in recruitment decisions.'

If UEA is anything to go by, 2001 should have been a watershed year in higher education.

Source: Extract from article by Carol Glover, "Raising Highbrows", published in *People Management*, 28th June 2001, and reproduced with kind permission.

Questions

1. What has led to the situation that UEA find themselves in now?

2. What are the potential problems facing recruiters?

3. What are the potential problems of providing a succession of short-term contracts to the same person?

SUMMARY OF KEY POINTS

- Effective Human Resource Management (HRM) ensures that the right people are in the right job at the right time.
- At the start of the recruitment process you need to identify the exact vacancy. It is not appropriate to simply recruit like-for-like, as the requirements of the job may have changed.
- A job analysis to produce a job description and person specification must be completed before the job is advertised or job holder sought.
- Ensure that the selection process is appropriately rigorous to check whether the candidates have the desirable qualities needed for the job.
- Select the candidate that best matches the requirements, including all the essential one's.
- Plan an induction programme that enables the candidate to feel part of the organisation, department and team, as well as to understand the requirements of the job, company policies and the reward system.

Improving and developing own learning

The following projects are designed to help you develop your knowledge and skills further, by carrying out some research yourself. Feedback is not provided for this type of learning because there are no "answers" to be found, but you may wish to discuss your findings with colleagues and fellow students.

Project A

Review the recruitment and selection process of your organisation, or one you know well. What suggestions for improvements can you make?

Project B

Find some recent job adverts. In particular look for:

- Posts recently advertised by your own organisation.
- Marketing roles.

> From the adverts, what can you infer about the person specification? What kind of people will be attracted to answer these adverts? Who would not answer the adverts?
>
> If you can, get access to the job description and person specification for the roles (ask for permission from your HR specialist). How well do you think the adverts were targeted? What would you have done differently?

> **Project C**
>
> Review the last induction process you went through. What suggestions for improvements can you make?

Feedback to activities

Activity 6.1 HRM and marketing

Depending on the companies you chose, you may have got some very different answers. For example:

- A bank may want to be seen as helpful, reliable, trustworthy and friendly. This may cause tension with performance management based on sales.
- A fast food company may see itself as efficient, clean, cheap and cheerful. They may see no need to retain staff over the long term, and may rely heavily on part-time and transient staff.

Activity 6.2 What do I do?

Sometimes what we see as the most important parts of our job and what we are setting out to achieve, may differ markedly from other people's views. Seek clarification if you are not sure what your priorities should be.

Activity 6.3 Recruiting marketing managers

A useful search engine is http://www.google.com. Your results will depend on which job sites you found, which countries they were based in, and what search terms you used.

You may have noticed that the job title alone is a poor guide to the amount and extent of management activity required. In addition, searching on a term such as "management" may not be useful on some sites – this can bring up many jobs from junior to senior. Occasionally, employers may be looking for specific management qualifications, such as an MBA. In other cases the experience they specify gives you an indication of the breadth and depth of management skills they are seeking.

Effective management is highly valued by most organisations.

Activity 6.4 Recruiting sales staff

Your investigation might have considered some of the following issues:

How effective is this process? A 50% wastage rate in the first year seems very high, but you would need to know how this compares with other organisations in the same industry and location before drawing any firm conclusions. Likewise for the ratios between replies/interviews/employment. You might also want to know the difference between the number of jobs offered and the number of people employed.

The cost of getting 20 people employed is on average £6,000, or £300 per employee. However:

- New employees make only £50,000 instead of £100,000 in their first year.
- Every employee lost in the first year costs the company a minimum of £51,300 (cost of recruiting and training someone else plus novice status). This is a minimum figure, based on people leaving just as the year is up.

It may therefore be more cost effective to spend more on recruitment and selection, if this will result in increased retention rates. The scope for doing so will depend on how well the company is performing at the moment – a recruitment agency may be able to help with data here. You will have spotted that the data given on retention rates and income generation is far from complete, and you may wish to ask for more detailed information before submitting your conclusions.

You might have concluded that the company should consider some of the following issues:

- The competition. What are the characteristics of the jobs offered by competitors? How do they compare on remuneration, prospects etc.? What is our organisation's positioning?
- The initial recruitment marketing. Are we attracting the right people for the job?

Is there a mismatch? It seems perhaps that we are employing people who are always seeking new challenges and to learn, to do a repetitive job with little development prospects.

- The selection procedures:
    - CV/Application screening. Are the right factors being used? What would the impact of using more stringent criteria be? Would telephone interviewing be useful?
    - Interviewing. Do candidates match the person specification? Would an assessment centre for shortlisted candidates be appropriate?
    - Would psychometric testing be a useful adjunct to the interview procedure?
- Staff induction, training, and other experiences on the job. What reasons are people giving for leaving?

Depending on your findings, you might consider piloting some of these ideas in the next campaign. For example, several different ways of screening CVs could be piloted alongside the present methods, and interview performance then compared with the results.

Activity 6.5 Job descriptions

The results of this will differ from organisation to organisation. You may have discovered the information under different headings, or that some of the information is in different places from the job description itself. This activity will have given you the opportunity to think carefully about your own job and the expectations of you and your employer.

Session 7

Effective teams

Introduction

This Session provides an introduction to teams and their development. Marketing managers will work in a number of teams – some of them permanent and others temporary (such as a project team). Some teams work better than others, and this Session explores some of the reasons why.

The final section discusses conflict and considers what to do when disagreements arise and things go wrong between individuals and within groups.

> **LEARNING OUTCOMES**
>
> At the end of this Session you will be able to:
>
> - Discuss the factors affecting team performance and effectiveness.
> - Understand how to set plans to improve team performance.
> - Identify preferred team roles.
> - Recognise how to deal with inter- and intra-group conflicts.

What is a team?

A team is a collection of individuals who actively work and interact together to meet a shared, common purpose.

- A rugby team during a match.
- An orchestra during a performance.
- A project team working to stage an exhibition.
- A sales team seeking to maximise their collective sales effort.

Teams are often fluid – they can form, dissolve and reform. For example, former freelance members of an orchestra can still be identified as a group, but are not however a team (see Figure 7.1 overleaf).

While a team always consists of a group of individuals, a group may not necessarily be a team. Groups may be defined by any common characteristic:

- People who like blue flowers.

- People who have birthdays in January.
- Marketing professionals.

Figure 7.1 Difference between a group and a team

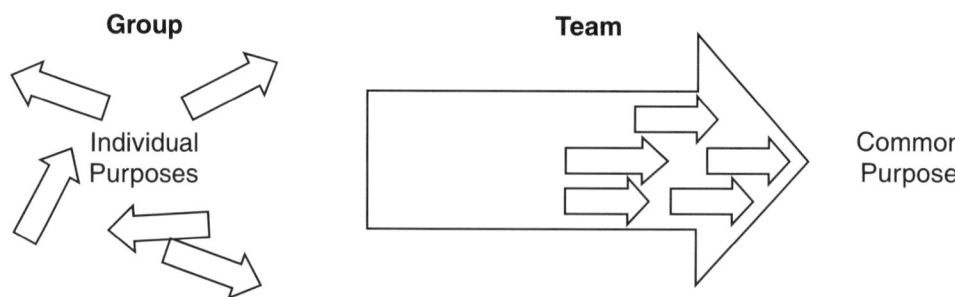

Benefits of effective teams

In theory at least, a team that is working effectively can achieve far more than a group of individuals can for the organisation.

- Depending on the task at hand, the team can self-organise itself for the best results. For example, leadership can change depending on the person with the most experience in that area.
- Team members can support each other during difficult situations.
- Team members learn from each other, supplementing and extending their own skills through sharing activities.
- Teams provide a means of gathering an extensive range of skills to bear on an issue. This can result in more innovative and wider ranging solutions than you would get from one individual. They are able to solve more complex problems than an individual working on their own.

As can be appreciated, there are also benefits for the individual, including social, learning and developmental benefits, which stem from being part of a successful and well-organised team. Some of these benefits (together with the fact that humans are naturally social animals) are behind the formation of informal teams, which can develop without the direct intervention of a manager.

Less desirable characteristics can also emerge in teams, such as working to a common purpose that is to the detriment of the organisation; creating unhelpful attitudes and behaviours that are imposed as the norm (change is unwelcome); shared responsibility comes to mean no-one takes responsibility. These need to be taken account of in both formal and informal teams. Some individuals may also see teams as a threat to their own autonomy and status.

Team processes

One useful model for looking at the way a team develops from a group of individuals is through the stages of forming, storming, norming and performing (Tuckman, 1965).

Figure 7.2 Forming, storming, norming and performing

Forming	Group comes together for the first time to learn about their shared purpose. Strong directional leadership is required, as individuals need a lot of information at this stage.
Storming	People begin to question their role and others contributions, and generally try to achieve more of what they want. Strong leadership is needed to unite them as a team, so it becomes cohesive.
Norming	Everyone is committed to the common goals and works together to achieve them. A strong sense of shared values exists, and people understand what is expected of them in terms of behaviour and contribution of skills and knowledge.
Performing	Effective collaboration is the norm, with people undertaking their own roles flexibly. Everyone is learning from the experience and the team is able to improve its performance.

As with any model, although useful, it needs to be used in the knowledge that it is not reality. Bear in mind that:

- Teams may move from one stage to another and back again very fast. For example, if a performing team loses one of its members, even temporarily, it may revert to storming, as the group needs to re-evaluate its interactions.

- All of the stages contain some necessary activity that builds the foundation for, and allows progression to, the next stage. If you believe you have joined a team that has gone directly to performing, it is likely that it is in fact still in the forming stage, with much still unresolved.

A fifth stage was added to the above model at a later date and refers to the break up of a team termed adjourning or sometimes called the mourning stage. The importance of this stage is often underestimated and neglected. When a team has ended its life, it is important to build in some sort of activity that allows people to celebrate its success and let it go e.g. award giving, ceremonial disposal of papers, a celebratory meal.

By understanding team processes a team leader can more effectively support the group at whatever stage it is at, enabling them to move onto the next stage.

Team effectiveness

Team effectiveness will be affected by:

- The extent to which a common purpose is clear.
- The extent to which the team is effectively organised to meet its intended purpose.
- The extent to which the team contains the necessary constituent elements (team roles, ASK factors).
- The effectiveness of team interactional processes, often referred to as group dynamics.

It is not possible to assess effectiveness by only observing team processes.

- A team that seems to be happy and to get a lot done may in fact be suppressing conflict and tolerating underperformance. For example, they may be "stuck" in the norming stage, and are actually running the team for the individuals rather than to meet the team's intended purpose.
- A team that is performing well may have an inappropriate purpose. For example, a marketing team might put all its efforts into ensuring beautifully produced advertising and literature – for products that customers no longer want!

Shared team SMART objectives and measurement of results are critical in promoting and monitoring team effectiveness. If team members do not know what they are trying to achieve, or how to measure progress, they may become disinterested in what they are doing.

> **Activity 7.1 Teams**
>
> Identify two different teams you belong to, such as a work team, a club, or a society.
>
> 1. To what extent does each one meet the definition of a team?
> 2. What stage do you think they are at? (From forming through to adjourning.)
> 3. How effective is the team?
>
> Find someone in each team to discuss these questions with, preferably someone who you think is quite different to you, either because of their role or because you tend to have different perspectives. Explain the definitions and issues to them, and then ask them for their assessment before you discuss yours. What differences in perception are there?

Team leadership

Effective leadership is essential in improving team performance. A model that is particularly useful in considering and planning improvements to team leadership is John Adair's Action Centred Leadership model. This is based on the need for leaders to have concern for three areas:

- Maintaining and developing the team.
- Taking account of individual needs.
- Achieving the tasks required to fulfil the common purpose.

These different areas are mutually supportive. Managers need to recognise and plan how to balance these three areas, ensuring that they support each other. At different times one or the other may come to the fore.

- A focus on the task may be perfectly appropriate coming up to a deadline. It then needs to be balanced with attention to individuals and the team.
- When forming a team, individual needs for acceptance and motivation towards the team purpose require a focus on the individual.

Identifying scope for performance improvements

Teams need to be encouraged to plan stretching objectives, to increase their performance not merely maintain it.

Teams may over or underperform due to any number of different factors, and interventions may focus on any one or more of Adair's team, task and individual areas. Effective planning and monitoring of performance and potential improvements involves:

- Monitoring how the team is operating, e.g. timing of move from one group process stage to the next, percentage of deadlines met, quality of work, quality of team interaction.
- Monitoring the actual results achieved when compared with the SMART objectives set for the team.

A balance needs to be struck between ensuring effective and early identification of issues and swamping the team with measures. Equally, a balance is required between how the team is operating (which may lead the results), and the results themselves. The bigger the team the more formal the performance monitoring systems are required.

One of the most effective ways to identify the areas that can be improved (or need to be improved) is by harnessing the ideas and thoughts of the team members. Encouraging and rewarding openness is critical, or issues may get pushed underground, only to surface again when it is too late to do anything but crisis manage.

Team, task and individual interventions are discussed below.

Planning team interventions

Team interventions cover a number of areas, and the ideas in Sessions 8, 9 and 10 on the management of motivation, performance, and training and development, also apply here. Having decided what specifically the intervention needs to achieve, and by when, there are a number of options for team intervention:

- Facilitate the team to come up with the solution. This has the considerable advantage that members automatically buy-in to the solution.
- Wait and see if the system will right itself, giving yourself deadlines for intervening if nothing changes. This only works if the team is aware of an issue (which they may be if there is clear setting and sharing of outcomes and

SMART objectives). Sometimes the need for control can cause a manager to intervene too early and too hard.

- Actively facilitate team development exercises to support team skills development. Often this is best introduced by an outside, skilled facilitator, as they are seen to be independent.

Planning task interventions

Organisation and reorganisation of the work is critical to the success of the team. While the principles of time management covered in Session 4 apply, additional project and process management skills are required to:

- Breakdown the overall goal into sub-goals, processes, activities and tasks, taking account of the interdependencies.
- Plan and allocate work between the team.
- Put in control measures to ensure progress and task completion.
- Plan appropriate measurement, monitoring and review.

Again, well-facilitated teams can be very effective in identifying and implementing task interventions.

Planning individual interventions

Intervening to improve individual motivation to increase performance is discussed in the next Session. In terms of meeting individual needs, the team manager will undertake actions such as praising, developing, listening to individuals and helping solve their problems.

Activity 7.2 Task, team and individual

1. Imagine you are coaching a new team leader, who will be leading a team planning an exhibition. While they have encountered John Adair's model before, they want an example of how they might use it in planning their approach with the team. Set out a table that could be used in discussion with the team leader on how over-reliance on team, task or individual might undermine the delivery of the exhibition. Over concern in one area may lead to neglect in another.

2. What else might you do to ensure their success in applying this model?

What is a team role?

In social science, a role is defined as a pattern of behaviours adopted by an individual that is based upon knowledge about the role, for example, its responsibilities. This Companion has already discussed what the role of a manager is, and hence the pattern of behaviour that a person undertaking that role will perform, such as planning, facilitating, deciding, communicating, organising. You will also have some expectations about the role of a marketer.

For those involved in a work team, there are additional behaviours that are important for it to function effectively (e.g. challenging ideas, ensuring the group keeps on task, diffusing tension), which fall outside of people's formal roles where expectations are often based on job titles. People have different preferences as to which pattern of behaviour they exhibit, and as a team develops through the storming stage, members will negotiate for, and learn their roles (this process is called role differentiation). For example, you may know people who habitually take on the behaviours to:

- Criticise ideas.
- Resolve conflict.
- Keep the group on topic.
- Draw quiet people out.
- Tell jokes when everything is getting tense.

There is a lot of research covering team roles and their impact on team effectiveness. The next section is going to concentrate on that of one researcher, Dr. R. Meredith Belbin, as his approach has been practically applied and is often used in management training.

Belbin's team roles

Belbin's team roles cover all the behaviours his research suggested were important in contributing to team performance. They are clustered into roles based on which behaviours tend to occur together in individuals.

The team roles identified by Belbin are:

- **Co-ordinator** (used to be called the Chair), who ensures everyone understands what needs to be achieved and encourages participation by all.
- **Shaper**, who acts as a driver, urging other members to complete a task, especially when deadlines are approaching.

- **Plant**, who comes up with lots of ideas about what should happen, but tends to leave others to develop them.
- **Completer/finisher**, who is meticulous about detail, so ensures that the team considers every option from all angles.
- **Resource investigator**, who is a good networker both internally and externally to the organisation.
- **Monitor/evaluator**, who is the team's critic and stops it reaching too hasty a decision.
- **Team worker**, who works hard to ensure that people work in harmony.
- **Implementer** (used to be called the company worker), who is a practical person who likes to look at how to achieve the task.

A ninth role, the **Specialist**, may or may not be present. This person contributes specialist knowledge and expertise, so may only be a temporary member. Teams do not need eight or nine members to be effective, as most people can take on more than one role according to the current strengths and weaknesses of the team.

Belbin's research suggested that problems in a team tend to occur when there is a lack of balance of roles, such as:

- Too many people competing for the same role. Several of Belbin's "shapers" may spend a lot of time challenging each other.
- No one taking on behaviours that are crucial to the team. If there is no "team worker" this may result in inter-team conflicts taking over from the task in hand.

People will have different preferences for Belbin's roles. As well as reading about the typical behaviour characteristic of each role, there are diagnostic instruments available that can help identify an individual's preferred role. Some people will be able to comfortably display a wider range of roles than others.

Implications

Considering team roles has implications for managers when they are:

- Building a team. If you select a team based only on specific skills that on paper look more than sufficient to complete the task, then the team may still struggle to perform. How well would a project team perform if they have no one interested in turning the ideas into reality and getting them completed to a high quality?

- Improving team performance. By identifying their preferred roles and discussing the implications, a team may be able to identify gaps and overlaps, and therefore renegotiate their roles. This could be used early on to facilitate the Storming stage.
- Improving individual flexibility and effectiveness. By understanding your own preferred (and least preferred) roles, you can identify development activity which will enable you to take on at least one other role effectively, and learn to value and look out for contributions from others in the team.

Activity 7.3 Team effectiveness

A colleague is starting working with a new marketing team, and knowing that you are undertaking a marketing qualification, has asked you for information on factors that affect team effectiveness. Write a memo outlining some of the main factors that your colleague should consider. You may wish to refer back to the background reading for this Session before undertaking this activity.

Activity 7.4 Virtual teams

Virtual teams are used more and more in organisations, yet many of the established theories and approaches are based on observations of teams that are physically present with each other.

Research the topic of virtual team processes and team roles using the Internet.

What implications does this research have for your organisation, either now (if it is using virtual teams) or in the future?

Conflict as a trigger for change

All managers need to be able to identify and deal with conflict, whether between themselves and colleagues, between members of their team, or with customers. Conflict can occur in many situations, such as when:

- A customer complains that their product arrived late and was not to the specification promised by the salesman.
- Members of a team have opposing views on a new product launch.

Effective teams

- In a team meeting one individual ignores or puts down another colleague's ideas, whilst being constructive about suggestions put forward by others.

Without conflict in some form, there would be few triggers for change, and individuals and organisations would become complacent and moribund. The best approach is to deal with conflict constructively, and see it as an opportunity to learn.

Identifying hidden or latent conflict

Ignoring signals that there may be an issue can result in a more significant problem. Signals can range from someone shifting in their chair during a meeting yet not contributing, to a previously articulate employee becoming uncommunicative.

Figure 7.3 Consequences of hidden conflict

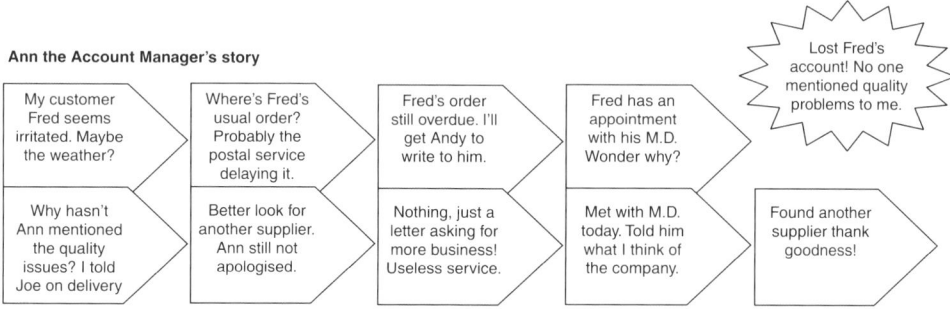

In the example above, if Ann had acted on the signals her customer sent out she could not only have strengthened her relationship with Fred, but also assisted the company in resolving quality issues for all its customers. Complaints are often a way of strengthening relationships if they are handled well.

Making yourself aware of subtle yet significant changes in behaviour from others is an important skill. Raising what you have observed tactfully, and if appropriate, privately with the individual(s) involved will become more natural with practise. As with any feedback:

- Comment on what you have observed without making judgements.
- State your concern that this behaviour may be the result of an unresolved issue, which may be significant for the organisation/your team/your working relationship. If it can't affect any of these, don't raise it.
- Listen carefully to the response, and question further (if appropriate) to gather more information.

Responses to conflict

For the manager who wishes to avoid rather than deal with conflict, ignoring the signals and hoping the issue will go away is only one of several options open to them. Other common approaches are:

- Imposing their preferred view because after all they are the manager.
- Giving way to people who seem to feel very strongly, so as to keep the peace.

As well as potentially causing problems of low morale and encouraging submissive or domineering behaviour (depending on the approach), the problem with all these responses is that they do not address the question "What is best for the organisation?" and "Is there a solution to this problem which meets everyone's needs?". By avoiding conflict, the manager is denying the opportunity to ensure that changes will benefit the organisation and the individuals within it. They are also potentially driving conflict underground and storing up problems for later on.

Managers need to develop the skill of standing back from an issue, listening and questioning to understand all perspectives, and then facilitate a problem-solving approach. These are the same skills already described in the "Negotiation Skills" section, under the "win-win" collaborative approach.

Mediating or facilitating conflict

For an optimal solution to be found, it is imperative that each perspective (or model) of a situation is understood and fully explored. For a simple issue this can just be a discussion between two people who then resolve the problem. However, depending on the individuals involved and the significance of the issue, it may be useful to have a third party to facilitate. For example, if a marketing team has different views on a new pricing strategy then a facilitator might:

- Ask for all the facts to be put on the table, with no judgements on their meaning.
- Get the team to agree on a set of criteria against which they will judge the options.

- Get the team to brainstorm all the possible strategies, and then narrow them down to the main options.
- Taking each option in turn, get the team to act as if they are 100% behind it and then 100% against it, recording all their responses against the criteria the team agreed.
- Facilitate the team to decide on the option that best meets their agreed criteria.

Activity 7.5 Conflict management

How do your colleagues deal with conflict?

Identify three colleagues in your organisation who are willing to talk to you about their approach to conflict, and about their views on the way the organisation handles conflict. Prepare your agenda and questions beforehand, and then either:

a. Hold interviews with each of them privately.

b. Hold one meeting with all of them.

Also answer the questions yourself (or get a colleague to interview you using your agenda and questions). If you are not in an organisation, select three of your contacts.

From your interviews, what observations can you make about:

1. The range of approaches taken by your colleagues.
2. The approaches to conflict in the organisation.
3. Actions that you think the organisation could take to encourage more effective handling of conflict.
4. Actions that you could take to improve your own approach to conflict, incorporating these into your personal development plan.

Role of conflict relating to groups

Conflict tends to arise when people believe that their goals are not aligned, and that by meeting one goal it will compromise others. In groups there are two main types of conflict to be managed:

- **Intra-group conflict**, where the conflict arises between members of the same group, such as:
  - A team member challenging a decision to reduce the number of product features available.
  - Half a group wanting to launch a service immediately, whilst the other half wants to wait.
- **Inter-group conflict**, where two different groups are not aligned, such as:
  - Operations believing that the sales team do not take account of costs when agreeing to special customer orders.
  - The sales team believing that operations are intransigent and inflexible.

As stated earlier, conflict can be a trigger for change, such as when it allows a team to move into and through the storming stage. However, it is also possible for unhealthy levels of conflict to arise, e.g. if the conflict is interfering with meeting organisational goals effectively, or if it remains unresolved. Managers need to think of conflict in relation to how it is serving or blocking effectiveness – it can do either or both.

Group decision making – why conflict is important

There are two group processes known as "**groupthink**" and "**group polarisation**", which help to illustrate why an element of conflict is important in improving the quality of group decision making. Note that these processes work at a subconscious level; they are not related to people's skills and abilities.

Groupthink (Janis, 1977) arises when groups make decisions prematurely, when they have not yet found all the available options or evaluated them fully. In a group that is at the norming stage, people may conform rather than raise concerns. Those who do raise concerns may be quashed by the rest of the group. Janis investigated groupthink in top-level teams and found that a number of factors contributed to their inability to make decisions. One alarming reason was that they became convinced of their own "superiority" and tended to filter out information that appeared "negative" or contradictory to their own views.

Group polarisation arises when groups make more extreme decisions than those an individual would make. If a group largely agrees on an issue, then their individual views become more and more united in favour as the discussion progresses. So a group of high-risk takers will make an even more risky decision, and a group of cautious individuals will make an even more cautious decision!

To make the most of individual contributions, and to ensure that the quality of group thinking is greater than the sum of its parts, it is important to combat these tendencies by introducing conflict:

- Ensure that a range of different opinions are represented, perhaps by bringing in an outsider to the group, or by asking a group member to take the role of someone opposed to the prevailing view, and of course by valuing different opinions.
- Keep the group very highly focused on its organisational purpose, so that this is embedded as their highest priority rather than interpersonal relationships.
- Although introducing conflict goes directly against many people's natural tendencies to want to surround themselves with like-minded individuals, managers must make the effort to include a range of viewpoints.

Unhealthy intra-group conflict

This can arise when the goals of individuals start to come into conflict with each other and with the goals of the group:

- Review Session 5 for ways of resolving conflict through negotiation.
- Sometimes such conflict may have been inadvertently introduced by the organisation.
  - Reward structures based on individual performance may result only in unhealthy competition. If no one is going to be rewarded for team performance then it obviously isn't important.
  - Two people going for a promotion may believe that unless they are seen to take the role of a "shaper" they will miss out.

Inter-group conflict

Such conflict may actually have positive consequences:

- Sales teams competing with each other (so long as they are not poaching each other's customers) may achieve more by being challenged in this way.
- Balancing different objectives, such as those of sales and operations, can result in better customer service, provided that both groups recognise they are contributing to a higher common goal on behalf of the organisation.

However, if the conflict is to the detriment of organisational goals then again the matter needs to be resolved. The type of intervention used will depend on the circumstances:

- Misunderstandings between individuals may just require a face-to-face meeting with open, honest dialogue.
- Personality clashes may require outside intervention to resolve if all other avenues have been explored.
- The issue may be treated as being "owned" by both groups involved (such as in a clash between operations and sales), and a joint facilitated meeting focused on understanding and problem solving may be the most appropriate course of action.

Activity 7.6 Conflicts with customers

Identify some recent conflicts between your organisation and its customers, such as customer complaints or clashes with consumer groups. For each one:

- What was the history of the conflict?
- What negative consequences did it have?
- What positive consequences did it have and for whom?
- Once resolved, will/was the organisation better or worse off than if the conflict had not arisen? Are the groups or individuals involved better or worse off? By how much?

How much do you think customer complaints are worth to your organisation? Are you gaining maximum value from them (e.g. in triggering learning and change in your organisation)?

Case Study – Managing mergers: the people issues

Mergers, acquisitions, buy-ins or buy-outs continue with growing frequency. Research shows that many of their desired benefits do not materialise, whilst the costs of integration are usually underestimated.

The most frequently cited reasons for poor results are people related. During the acquisition phase, most deals focus on financial, legal and sometimes technical or marketing factors, but rarely on the human issues.

In 1999 the total value of cross-border mergers and acquisitions reached over 1.1 trillion dollars, a tenfold increase in eight years (source: UN 2000). The OECD says that this often does not actually yield any benefits, owing to the costs of merging different organisational cultures. To address this, merging companies need to consider developing a process for post-merger integration, which focuses on the human aspects of the organisation. The aim is to ensure that all facets of people's roles and contributions to the organisation are thoroughly investigated, within the context of the emerging business strategy.

Before the merger this includes culture, climate and communications, competence (the quality of skills, leadership and teamwork) and the management of core information and data.

After the merger, the new organisation needs to assess candidates to create new teams and set up team building events; carry out a cultural analysis, roll out a new vision, values, culture and strategy; and further develop competency profiles and appraisal processes.

Compensation and benefits will need to be integrated and new Human Resource (HR) strategies and policies put into place. Support for the HR function itself should be considered. Lastly, there is likely to be an outplacement programme to manage. In everything that is done, internal communications are crucial.

Many companies have achieved significant improvements to mergers by adopting some of these ideas. But, as yet, no organisation has adopted an entirely integrated approach.

The number and value of mergers is growing rapidly, particularly in cross-border acquisitions within the European Union. There were 195 deals completed in the UK in 2000. Yet a recent survey of 58 mergers in the UK found that only 14 had considered cultural issues before the purchase decision was made.

Source: Effective Management for Marketing examination paper, December, 2001. Adapted from *People Management*.

Questions

You are the Marketing Manager for a car manufacturing company that is considering merging with another car manufacturer (in the same country). Your Chief Executive has read the above article and is concerned about how this merger can be managed successfully. He has asked you to set out your ideas about how to create new marketing teams across the new organisation and set up team building events. Write some notes for yourself, prior to a meeting with the Chief Executive.

SUMMARY OF KEY POINTS

- Teams are different to groups in that they work towards a common, shared purpose (goals/objectives), and they need to interact effectively to achieve a performance that is greater than the sum of the individual parts (synergy).
- Teams go through stages in their development, which include the forming, storming, norming and performing stages. A fifth stage termed adjourning refers to team break up.
- Balanced teams (according to Belbin) are more effective because they hold all the behaviours that enable teams to solve problems effectively and make good decisions.
- There are many factors influencing the effectiveness of teams, including knowledge of shared goals, effective leadership, balance of team roles, knowledge and skills, and commitment to the task.
- Virtual teams have little opportunity to meet face to face, but this is very important at key stages, such as at the beginning and at significant achievement points.
- Conflict can be a positive force triggering change.
- Mediators and facilitators may be required to resolve conflict in teams and between teams.

Improving and developing own learning

The following projects are designed to help you develop your knowledge and skills further, by carrying out some research yourself. Feedback is not provided for this type of learning because there are no "answers" to be found, but you may wish to discuss your findings with colleagues and fellow students.

Project A

Review what stage of development your team is at. How can you move forward?

Identify team roles (according to Belbin) and evaluate how "balanced" the team appears to be.

Effective teams

> **Project B**
>
> Observe different teams at work. What factors influence their effectiveness and what prevents them from performing well?

> **Project C**
>
> If you are able to, sit in with a facilitator as they work with a team to solve a problem or identify the issues that are hindering performance. Facilitators, due to their neutral position, are often used at meetings between representatives from different organisations, where problems with projects need to be resolved.

Feedback to activities

Activity 7.1 Teams

1. You will probably have considered:

   - Whether the group had a common, shared purpose.
   - Whether they are interacting co-operatively or working as individuals.

2. Your assessment will be dependent upon the behaviours you have observed. Sometimes people are surprised at the answer they have, as it differs from their expectations.

Stage	Example behaviours
Forming	- Politeness and suspicion. - Getting to know people. - Finding out what is expected of individuals, and of the team. - Looking for direction from the senior member of the team. - Self positioning e.g. statements of ability.

Stage	Example behaviours
Storming	- Competition. - Arguments. - Challenges. - Staking claims. - Forming alliances and factions.
Norming	- Emergence of group values and beliefs. - Tendency to defend "the team" – staking out the team's territory. - Emergence of accepted behaviours e.g. taking turns to make the tea, in-jokes and jargon. - Established relationships and roles.
Performing	- All behaviour directed towards team results and learning how to improve results. - Co-coaching and facilitating. - Flexibly adopt different roles depending on circumstances e.g. leadership changes. - Challenge each other and the team constructively and openly.
Adjourning	- Loss of purpose and direction. - Referring to past successes. - Hanging on as long as possible.

3. To answer this question, you would have needed to know what the outcome of the team was meant to be. Did you?

You may have got some interesting insights from comparing your answers with those of other team members. Differences in attitudes and perceptions, and differences in when you have had an opportunity to observe, are all relevant. A third party observing the team from the outside might have had other observations. For example, it is common for a team to think they are Performing, when in fact they are Norming, particularly where they do not have clear outcomes and results.

Activity 7.2 Task, team and individual

1. One way of doing this is as follows. You may have come up with additional points and ideas. The example of preparing for an exhibition is used to highlight potential results of over-concern and neglect.

Area	Over-concern may result in:	Neglect may result in:
Task	■ Dictatorial management; direction remains unchallenged. ■ No interaction – team doesn't get past forming. ■ Individuals are unsupported and unhappy, and mistakes are made. Result: Exhibition uninspired and dull.	■ Team gradually subverts purpose for their own ends. ■ Team never gets past norming, deadlines are missed, and work is sloppy. ■ Individuals are bored and underperform. Team members leave. Result: Exhibition is poorly realised.
Team	■ Team processes are excellent. However, there is little concern for the task and deadlines are missed. ■ Individuals do not develop. Result: Exhibition is just in time and rather slapdash.	■ Individuals follow their own agendas at the expense of colleagues. Mistakes are made as no one is interested in supporting each other. ■ Team never performs. Arguments and blame interfere with the task in hand. Result: Exhibition gets done on time, but no one speaks to each other again!

Area	Over-concern may result in:	Neglect may result in:
Individual	■ Tackling individual needs even where this severely interferes with the team and the work in hand. ■ Team stuck at forming. ■ Deadlines missed. Result: Exhibition is delayed.	■ Individual goals and aspirations are ignored, so people never feel inspired to meet team goals. ■ People leave, get sick, etc. Result: Exhibition is delayed.

2. In practice, you would want to develop the discussion with the team leader to get them to plan what they will do to appropriately use team, task, individual to manage their team.

If they only know what they don't want to do, they may concentrate on avoiding it rather than on applying the model and achieving positive results. Alternatively, if you had only shown them how it could help, they might not be sufficiently motivated to apply it. Negative consequences can be a useful motivating factor for some.

You want to ensure you leave the team leader with a plan of what they want to do, hence you would always carry out this coaching session by presenting the negative consequences first and then introducing the positive aspects.

Activity 7.3 Team effectiveness

MEMO

To: J. Slack
Brand Manager

From: R. Fletcher
Marketing Manager

Date: 4th November 2002

Subject: Factors affecting team effectiveness

Good luck with your new team! I am sure that you are equal to the challenge. You asked about the factors that can influence the effectiveness and performance of teams. In my opinion the main factors include:

- **Sharing a common understanding of purpose, objectives and approach.** Everyone must understand what the team needs to achieve, the individual contributions that must be made, what the long-term goals and short-term targets are, and the manner in which the team will operate. In addition, everyone must feel mutually accountable – in other words only the team succeeds or fails, there is an absence of a blame culture.
- **Group size.** The smallest number of team members that contain the range of knowledge and skills you require is most likely to solve problems and make decisions quickly. Optimum size depends on the nature of the work.
- **Group cohesiveness.** If the team "gels" then conflict will be positive and will produce constructive debate not defensiveness and disagreement. Groups that become too cohesive may develop groupthink (Janis 1977).
- **Member characteristics.** Belbin suggests eight team roles that need to be present if management teams are to produce results. These are: co-ordinator or chair; team worker; implementer or company worker; plant to generate ideas; monitor/evaluator, to prevent the team from making hasty decisions; resource investigator, who is a good networker with useful contacts outside the team; shaper, who drives the team to meet deadlines; and completer/finisher, who ensures relevant details are not overlooked. An optional member is the specialist, who may be present due to their particular expert knowledge.
- **Member commitment.** Your project team may contain people who are part of more than one team, so suffer from conflict of interests. They may find it difficult to prioritise activities or meet deadlines.
- **Level of face-to-face interaction, particularly in fast moving environments.** When priorities change rapidly it is useful for teams to be able to meet frequently to discuss any problems relating to this and to reorganise responsibilities. Some teams, such as international project teams, are separated by distance and time, but it is still important for them to meet face to face.
  - At the start of the project to "form, storm and norm".
  - At milestones or critical points in the project to ensure they continue to perform.
  - At the end to celebrate success and learn from the experience.

I understand that you may be faced with this situation later in the project.

- **Leadership.** Your style must be aligned with the situation. The leader needs to be strong but fair and willing to listen. Appropriate styles range from tell and sell, through consultative, to delegation and empowerment.

There are many other factors that influence effectiveness, such as the nature and importance of the task, the availability of resources, the ability of the team to communicate with other parts of the organisation, and the way in which the company recognises and rewards team success.

In my experience, teams need to be presented with a significant challenge if they are to become high-performing teams. In addition, they must perceive value in what they do. If no one cares if they succeed or fail then commitment and motivation are likely to be low and people will concentrate on more important individual tasks.

I hope the above is useful. I look forward to hearing from you about how things are going. Once again, good luck!

Activity 7.4 Virtual teams

Your findings will depend on the sites you used. Try using the search engine http://www.google.com. Just typing in "virtual team" results in a lot of useful links. If you add "roles" as an extra search term (and then add "processes" instead) it will bring different sites to the top of your list.

One of the main themes revolves around explicit agreements and clarity being even more crucial for virtual teams than face-to-face teams. It is much harder to identify and negotiate misunderstandings than it is when you are present with each other. Some of the points you might have found are:

- Making the purpose extremely clear.
- Making people's roles and reporting explicit.
- The impact the working environment has. How will you structure online interaction? What group norms are you encouraging?
- How you facilitate group processes. Reverting to a group rather than a team is a risk.
- Best practice for electronic communication. What may have been meant as a joke or as constructive feedback, may be taken badly by the recipient. As you can't see their face or hear their voice, how will you know?

Activity 7.5 Conflict management

You may have included different items in your agenda, depending on your interests and concerns. One approach within an organisation would be:

Agenda

1. Introduction

   Explanation of purpose of interview/meeting, plus agreement to confidentiality of information given (10 minutes).

2. Approach to conflict situations

   What conflicts have you been involved in recently? For each of these (take up to three) what happened? How was the approach effective? What could have made it more effective?

3. Cultural Norms

   How do you believe conflict is usually dealt with in your area? What seems to be the accepted way of handling conflict in your area? What are the differences (if any) between the way your area and other areas of the organisation handle conflict? What are the similarities (if any) between the way your area handles conflict compared to other areas of the organisation? What would be an unacceptable or unexpected way of handling conflict in your area? In the rest of the organisation?

4. Summarise and close.

You may notice that sometimes someone's memories of an event differ considerably from what actually did happen. They may remember it differently from how it happened, or they may want to show themselves in the best light (consciously or unconsciously), so your findings may not be entirely accurate.

You only interviewed a small sample of people, so it would be inadvisable to draw definite conclusions from this sample. As you begin to notice the handling of conflict in the future, you may well find differences between what you observe and what was said at the interviews – and indeed how you answered the questions yourself!

Activity 7.6 Conflicts with customers

Here is an example for a hypothetical customer and organisation. The mental model which organisations use to deal with customer complaints can have a big impact on their success with dealing with them.

1. Situation: a customer buys a vegetarian meal and finds meat inside. The customer complains to the store and head office, and the store gives vouchers out of the till immediately, the product is recalled, and the customer later gets sent a cheque. The store does not require the customer to write a letter; instead it takes over the complaint on their behalf.

2. The customer lost faith in the product. The organisation paid out £50 per customer affected (£1,000), and the retail price of all the destroyed faulty goods amounted to £4,000. Much of this was passed on to the supplier.

3. The organisation got the product off the shelf quickly. Because of this only twenty customers were affected, hence limiting the organisation's losses. Most customers were very happy with the compensation (which far outweighed the value of the product), and the timely response by the store impressed them. The satisfied customers told others about the good service, so the organisation's reputation was slightly increased or at least left intact. The supplier tightened up its processes, so a by-product was less overall wastage and reduced costs.

4. In the longer term, the organisation was better off:

    - Better processes by the supplier resulted in reduced costs. Those savings passed on to the organisation amounted to £2,500 per annum.
    - The issue helped reduce the risk of similar incidents in the future.
    - The customer's early warning significantly reduced the losses from the incident.
    - The affected customers actually bought more than before, and told their friends. The organisation's reputation went up amongst this group.

The organisation valued its customer complaints, and reduced the barriers to making any complaints. Barriers to customer complaints cost some organisations a lot of money. Consider how the impact might have been different if the store had refused to do anything without a letter from the customer.

Session 8

Managing motivation

Introduction

This Session explores motivation and job satisfaction. There is no direct link between the two – highly motivated people do not necessarily achieve high levels of job satisfaction and vice versa. In addition, what motivates one person will be different for another, but the theories that are explored indicate how managers can identify important drivers that can be used to encourage people to work more enthusiastically.

The different theories of motivation are briefly described, with examples given to help marketers understand what they mean in the work place. As a marketing manager, you can use the discussion used in this Session to help you create a work place environment where people are encouraged to give of their best.

> ### LEARNING OUTCOMES
> At the end of this Session you will be able to:
> - Discuss the factors that contribute to individual motivation and job satisfaction.
> - Explain the theories that underpin the motivation of individuals.
> - Identify how to plan to motivate individuals.

What is motivation?

When people do something, like writing a report, there is a cause. There is a force that impels them to work towards a goal and sustains their action until the goal is reached. This force is referred to as "motivation". The different theories of motivation that seek to explain this hypothetical force begin in different places:

- Inbuilt drivers and needs, which cause people to seek out certain experiences.
- How jobs are designed.
- The consequences of people's behaviours.
- The way people make decisions.

In this search, theorists and researchers have been more or less successful. However, whilst providing useful insights and guidance into what influences work motivation, there has been no absolute truth discovered. Different people are motivated by different forces at different times. The factors affecting their motivation are many and varied and may be deep-rooted.

Motivating by satisfying needs

Maslow's hierarchy of needs model is well known. It ranges from the lower order needs, such as survival and security needs, through to the social needs of self-esteem and self-actualisation. Maslow states that people are motivated by attempting to satisfy distinct sets of needs, the importance of which are driven by how well they are being satisfied at the moment, and where they are on a hierarchy.

- Most people will not be motivated by a set of needs unless they have reasonable satisfaction in the set immediately below them. Extreme hunger or thirst may make your performance in a meeting seem rather irrelevant. Lower order needs must be satisfied first.

- The hierarchy is based on Maslow's experience with his patients, and has not been rigorously validated. Later researchers (such as Alderfer) have challenged its assumptions, particularly whether there is actually a hierarchy.

McClelland's achievement motivation theory proposes that there are three important needs for work motivation: affiliation, power and achievement. He proposes that the mix is different for each individual, and that the highest motivation is seen when the needs of the job match the motivational needs of the individual.

Herzberg's research was based on job satisfaction. What causes people to be satisfied or dissatisfied? He came up with two factors (hence his "two-factor" theory):

- Factors which, if not present, will cause dissatisfaction (hygienes), related to working context e.g. salary, working environment.

- Factors which, if present, will cause satisfaction (motivators), associated with performing the work e.g. achievement, development opportunities.

Further research has not tended to support Herzberg's findings, in particular the case for two distinct factor types. One person may be highly motivated by the thought of getting a better chair, whilst another may think this is irrelevant, unless they have an uncomfortable chair, in which case the second person may well be dissatisfied not motivated.

Job design

Other models such as the **job characteristics model** (Hackman and Oldman) have also pointed to the importance of considering job design in motivation. This model suggests that people will be satisfied if they can achieve three psychological states in work (knowing the results achieved, meaningful work, and being responsible for own performance), and suggests that this can be predicted through five different job characteristics.

Behavioural consequences

Behaviourist theories of motivation **(B. F. Skinner)** are based on people's tendency to exhibit behaviours that either enable further rewards or avoid something undesirable. For example:

- Praising someone for accurate work may cause them to repeat the behaviour.
- If getting home on time avoids rows, someone may consistently leave early.

Rewarding someone is considered a better strategy than punishing them.

- Attention can be a reward. A manager who only speaks to employees as a reprimand may increase undesirable behaviour. People feel more valued if they feel that a manager is aware of them and what they do.
- Behaviours that are not rewarded will reduce and eventually cease, so a good manager should reinforce the behaviours they want to see through praise, and get rid of those they don't by supporting people to change their behaviour.

The goal setting theory (Locke) is also based on the idea of linking specific behaviours with specific consequences. This is where the idea of SMART goal setting fits in. Vague goals that are open to interpretation are not as motivating as SMART goals that have clear consequences.

Decision making

These theories take account of people's cognitive capacity – their reasoning processes.

- **Equity theory** (Adams) suggests that people are motivated to take action or change their mindset to increase the perceived fairness of their treatment. For example, they may work harder if they feel overpaid, spend less time on a report if they feel underpaid, or produce work of higher quality to justify their bonus.

- **Expectancy theory** (Vroom) suggests that people's actions depend on their perception of the probable effort involved in attaining a specific level of performance, the probable outcome of that performance, and the value of the outcome for them. If you think that by making a certain effort it is almost certain you will perform well, thus achieving something important to you, then you are more likely to act.

> **Activity 8.1 Motivational drivers**
>
> The concept of motivation and the theories of motivation are based on mental models of how people act. Some of the underlying concepts may have more to do with the culture of the organisation than they do with simply being human. With one or two colleagues, consider the different theories of motivation outlined previously:
>
> - What methods of encouraging better performance are used in your organisation that you think are derived from these theories?
> - How much of this theory is personally applicable to the way you are managed, and the way that you manage?
> - What culturally based assumptions may not be true in either your organisation, your country, or in a different country?

Applying the theory

Motivation is an important factor in someone's productivity, and therefore in meeting a team's targets.

As marketers, you may also have recognised some of the concepts from product buying and marketing strategies. Making sure someone recognises a need, takes action to buy your product based on that need, and having experienced the product wants to buy it again, all require an underlying motivation.

Theories of motivation are useful for practising marketing managers because they provide frameworks from which to consider how to increase employee motivation – and indeed your own motivation. The next sections provide some practical examples of how the theories have been applied in organisations.

Designing jobs

One way of using the theories of motivation is to redesign jobs so that they better meet psychological needs. The two-factor model (Herzberg) and the job characteristics model (Hackman and Oldman) have both been influential in this approach. Some of the various strategies used are shown below.

Figure 8.1 Motivational strategies – job design

Strategy	Approach	Example(s)
Job rotation	Ensure that a range of abilities and skills are used and developed, leading to greater variety and greater job satisfaction.	Changing from a traditional assembly line approach, to an approach where job holders are trained in and move between different jobs.
Job enrichment	Make sure that the job holder can see the outcome of their efforts, taking on end-to-end tasks rather than just part of a task. Link the role to the impact it has on people e.g. customers, colleagues. Increase the extent to which the job holder can manage their own time and decide how to do tasks. Ensure the job holder receives clear information about the effectiveness of their performance.	Providing queries staff with the capability to see customer requests through from inception to fulfilment, rather than just handing the request on to someone else never to be seen again. Moving from an emphasis on how the task should be done, to what results the task should achieve. Providing feedback that is clearly linked to performance, and encouraging the employee to take action on the results.
Job enlargement	Encourage the employee to take on a wider role.	Getting a sales assistant to set targets for, and get customer meetings in the diary, instead of just following the lead of the sales manager.

Understanding the individual

You may already have noticed that the type of job design changes discussed in Figure 8.1 will suit some people more than others. In addition, some programmes are more successful than others. Part of this may be down to how well a programme has been implemented, but it will also be down to individual differences. Interventions here concentrate on matching the person with the job they are expected to do.

Figure 8.2 Motivational strategies – taking account of individual needs

Strategy	Approach	Example(s)
Job design	Design the characteristics of the job to motivate the people most likely to have the ASK factors required.	Product managers want creativity. Ensuring job variety and autonomy are more likely to meet this desire than asking for adherence to specific procedures.
Matching people to jobs	Identify employee's motivational profiles and match them to the job profiles.	Use of Thematic Apperception Test (version derived from Achievement Motivation Theory). For example, people who need friendship and social interaction are more likely to enjoy a team role than one that requires them to work in isolation.
Managing perceptions	Link employee's identified needs to those of the job.	Demonstrate that by improving their influencing skills to the standards required to perform well on the job, an employee will be considered for promotion, thus meeting their achievement needs.

Effective Management for Marketing

Strategy	Approach	Example(s)
	Understand and honour employee's perception of equity or expectancy.	Ensuring that work related goals are explicit, understood, considered to be attainable, and bought into. Rewards tailored to individual, and demonstrably fair.

Changing management approach

Behaviourist theories have been widely used in management training and in organisational programmes, and are considered to be successful. While much early work concentrated on external (extrinsic) rewards, it is now recognised that personal (intrinsic) rewards, such as challenging work completed successfully, are also central to employee motivation.

Figure 8.3 Motivational strategies – management approach

Strategy	Approach	Example(s)
Behaviour reinforcement	Increasing reinforcement of desired behaviours. Reducing reinforcement of negative behaviours.	Pay is based on performance e.g. sales, productivity. Regular, genuinely appreciative feedback. Ensuring individual performance rewards are also linked to team rewards.
Goal setting	SMART goals. Management by objectives.	Supporting job holders in setting stretching, achievable, SMART objectives, linked to performance.

Activity 8.2 Management By Objectives (MBO)

Your Marketing Manager, Gill Laurel, is known to value employee job satisfaction very highly, and she believes that she has a very highly motivated team. She is very concerned about the impact of the organisation's "Management By Objectives" programme on the team, so she has asked you to research it on her behalf. She believes it may be seen as manipulative. The intention is to:

- Get employees and their manager to jointly set SMART performance targets, to be assessed yearly for remuneration purposes.
- To have regular meetings at which the progress towards the goals is assessed and managers give guidance and support to assist in meeting the targets.
- To ensure that the process supports individual, team and organisational goals.

Write her a note setting out the benefits of introducing such a programme.

Until now, the emphasis has been on rewarding employees for how they do the job – rewards based on ASK factors (Attitudes, Skills and Knowledge) and procedures rather than on results. You believe that the programme can bring a lot of benefits and want to support Gill in making the most of this opportunity.

Possible symptoms of poor motivation

You cannot physically see someone's lack of motivation. Instead you may observe symptoms as varied as disinterest, low productivity, or increased levels of sickness. The figure overleaf shows just some of the possible consequences of poor work motivation.

Effective Management for Marketing

Figure 8.4 Some possible symptoms of poor motivation

```
                    Become              Sickness
                    stressed            levels rise
                       ↑                    ↓
    Poorly                                              Causes
    motivated   →   Boredom      →     Productivity     further
    employee        sets in             decreases       decreases
                                           ↑↓           in motivation
                    Work                Satisfaction
                    relationships  ⇄    deteriorates
                    deteriorate         further
```

Bear in mind that some of these symptoms may be caused by factors other than job satisfaction:

- Sickness levels may increase due to a flu epidemic etc.
- Productivity may decrease due to the demands of learning a new procedure or system.

As a manager, you cannot know for sure what the cause is without evidence. However, if you see such symptoms as in Figure 8.4 appearing then poor motivation is one of the areas you will want to investigate.

Identifying the root cause

If you are in a situation where one or more people seem demotivated, then the only way you can be sure of the reasons for the symptoms is to ask. You may have some ideas as to why this may be the case, based on:

- What you know about the person, their needs and goals, changes in their personal circumstances.
- Their job. Have there been any recent changes that may have had an impact? Have they been struggling with some aspect of it?
- Their relationships with their manager and colleagues. Do they get a lot of criticism yet little praise? Are they well supported in achieving their goals?
- Recent or proposed changes in the organisation. Has the organisation been

getting a bad press lately and internal PR not dealt with the crisis situation effectively? Are there rumours of reorganisation?

Managers have been known to come up with some fantastic theories that actually have no basis in fact. Acting on these may be destructive rather than helpful. For example:

- Inviting someone in who you think may have given up on promotion, to give them a motivational chat about how close they are if they can just increase their performance. In fact, they have been soldiering on after having recently been diagnosed with a serious illness, and this is the last thing they want to hear.

- After a recent round of redundancies, calling a valuable employee in to tell them how important they are, and how they are safe from the axe, because you think they are worried about their job. In fact, they are still in mourning after the loss of most of their close colleagues and friends through redundancy, and couldn't care less about the job. Your intervention makes it more likely they will resign.

Discovering the causes of apparent low levels of motivation is best carried out:

- During one-on-one interviews.
- As a team discussion, if the performance of the whole team seems to be suffering.
- By survey if found in a larger group (as with marketing research, this type of survey needs to be carried out by professionals. Companies who specialise in these tools can provide comparisons with other groups in the same industry for norming purposes).

Possible causes of poor motivation

By being more aware of some of the causes of poor motivation, and taking these into account when you plan or react to changes, can help you mitigate some of the risks to your team and the organisation. Figure 8.5 (overleaf) shows just some of the possible causes. You may notice how some of the theories of motivation can be realised in organisations.

Effective Management for Marketing

Figure 8.5 Some possible causes of poor motivation

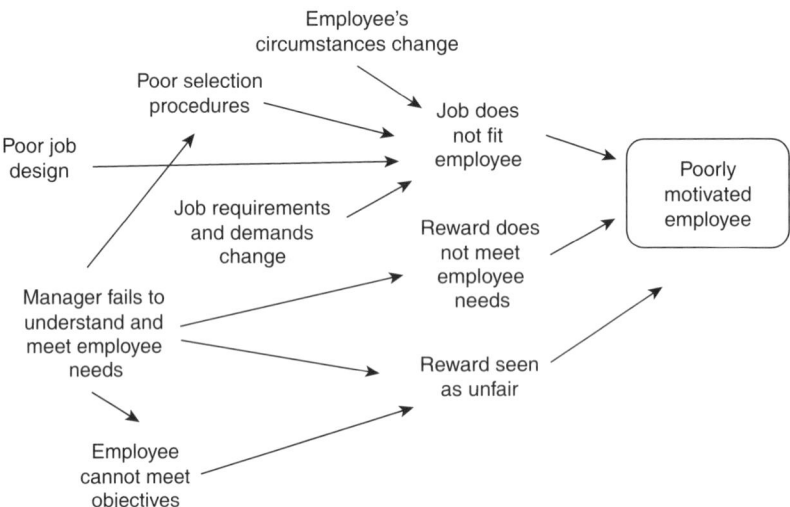

Activity 8.3 The good and the bad!

1. On a diagram similar to the one above, map the causes and consequences of poor motivation for you, for your job, or perhaps for completing this course of study! Now map another diagram for good motivation. Estimate the impact of each chain of events on your productivity (in %). What actions can you take to increase your motivation?

2. With no more than two other colleagues, carry out the same exercise for a group of people in your organisation, such as your team or a group of sales staff. Choose a group which you all have knowledge of.

Shutting the stable door before the horse has bolted

The previous sections looked at how to identify and diagnose the symptoms of poor motivation. However, prevention is usually better than cure. If a manager has a good understanding of people's needs and goals, is aware of the changes in jobs and the organisation and their potential impact on people, and uses a range of motivation theories in their management practice, then many motivational issues can be foreseen and planned for.

Here are some examples of poor motivation which, through better planning, could have been removed or at least alleviated. They are based on real life examples.

Situation	Early interventions
A marketing assistant, highly motivated to succeed, believed that they deserved a promotion over another colleague. Their colleague was promoted first. The reward they wanted (that of promotion) had not been achieved in the timescale they anticipated, and therefore they became demotivated. When another position became available, they had already resigned.	If the manager had kept a close eye on the individual's expectations, they could have identified the situation beforehand, kept the employee motivated and informed, and asked them to apply for the new position.
A badly designed selection process resulted in the appointment of someone who thrives on a lot of social interaction, to a job that required them to work alone and offsite for long periods. This caused them to become very stressed and demotivated.	See Session 6. Someone didn't establish a good person specification, or maybe they "sold" the job incorrectly at the interview.
Customer service staff were given sales targets for the first time. Up until now, they had been recognised for the way they dealt with customers and followed procedures – some of them even saw sales as intrusive to the customer. With the new sales targets many became stressed, divided between what they saw as good service versus sales, and sickness levels rose.	Good marketing could have alleviated the issue. How does sales equate to good customer service? Another approach would have been to redesign and re-allocate jobs, selecting those suited to sales and allowing the others to focus on maintenance tasks.

Situation	Early interventions
Times were hard and the organisation decided to cut back on its costs. It started charging staff for their tea and coffee, stopped any personal use of work phones, and ended the practice of having refreshments provided at meetings. However, senior staff continued to be provided with free refreshments, large cars, mobile phones, and first-class travel. This was seen as very unfair, so after a while staff started charging expenses by the book (which resulted in greater costs), and reduced their work rates – still performing to the demands of their job, but overall dropping productivity.	This is a good example of equity theory in action. Why would people be happy cutting back when others on far higher salaries are not doing the same? Starting any cost cutting at the top of the organisation would have demonstrated the seriousness of the situation and the willingness to spread the burden fairly.

Planning interventions to change motivation

Having set out SMART objectives for an intervention, you may want to consider interventions aimed at:

- Promoting or enhancing motivation.
- Maintaining motivation. For example, on a long project people may become stale after a while, and will need interventions to keep them motivated.
- Renewing reduced motivation.

It is important to evaluate the various options available to you:

- How well will it achieve the outcome?
- How long will it take?
- How much will it cost (including the impact of any absences on the business)?
- What value will it bring? Over what period?
- Is it appropriate for this individual or group? What are the knock-on consequences? Promising someone a promotion may result in an immediate increase in motivation, but unless it is deserved they may be seen to be treated unfairly, causing demotivation amongst colleagues.

When planning an intervention, you also need to consider the value of involving the group or individual for whom the intervention is planned. As with all interventions, some form of monitoring needs to be carried out to assess the success of the intervention relative to your outcome.

Activity 8.4 Theory and practice

Think of something that you really want to buy, like a book on a certain topic, flight tickets, clothing, or a computer game.

Search on the Internet for different options, using at least five sites, and select just one.

As you carry out this activity, notice:

- What factors motivate you to want the item? What needs are you attempting to satisfy?
- How do the various sites you visit attempt to motivate you to buy it? How well do they match your needs?
- What demotivates you as you search? Do you notice "hygeines" and "motivators"?
- To what extent are you motivated by rational factors such as price? To what extent by the look and feel of the site?
- How would your answers differ depending on the nature of the purchase?

Case Study – The employees and the brand: the importance of communications and motivation

Reform in the arts has not experienced the same management revolution as, for example, the health service or public utilities. In the world of entertainment, particularly the theatre, the role of management is often misunderstood and undervalued. The Royal Shakespeare Company (RSC) is a company well known for its performances in the theatre. It has now experienced a management revolution that has changed the way it works. This is to ensure it delivers the highest standards of quality, maximises accessibility to the public, and adds value to the lives of those who come into contact with the company.

The RSC has its own special problems, including pay that cannot compete with commercial theatre or television, and the 18-month contract period that deters many big screen actors (who need to be able to undertake filming assignments at relatively short notice).

To overcome these problems new contracts have been written to allow more flexibility, and increased training and development opportunities have added value to the time people spend with the company. The new approach is reaping its rewards, with major British actors appearing with the RSC, some after a 20-year absence. A shorter London season and more resources put into regional partnerships and tours has ensured that 80% of the UK's population now live within an hour's drive of a RSC production.

While those that provide funds and many other external stakeholders have welcomed the changes, media interviews with RSC actors uncovered uncertainties about RSC's vision and reasons behind the changes.

Staff surveys were conducted and it emerged that too little consultation had taken place with the actors before the changes were implemented. Internal communications were to blame and management agreed that an objective analysis was needed.

Findings from the staff surveys revealed that actors' perceptions of the company were confused. For example, management and the board were seen to be elusive and their role was not understood.

It raised the question of how to create effective communications between management and actors, and how to communicate the corporate goals (beyond those of making a success of each RSC production). Management specifically wanted to know why artists wanted to work with the RSC, and how they could make the company as attractive as possible to them. It also emerged that few actors who joined the RSC knew what to expect. Rehearsal schedules are demanding – followed by an evening performance (6 each week, plus 2 matinees). Actors can be performing in up to three different productions simultaneously. Touring makes different demands, with actors living in temporary accommodation from week to week, enduring months away from their families. This also makes them feel remote from the organisation.

There is recognition by the management that the RSC brand is crucial to success, and that the brand is the people involved with the company, particularly the actors.

Source: Effective Management for Marketing examination paper, December, 2000. Adapted from an article in *People Management*.

Questions

1. How would you develop and implement an internal communications plan that improves the process of communications, motivation and team spirit?

2. Briefly explain how this would contribute towards the brand.

SUMMARY OF KEY POINTS

- Theories of motivation consider what drives people to work harder and faster, from a number of different perspectives, including satisfying needs, identifying drivers and influencing behaviour.

- Different people are motivated by different drivers at different times in their career.

- Identifying the causes of poor motivation may be complex but are essential if individual and team performances are to be optimised.

- Planning successful intervention depends on an accurate diagnosis of the problem and the related issues, setting SMART objectives, and reviewing the possible options against the probable achievement of the desired outcome.

- When planning how to motivate individuals or your team, identify how to create an environment where people feel able to give of their best and support each other.

Improving and developing own learning

The following projects are designed to help you develop your knowledge and skills further, by carrying out some research yourself. Feedback is not provided for this type of learning because there are no "answers" to be found, but you may wish to discuss your findings with colleagues and fellow students.

> **Project A**
>
> Identify your motivational drivers. What makes you work with more enthusiasm and willingness? What causes you dissatisfaction and causes you to work less energetically?

> **Project B**
>
> What are the factors within your working environment that lead to poor job satisfaction? How can these barriers to effectiveness be removed or minimised?

> **Project C**
>
> How effectively are people rewarded and achievement recognised in your organisation? What effect does this have on performance? What improvements can you suggest that might lead to improved performance in the short and the long-term?

Feedback to activities

Activity 8.1 Motivational drivers

You may have considered issues such as:

- The extent to which theories can be seen as immediately applicable. Applications based on Skinner's work are seen more often than those of Maslow's.
- Incentives that are used to boost performance short term, and management styles and behaviours (such as praise and other forms of recognition) that are designed to enhance long-term results.
- How management approaches can sometimes result in different consequences than those anticipated. For example, an ex-salesforce manager may attempt to use money and public "prize giving" to motivate his new strategic marketing department, who are actually more motivated by the opportunity to do stimulating work.

- How people's needs may vary in different cultures. Western cultures tend to place a higher value on individual achievement than Asian cultures do.

Activity 8.2 Management By Objectives (MBO)

The purpose of your note was to motivate Gill to implement the programme in a way that will produce the best possible results. What different motivation strategies did you use?

In your note, you should have explicitly linked the benefits of MBO to Gill's concern for continuing job satisfaction and supporting team motivation, and not just set out the benefits of MBO. For example:

- Setting challenging yet achievable SMART objectives has been shown to increase motivation and hence satisfaction.
- Employees will have greater freedom to manage their jobs to achieve specific results (job enrichment), hence increasing satisfaction.
- Benefits can only be realised if people are totally involved and committed to setting and meeting their own objectives, if the objectives set are SMART, if rewards are seen to take account of the individual's needs, and if Gill is involved in supporting her employees to meet their objectives. Under these circumstances the system is highly unlikely to be seen as manipulative.
- Gill has an opportunity to gain even more information about her employees job satisfaction as part of the MBO discussion process, information that she can use to mutual benefit to increase job satisfaction and motivation.

Activity 8.3 The good and the bad!

A rough estimate is all that is required by this exercise. It is offered as a way of exploring the issues of motivation and of understanding your mental model of the most important factors. As a problem-solving tool, it can provide you with a way of prioritising which issues to address first. You may well have:

- Left out factors. Did you look back and check against the theories set out in this Session?
- Under or overestimated the importance of factors.
- Included factors that actually have no influence.

By using this type of technique within a team, you can come to a shared understanding of the issues and create an action plan to address them.

Activity 8.4 Theory and practice

Some online marketers have paid more attention to customer motivation than others. Having to wade through several site pages, via impenetrable navigation and difficult text, tends not to motivate someone to buy!

Session 9

Managing employee performance

Introduction

Managing the performance of individuals and teams is a key management activity for marketers. The previous two Sessions have begun to explore this topic, so this Session concentrates on performance review and appraisal. It is a very practical Session and encourages you to review your own performance in this area!

> **LEARNING OUTCOMES**
>
> At the end of this Session you will be able to:
>
> - Explain the role of appraisals in performance management.
> - Prepare and plan for appraisal interviews.
> - Carry out effective appraisal interviews.
> - Set performance objectives and targets.
> - Manage individuals to improve their effectiveness.
> - Recognise how to follow-up appraisal interviews.

Performance management

Performance management of an individual involves a number of activities, including:

- Assessing performance against accountability for results.
- Taking corrective action in cases of underperformance, for example disciplinary interviews (Session 5).
- Providing an environment that motivates staff to perform well in their jobs (Session 8).
- Enabling staff to identify and address personal development needs, in support of their job performance, career potential and aspirations.

The domain of appraisals is the last of these areas.

Purpose of appraisals

The purpose of an appraisal may be one or more of the following:

- To review employee performance from the time between the previous appraisal and current.
- To review the achievement of objectives set at the previous appraisal and set new objectives for the future.
- To identify employee training and development needs.
- To inform the pay review.

Benefits of appraisals

Some benefits of appraisals are as follows.

For the individual it should help them:

- Understand their strengths and development needs, from their perspective and those of their colleagues.
- Identify plans for addressing their development needs.
- Understand the relationship between how they do things and their job and career prospects, both short and long-term.
- Have an input into their own development plan.

For the manager it should help them:

- Understand the individual's aspirations, hence how best to motivate them.
- Find a structured way of addressing development needs, separate from discussions on assessment and pay.
- Encourage self-assessment by the individual, who is encouraged to take on responsibility for managing their own development.

For the organisation it should help it:

- Empower and encourage its employees to self develop, thus improving overall performance.
- Discover additional information about employees' aggregate development

needs, enabling more accurate human resource development planning and management.

If an appraisal system is to work effectively it needs to be carefully designed and marketed to meet the current needs of the organisation and the individuals within it. For example, an organisation without any appraisal system would probably be ill-advised to introduce a full-blown, competency driven, 360° appraisal system immediately!

Forms of appraisal

Formal appraisal systems can differ in a number of areas:

- Who (other than the individual) provides feedback? A 360° appraisal system involves soliciting feedback from an individual's peers, staff who report to them, and their line manager.
- Who collects and delivers the feedback? This is usually the line manager, although feedback from reports and colleagues may be collated and delivered by a representative.
- What areas are appraised? Competencies? Skills? Knowledge?
- How are areas appraised? Is there a set of standards, or is feedback free-format, under a series of headings?
- How does the individual provide their impressions? On a self-appraisal form first? By responding to feedback?
- How is the development plan put in place? By the individual? In discussions between the individual and their line manager?
- What information is provided outside the appraisal interview? Is it private to the individual? Is it filed in their personnel file?

Activity 9.1 Appraisal review!

Go and talk to someone in your organisation who is well acquainted with the systems of performance management and appraisal, such as your HR specialist. If possible, also interview someone in another organisation about their company appraisal system.

- How is the system intended to perform?
- How does it perform in practice?

- What are the realised benefits for performance management?
- What are your personal experiences of being appraised? What was good/less good about these experiences?
- What recommendations do you have about the way your organisations' appraisal system is used and internally marketed?

Information requirements

Prior to the interview, the appraiser and appraisee need to know:

- The basis for the appraisal. What is being appraised and in relation to what?
- The aspirations of the individual (which can be found in past interviews or may form part of a pre self-appraisal completed by the appraisee).
- The results of previous appraisals. Review the individual's performance development plan, and consider any feedback gathered since the last appraisal.

The appraiser should also have:

- Up-to-date, behaviourally based feedback against each area to be appraised, obtained from specified individuals.
- Information on the development support available from the organisation, in order to identify opportunities for the individual.

As an appraiser, it is essential that you check any feedback on the individual's performance very carefully. You must ensure that it is:

- **Specific**. What were they seen doing or heard to say, when, and by whom?
- **First hand**. 'I overheard so-and-so saying that Gavin told them that Sarah's report had some spelling mistakes.' You need to track down the person who made the observation, otherwise this is simply gossip and hearsay.
- **Within the relevant period**. 'Well now I come to think of it, that was two years ago'. Make sure that your interviewees have been in a position to make recent, meaningful observations of the appraisee.
- **Relevant**. Which appraisal area does this relate to? How does it impact the

area being appraised? How is this information important for them?

- **Able to be acted upon**. Is it possible in principle that they can do something differently to enhance their performance, or that they can continue to exhibit a behaviour that assists their performance?

Asking for comments on strengths, development needs, and what the employee will need to do to achieve their aspirations, will help to get a rounded perspective. When gathering information for the appraisal of another individual, make sure that the interviewee (person giving the feedback) is well briefed and prepared beforehand. Make detailed records of what you are told, checking their accuracy at the time of the interview.

Self-appraisal

As previously mentioned, the appraisee may be asked to do their own appraisal, either to be supplied to the appraiser or to be brought to an interview. Whether this is required or not, it is recommend that the appraisee spends time collating:

- Feedback they have already had.
- Their assessment of their own progress since the last appraisal.
- Their assessment of their own strengths and development areas, in particular where they want to make the case for a development activity, such as a training course.

Self-appraisal is useful because it gives the appraisee the opportunity to reflect and assess their own performance.

- Individuals who are new to the appraisal system may either overestimate or underestimate their **development needs**, so may need more guidance.
- Experienced self-appraisers will be able to self-appraise and self-correct more accurately.
- Self-appraisal emphasises support and development, as opposed to managerial **assessment**.

Planning the interview

For the interview the appraiser needs to ensure that:

- There is enough preparation time to allow all the information to be collected.
- The interview location is private and comfortable.

- There will be no interruptions.
- Any cancellation or movement of the interview is extremely rare.
- The appraisee is well briefed.
- Plenty of time is allowed, given the material to be covered. (You may want to build in half an hour to an hour contingency time, which will also give you the opportunity to write-up the meeting immediately afterwards.)

Structure of the interview

The basic elements of an appraisal interview are:

Opening:

- Put the appraisee at ease and establish a rapport.
- Check that it is an appropriate time.
- Reconfirm the purpose and agenda.

Discuss the results of the self-appraisal. } In parallel, following the
Give feedback. } structure of the appraisal
Review goals and aspirations. } report.

You should take care not to turn the appraisal into a guessing game, or as an excuse to defer difficult feedback ('If I can get them to say this first, then I won't have to tell them what Nick said'). To avoid this, one way of structuring the approach is to ask the individual to provide their views of one area, which you then question and give feedback on before moving on to the next point.

Agree development actions.

Closing:

- Summarise.
- Agree follow-up.

An organisation with a mature appraisal system might have quarterly or half-yearly update meetings for interim appraisals, with a full review once a year. This is useful in ensuring that the manager does not store up all their feedback and hit the individual with the lot at once.

Giving feedback during appraisal interviews

If you have prepared as recommended, you will already have very specific feedback, based on observations of behaviour and not just opinions. The purpose of delivering the feedback is to motivate the individual to understand and act on it. This comes down to good marketing, linking the feedback to the individuals needs. For example:

'Rachel, when we last met you said that it was important for you to be considered for a promotion in the next six months. Sadat's observations on your time management skills are very relevant to how you are perceived as a promotion candidate. On two occasions in the last couple of months you have delivered work late with no explanation.'

This relies on the manager having sufficient information about the goals and aspirations of the appraisee to make this link.

There are various methods for attempting to ensure that the interviewee hears both positive and negative feedback:

- Feedback sandwich – positive/negative/positive (to ensure the person is receptive, and is left with a positive thought).
- Giving positive feedback first (to put at ease), then negative.
- Giving negative feedback first (as people are always waiting for it), then finishing with the positive (as they will definitely hear it now that the negative is out of the way).

What works well depends on the motivation and skill of the feedback giver as much as it does on the method used. Avoid the following types of feedback:

- Insincere. You need to believe it or why will they?
- Given to make the giver feel better. Giving feedback is for their needs not yours.
- Irrelevant to the receiver. If it can't be linked to their goals why would they be interested in hearing it?
- Attempting to mind-read their motivation. Stick to verifiable observations.

Agreeing development actions

Session 3 has already given a suggested format for a personal development plan, together with guidelines for setting development actions. Some organisations have their own forms, and individuals may also want to customise their own form. The appraisee should be encouraged as far as possible to come up with their own actions and priorities, with the appraiser helping to ensure that:

- The actions are considered in the context of their impact on the appraisee meeting their goals and aspirations. This is particularly relevant if an appraisee shows a tendency to want to tackle what is easy for them, rather than what will have the biggest performance impact.
- The individual receives appropriate support from the organisation and the appraiser in meeting their goals.

Activity 9.2 Role play

Find a colleague to assist you in practising your feedback skills. Identify a couple of individuals who you work with, and who you would like to give some feedback to on a particular area (but haven't yet). Prepare the feedback you will give in writing. Brief your colleague about the person they will be role playing, and practise delivering the feedback and getting agreement to development actions, getting information about what works and what doesn't. Then reverse the roles.

Use the opportunity to investigate the impact of poorly given feedback as well. There is nothing like being on the receiving end of the "don'ts" to realise how annoying it can be. Once the exercise is complete, use the opportunity to give feedback to each other about your feedback skills!

The role of performance objectives in performance management

It is usually more appropriate to link remuneration with the results someone achieves than with how well they do the activities comprising their job. In many organisations there is a direct link between results and an individual's pay (performance-related pay).

Determining objectives and target areas

Put simply, objectives can be defined as what you are attempting to achieve, and should be SMART (Specific, Measurable, Achievable, Relevant and Time bound).

For example:

- **Aim** (financial): to meet or exceed all my sales targets for this year.
- **Specific objectives:** sell 8,000 units of product A, and 10,000 units of product B by the end of Q4.

- **Aim** (customer): to increase my customer satisfaction ratings by one point.
- **Specific objective:** achieve Level 4 in all categories by Q4.

- **Aim** (team development): to transfer my knowledge of sales processes to the team.
- **Specific objective:** run seminars for all team members, and achieve "good" or "very good" ratings for their usefulness, as measured by my peers, by year end.

Setting objectives

It is important that the objectives set for individuals, teams, departments, etc. are aligned with the overall aims of the organisation. Managers need to be very clear on the objectives and targets for their area, and ensure that the aggregate of individual and team objectives support these.

When setting objectives, remember to word them positively, so that meeting an objective is about achieving rather than avoiding something. Try '95% of customers surveyed in end year review are "happy" or "very happy" with service' rather than 'Less than 5% of customers surveyed in end year review are not happy with service'. Also remember that quality is better than quantity. 6-8 objectives spread over 3-4 different areas is probably the absolute maximum an individual can focus on effectively at any one time.

Some additional points in setting objectives:

- Objectives must be SMART.
- Best practice is to set objectives with the individuals input and agreement, rather than imposing them. In Figure 9.2 this might be achieved by negotiation. Naturally, such targets must as a minimum meet the demands of the job description.
- If an objective is 'to educate the Finance Department about what Internal Marketing can achieve for them by end year', then a measurement of 'hold at

least three meetings with them' is insufficient. There needs to be a measu
the quality of achievement in there as well – meetings rated as good or
good by attendees, three opportunities to assist them identified and ag
with them by end year.

- Too great a focus on individual achievement might be to the detriment of the team. Likewise, too great an emphasis on team objectives might reduce individual performance.

- Purely financial objectives may result in a focus on sales and cost cutting, to the detriment of customer satisfaction and service, which may adversely affect the organisation in the long term. They might also impact negatively on employee satisfaction and stress levels.

Links between targets and remuneration

If performance objectives are closely linked to remuneration, there can be a perceived tension between setting stretching and meaningful individual objectives, and the desire to get a good performance-related pay rise. Some organisations help mitigate this problem by ensuring that the results an individual achieves are compared with:

- The standards for their job and/or
- The results achieved by other individuals in the same or similar roles.

Activity 9.3 Setting measurable objectives

Go and talk to a HR representative in your organisation about the way in which performance objectives and targets are set and achievement rewarded:

- What are the current benefits and issues with the way this is achieved?
- What is considered best practice in your organisation?

The follow-up role in appraisal

The manager's role does not finish once SMART objectives have been set:

- Individuals may have difficulty in realising the objectives. For example, they may require coaching and other support in order to achieve them.
- People respond to recognition for their achievements, so the manager must be

constantly monitoring performance to find opportunities to give praise and positive feedback.
- Circumstances may change making certain objectives outdated, such as an objective to carry out internal marketing to a department that ceases to exist.
- Assumptions behind the objectives may change, again requiring objectives to be updated. If a product or service is withdrawn, then the sales objectives and targets will need to be updated.

Progress towards achievement needs to be monitored and reviewed regularly:
- Dealing with issues before they become problems.
- Identifying and acknowledging achievement.

Performance review meetings

Regular review meetings are an important tool in identifying and overcoming problems. Depending on the organisation's performance system, these meetings will naturally cover the assessment of results against objectives. However, in diagnosing issues and building on success, there will also be an emphasis on the link between appraisal and the results achieved:

- Managers need to ensure they have access to an individuals appraisal information.
- Having reviewed results, it will usually be appropriate (except in disciplinary interviews) to adopt an informal approach. Some managers emphasis this change by altering seating arrangements or with a break for refreshments.
- Where possible, it is for the employee being assessed to put forward suggestions rather than the manager.

Good questioning and listening skills are critical (Session 5):
- Do not jump to conclusions as to why someone has missed or exceeded an objective – you may be wrong.
- The ownership for action needs to be with the staff member being reviewed, not with you. Unless of course you turn out to be a major contributory factor!
- Ask questions designed to assist your staff member in exploring the issues, such as:
    - So what do you think contributed to this shortfall/your achievement?

- Considering your last appraisal, can you think of any other factors that may have contributed to this result?
- What ideally would you like to happen now? How are you going to achieve that?
- How can you use your strengths to improve your performance in this area? How have you successfully overcome issues such as this in the past?
- Who else do you know who is performing strongly in this area at the moment? What would they do in these circumstances?
- What are you doing to achieve such great results in this area? How can you transfer this excellence across to other areas?
- What else can I do to support you in achieving this target?

Through this type of questioning you may uncover someone's personal barriers to achievement, such as a lack of confidence in their ability. You may also uncover what are perceived to be external barriers to achievement, such as sales training was poorly delivered or someone else didn't deliver on their promises.

When exploring these, take care to bring the focus back to the actions that can be taken by the person. 'How can you ensure in the future that when someone promises something, you can follow it up in time to take corrective action if there are problems?' There may also be some actions you need to take. However, it is still worth exploring whether the issue should have been raised earlier.

Objectives should be changed as an exception rather than a rule:

- Some organisations set objectives and targets on a quarterly basis. If these are well considered when set, they are unlikely to become out of date.
- Managers need to take great care not to be perceived as "moving the goalposts" unfairly:
    - This causes unnecessary pressure on the employee, reduces trust, and should be avoided.
    - It may be considered grounds for constructive dismissal.
- Objectives set with regard to possible changes in circumstances and assumptions are less likely to require frequent change. For example, compare '10% reduction in budgeted costs' with '10% reduction in unit cost of services provided compared with last year's actuals'.

Informal feedback

Managers need to ensure that the results from the appraisal interview and development plan are used actively to support employees in their development. They will only achieve this if the information is kept live, and informal feedback is an invaluable way of ensuring this:

- Managers need to be sufficiently familiar with their employees' development goals to offer relevant feedback.
- Feedback needs to be offered in a constructive way.
- Remember to offer positive feedback and reinforcement. This is important for both development achievements and for existing strengths. If you want people to continue to exhibit what they are good at, and to take risks in experimenting with unfamiliar behaviours, then give them recognition.

Regular formal appraisal meetings and follow-up can to some degree help managers overcome a reluctance to offer informal feedback, but they are no substitute for it. Giving informal feedback is an essential managerial skill.

Case Study – Siemens relies on HR's input into global leader's initiative

HR will be taking the driving seat in an ambitious global leadership campaign that aims to transform the way business is conducted at German multinational Siemens.

Christian Lasch, from the Siemens Centre of Competence, told delegates at the Chartered Institute of Professional Development (CIPD) Northern European Exchange meeting in Derby, May 2001, that the leadership model had been 'developed by HR specialists from all over the world'.

Siemens, which has 440,000 employees, and offices in 190 countries, has already piloted the system in Switzerland. Subject to final alterations and approval, the company will be applying the programme worldwide the meeting was told.

Its rationale was based on inspirational leadership Lasch said, because motivated staff led to increased customer satisfaction and better results.

To get employees committed and enthusiastic, managers needed to create an inspiring vision, develop shared plans with employees, lead the action, and then stand back and review performance. Managers would also be evaluated on their employees' performance, and the key to the system was dialogue he added.

'You have to have a culture where employees can bring their opinions to the table,'

Lasch said. 'Everything comes together in staff dialogue. Try asking the employees what they really think of their manager and then link the manager's income to the results. It's a revolution – you should take a look at the results.'

All leaders would have to pass a mandatory dialogue training scheme he told delegates. Although many of the new scheme's methods were shared, Siemens was not imposing a corporate identity Lasch said. 'There is intelligence outside Germany. That's what we discovered at Siemens in other countries, and that's what we seek to bring into the company.'

Source: Article by Chris Taylor, People Management, 31st May 2001.

Questions

1. Discuss the potential problems of linking an annual performance appraisal to the pay structure.
2. What are the benefits that Siemens hopes to gain from employee dialogue?
3. How is employee dialogue linked to performance review at Siemens?

SUMMARY OF KEY POINTS

- Effective appraisals need to be planned in advance, so that the right information is available and the appraisee understands the purpose of the appraisal.
- Plan the interview time and date so it is convenient for both parties and make it a priority.
- Ensure discussion is relevant and focused on meeting the purpose of the appraisal.
- Set SMART objectives and identify clear and measurable targets to help the appraisee monitor their own progress.
- Follow up appraisal interviews to identify how well the appraisee is able to achieve the set objectives.
- Use informal feedback to continually support the individual in his/her efforts to improve performance.

Improving and developing own learning

The following projects are designed to help you develop your knowledge and skills further, by carrying out some research yourself. Feedback is not provided for this type of learning because there are no "answers" to be found, but you may wish to discuss your findings with colleagues and fellow students.

> **Project A**
>
> If you conduct appraisals for your staff, review the skills you need and assess your strengths and weaknesses. Identify any opportunities to develop the skills you require. If you do not give appraisals, then role play giving feedback with one or more colleagues to help you assess your skills level in this area.

> **Project B**
>
> Generate a list of possible SMART objectives and targets for internal and external marketing jobs in your organisation. Choose two jobs that are very different in their job description and level. Where possible, compare these with the actual objectives and targets set. What are some of the issues you encountered? What are some of the issues you might encounter if these were used for performance management?

> **Project C**
>
> Using the Internet, research guidelines for giving informal positive and developmental feedback. From these, prepare your own checklist and take at least three opportunities to practise and extend your informal feedback skills in the next week. Solicit feedback on your development of these skills.

Feedback to activities

Activity 9.1 Appraisal review!

In this activity you may have identified several blocks to the effectiveness of appraisals. Some of the areas you may have considered are:

- How aligned is the system with the culture?

- What training and development is required to use it effectively?
- What personal blocks do people have to appraisals?
- What priority is it given? Are appraisal interviews often cancelled, or are they always given priority?

You may have also have considered the following costs:

- Staff time in preparation, planning, carrying out, and recording the interviews.
- Opportunity costs of not carrying out other activities, e.g. sales.

You may have considered the potential impact on staff retention if appraisals are carried out well, or if they are carried out badly.

We hope this activity has provided you with an insight into the importance of ensuring an appraisal system is run effectively. It may be better to dispense with the system altogether than to run it ineffectively, as running it ineffectively may be to the detriment of the organisation.

Activity 9.2 Role play

You should have considered the contents of Session 5 on communication in this exercise. Other interpersonal skills issues may also have arisen (e.g. questioning, listening, gaining rapport), which you may want to address.

Activity 9.3 Setting measurable objectives

Areas you might have discussed include:

- Dependency of the current system on managerial expertise.
- The effectiveness of a performance system depends on the people operating it.
- Managers who are unpractised in setting good objectives may get more from a standardised system that has less room for individually tailored objectives. Highly skilled managers might find such a system restrictive.
- Willingness of managers to reflect underperformance (or excellent performance) in assessments.
- In some organisations managers avoid giving poor assessments even when perfectly justified. This makes it almost impossible to dismiss employees for underperformance.

- Achieving consistency of assessment is often a challenge. Setting clear and independently assessable objectives plays an important role.
- Differentiating between levels of achievement can be hard.
- Excellent performers can become demotivated if they believe their achievement goes unrecognised, e.g. if differences in the rewards for excellent and average performances is minimal.
- Competition between team members may be to the detriment of the business if individual rewards are not also linked to team performance.
- There needs to be a balance between long-term and short-term focus.
- Too many short-term financial objectives can undermine the business longer-term.
- An excessive focus on long-term objectives can result in people neglecting to make a profit this year.

Session 10

Training and development

Introduction

This Session explores how to organise management training and development from the time someone enters the organisation – induction. It discusses the merits of different ways of delivering training and how to evaluate their effectiveness.

> **LEARNING OUTCOMES**
>
> At the end of this Session you will be able to:
>
> - Explain the importance of induction and how to implement an induction system.
> - Discuss how to identify training needs and set plans to meet those needs.
> - Describe different methods of delivering training.
> - Describe how to evaluate the effectiveness of training.
> - Explain how to identify opportunities for management development.

Purpose of induction

Before planning any induction process, as with all activities, it is important to know the desired outcome of the process. The overall goals were outlined in Session 6, and included assisting someone with fitting in, as well as developing them to meet the job requirements. Objectives are likely to cover areas such as:

- Being supplied with the physical environment they need to do the job (this is sometimes overlooked and can make someone feel very unwelcome).
- Familiarising themselves with colleagues, their working area and facilities.
- Gaining organisational knowledge of both their department or area and the wider organisation e.g. history, structure, mission, goals and values.
- Understanding the job requirements, including performance management systems such as assessment and appraisal.
- Undertaking development activity (based on the ASK requirements of their job).
- Enabling them to raise any questions they have and obtain answers to these.

Training and development

These objectives need to be properly thought out and sufficiently detailed, so that you will be able to recognise when they have been met, i.e. they need to be SMART (essential for any planning activity).

Planning induction

Figure 10.1 Extract from induction plan

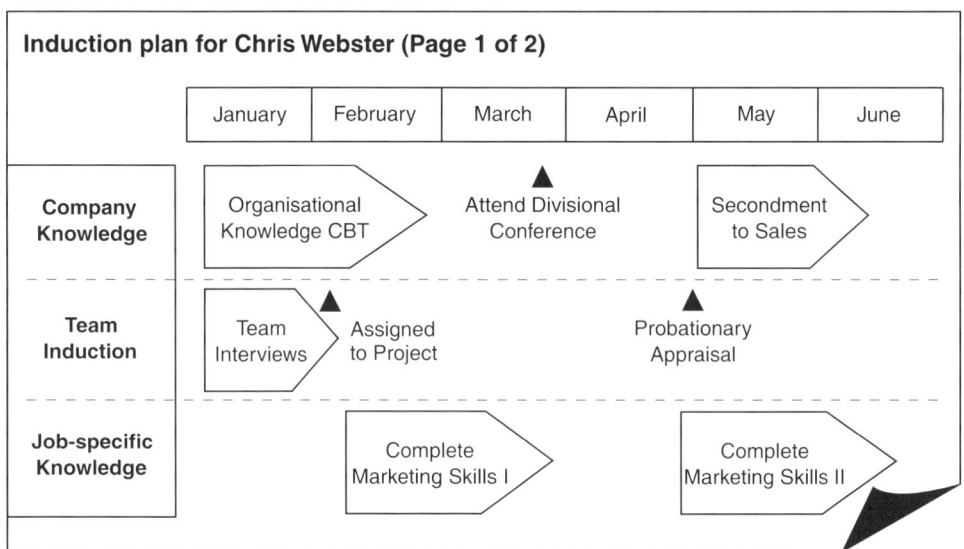

Once you have identified precisely what is wanted and by when, you can then plan the activities required (see Figure 10.1 for a simple chart). Some of this activity may be more appropriate once the person has joined, so that they can be involved in the plan. Activities could be a combination of several approaches, such as training, meetings with key members of staff, spending time shadowing someone.

In larger organisations in particular, there may be existing activities that can meet some of the induction needs. For example, some organisations have "organisational knowledge" courses, which cover issues such as organisation mission, goals and values, and standard procedures. In others, the development activity may be more specific and will therefore need to be tailored to the individual.

From the perspective of efficiency, and in particular where recruitment is a regular occurrence, marketing managers may prepare an induction template, which can be altered to fit each individual. This is likely to be more effective than starting afresh each time, as lessons from one induction can be transferred to the next.

Consider carefully the mix of activities and their likely short and long-term impact on the individual.

- Skills training is best followed by putting the skills into practise immediately. Whilst it may be tempting to send someone on back-to-back courses to get them up-to-speed quickly, it is unlikely to be effective.
- Asking someone to spend a long time reading organisational documents is a great way of making most people very bored, very fast. They are also highly unlikely to retain anything of value.
- Think carefully about who it is useful for the person to meet and, if appropriate, give them an active role in the induction. An explanation of the history of the team could be done by a team member rather than by you as team leader. This will assist them in getting to know people, and people getting to know them.
- Asking one of their peers to shepherd them through the process and be available to answer any queries, and also tell them about the undocumented side of the organisation can be very effective. People can be very inhibited from asking the boss "silly questions".

Activity 10.1 Induction

Prepare a twenty-minute presentation on your organisation that could be delivered to new recruits as part of their induction.

Where possible, talk this through with recent or new employees, your manager, or human resources to get feedback.

After listening to their advice, what would you change about your presentation?

Reviewing the effectiveness of induction

Effectiveness needs to be reviewed from both the perspective of the employee and the perspective of the organisation.

The basis for a review is the SMART objectives you set prior to planning.

Reviews need to be undertaken from a value/cost perspective:

- While the inductee may recommend a more tailored organisational knowledge programme, the time and cost may be prohibitive.
- Even though you have been seconding people to the sales department for many years, if this approach does not meet the stated objectives then it needs to be reassessed.

As with all appraisal and development activity, if you wait until everything is completed then it is usually more costly and ineffective to address the issues, so set monitoring and review activities into the plan from the outset. In addition, ensure that the inductee is familiar with the objectives set and ask them to raise any issues that are not met. This provides a good induction into appraisal procedures, as well as assisting in improving the induction programme.

Effective induction is the start of the training and development programme that individuals undertake, which is the focus of this Session.

Identifying training needs – purpose of a TNA

A Training Needs Analysis (TNA) enables an organisation to identify desired development outcomes and a recommended development approach. This analysis can be carried out at any level, from the whole organisation down to one individual.

By aggregating the needs of several people, the organisation aims to plan and manage its development activity more effectively, primarily by exploiting economies of scale. Managers are also better able to identify and address any cross-organisational development gaps, which are unlikely to have been picked up by examining one person's needs at a time.

Developing a TNA

A Training Needs Analysis will include:

- Where the organisation wants people to be? Analysed via ASK; relative to the desired organisational culture; defined in SMART terms, etc.
- Where people are at the moment? What knowledge and skills they already have.
- The benefit to the organisation of closing the gap.

Effective Management for Marketing

- The options for closing the gap.
- Recommended approach.

As with a marketing plan, a TNA needs to distinguish between people with different needs:

- ASK requirements – for different jobs, in different locations.
- Developmental gaps, such as different levels of IT awareness.
- Cultural groups, for example USA versus European.
- Implementation considerations – it may be easier for Head Office staff to attend several days off-site training sessions than it is to try and assemble all the sales staff together!

Note that any TNA must include a cost/benefit analysis to the organisation of closing the gap, and consider all the options for closing the gap. Despite the name, it must not be assumed that training is the answer. Without the analysis, the effectiveness of interventions can neither be predicted nor evaluated. SMART objectives for the recommendations need to be included.

Compiling a training plan

A training plan is a dynamic document in that it is a record of what individuals need in terms of training and what training they have already received. Therefore it must be constantly updated. In it's simplest form it can exist as a matrix with training activities along the top and names vertically as shown below:

Figure 10. 2 Training plan for marketing executives

	Induction	Report writing	Communication skills	Time management	Introduction to marketing	Advanced marketing
Margaret Beckett	✓	✓		✓	✓	
Duncan Fletcher	✓		✓		✓	
Hilary Highfield	✓	✗			✓	✗
Mark Stuart	✓	✗			✓	✗

Training and development

	Induction	Report writing	Communication skills	Time management	Introduction to marketing	Advanced marketing
John Ling	✓	✓		✓	✓	✗
Kevin Campbell	✓	✓			✓	
Belinda King	✓	✓	✓		✓	✗
Training numbers	0	1	5	5	0	3
Date of next course	10/01/03	03/02/03	14/01/03	15/04/03	26/02/03	27/06/03

Key:

Blank = training requirement
✓ = competent
✗ = further development needed

Planning a training session

Where a training session is planned to meet a need identified in a TNA it must:

- Be set up with SMART objectives derived from the TNA and individual learning objectives.
- Be tailored to meet the learning preferences of the attendees, so for example it should use activities that meet the needs of the activist, reflector, theorist and pragmatist.
- Build in activities which ensure learners actively plan strategies for using the material in the work place (and if possible, a means of following this up to ensure implementation).
- Include plenty of breaks and energisers to ensure that energy levels remain high.
- Take account of the subject matter, and ensure that the principles are demonstrated in the design of the training. For example, customer service training needs to demonstrate implicitly how it takes customer needs (i.e. that of the trainees) into account. Failure to do this can undermine the training on offer.

Effective Management for Marketing

> **Activity 10.2 Training Needs Analysis (TNA)**
>
> Talk to people in your organisation to discover how the different activities involved in Training Needs Analysis are carried out. How formalised are the processes used? Have there been any organisation-wide initiatives?

Advantages of using different methods for development

In some organisations, the response to any developmental issue is "send them on a training course", leaving the responsibility for development with the trainer. Whilst this attitude can still be found in some managers, it is now widely recognised that:

- Training is often not the only or the most effective answer to a development need.

- In some circumstances training can be counterproductive. For example, if someone believes that they are simply not creative, no amount of skills training will help and it may even add to the problem. They may need one-to-one coaching and counselling to overcome the issue. Alternatively, they may already have the skills, just no way of accessing and applying them.

There are many options for development, and their advantages and disadvantages depend on the precise situation, the desired outcome, and its value.

Figure 10.3 Examples of development options

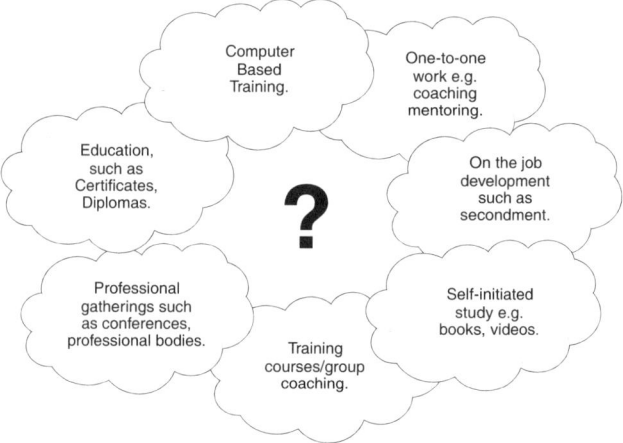

In deciding what to use, there are five important questions to ask:

- How well will it achieve the outcome we want?
- How long will it take?
- How much will it cost (including the impact of any absences for the business)?
- What value will it bring? Over what period?
- Is it appropriate for the individual or group?

Formal and informal development activities

Figure 10.3 shows some development activities that are formally structured, and which tend to be standardised with specific amounts of time set aside and specific modules to complete, such as open training courses on marketing skills, MBA courses etc.

It also shows other activities that, whilst having clear outcomes/SMART objectives, are less formally structured:

- Coaching or mentoring could be used to support someone settling in to a new job.
- Industry and professional knowledge may be best extended by reading, watching television programmes and videos, and by attending conferences, rather than with a formal training programme.

Development opportunities in the work place

If the individual and their manager are clear about their developmental objectives, opportunities often present themselves at work that can be taken advantage of. For example:

- Shadowing someone who is an expert in a particular area (be aware that bad habits can be modelled just as easily as good ones – one of the flaws in the old training system of "sitting by Nellie").
- Being given ongoing appraisal and feedback by a colleague (manager, peer, or junior staff, depending on the issue) who may use a combination of:
    - Questions aimed at assisting the individual to explore their own issues and find solutions.
    - Coaching to assist in skills development.
    - Counselling to identify and overcome personal blocks.
    - Advice where this is appropriate.

- Secondment to another part of the organisation.
- Being given additional or different responsibilities, such as special projects, supervising staff, researching and presenting back to the team on a key industry issue or professional skill, etc.
- Mentoring, where a senior individual acts as a sounding board and source of ideas and career advice.

> **Activity 10.3 Planning development of skills**
>
> You have observed that one of your senior market analysts needs to develop their influencing skills more. Currently they find it difficult to sell their ideas to other people – they tend to do so in their own terms, using a lot of jargon, and get highly defensive when challenged. In the past they have had little experience of having to sell ideas and have relied on others to do this for them. The employee has now recognised that they have a problem and wants to address it. In the past, the employee has responded enthusiastically to developing and using additional skills, particularly where these have come from a source external to the organisation.
>
> Prepare a grid to evaluate the available options to address this employee's development needs. Complete the grid with comments, stating any assumptions you make or information you would require.

Evaluating training effectiveness

When planning to evaluate any activity, you should consider:

- What is the evaluation for?
- What is the basis for the evaluation?
- Who is doing the evaluating?
- What are they evaluating?
- When is the evaluation taking place?

SMART objectives should have been set by the organisation right from the start of the training or development, and should form the main basis for the evaluation. The evaluation also needs to answer the following questions:

- What will be observably different in the individuals at the end of the training? (What will the trainees be able to demonstrate that they could not prior to the training?)
- What value will the training achieve? (What results can be linked back to the training? How cost effective is it?)

The latter is difficult to assess. An organisation must convince itself that there is a value in the training, even if it cannot be realised until far into the future and can only ever be assessed qualitatively. Some training, such as leadership development, does not obviously produce immediate quantitative results, but is still of great value to the organisation.

Depending on the development activity, an individual may have objectives that are not directly related to the training taking place, or may even have different objectives:

- Whilst attending an open training course on Advanced Marketing Skills, a personal objective may be networking with other delegates. This is unlikely to be explicitly stated in the course outcomes or managed by the trainer.
- An experienced presenter may get a different personal outcome than that of a novice when attending a presentation skills workshop.

This means that an activity that is considered "ineffective" by one individual may be "effective" for another. Evaluation only makes sense when compared against the objectives of the activity. It also means that individuals have 100% responsibility for managing their own development outcomes – it is not solely the responsibility of the organisation or individual planning and delivering the activity.

Training evaluation can be done in many ways, including:

- By trainees completing a post-course questionnaire and at intervals on their return to work.
- By setting trainees a test.
- By the trainer completing a report on the perceived impact of the training.
- Interviewing line managers about any improvements in the trainees work. Alternatively the line manager could produce a report, which might actually be a more cost-effective way of assessing the impact of the training than by individual interviews.

A full evaluation should include all those affected by the training. Appropriate methods include self-report, questionnaire, observation and interview. Each should be considered according to its ability to gather the information required, its ease of administration, and the cost effectiveness of its implementation.

Who evaluates?

Different perspectives may be required to evaluate training effectiveness properly:

- Trainees can evaluate against their own personal objectives.
- Line managers of trainees may have a different perspective on what difference a development activity has made to an individual's effectiveness in the work place.
- The trainer or developer can also help evaluate the impact of the trainee briefing (or sometimes lack of it), the suitability of people taking part in the activity, and suggest any changes to meet the stated objectives.

Evaluation is of no use unless it is forward looking and can be used for diagnosis and improvement. Getting several perspectives and inputs is essential to achieving this goal.

What to evaluate

The development process consists of several steps:

Figure 10.4 Outline development process

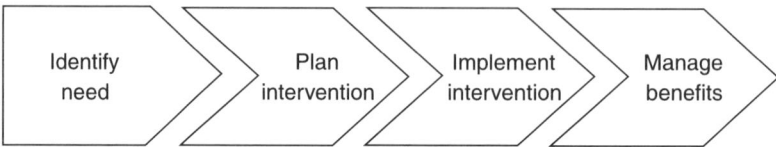

Training effectiveness can be undermined at any of these stages, and a poor evaluation may reflect problems at the earlier stages. Evaluation often takes place either just after and/or during implementation, or else after and/or during the final stage, "manage benefits".

Training evaluation usually takes place at or just after the "implement intervention" stage. However, as previously mentioned, it is also valuable to evaluate effectiveness after trainees have returned to the work place:

- When participants have had a chance to put their new skills into practice.
- After several months, to determine if behavioural changes are lasting.

Training and development

Activity 10.4 Evaluating training effectiveness

Identify three development activities you have undertaken in the last year. Using a spreadsheet set out:

- The basis for evaluating training effectiveness. If you do not already have all the information to do this, think back and reconstruct the thinking as best you can.
- Your evaluation:
  - Include an estimate of the value to the organisation of your training.
  - State your assumptions clearly. As a marketer you may be able to draw on your knowledge of evaluating advertising effectiveness.

What could have made the development you took part in even more effective? What will you do differently in the future?

Activity 10.5 Planning training

Your Marketing Manager knows that you are undertaking a course on marketing management and has asked you for some ideas for a team building programme. Write some notes to help you prepare for a meeting where plans for the proposed team building training will be discussed.

Case Study – The sharper focus group

It all began when Elaine Moore, NOP's (a business information group) Director of Training and Development, spotted an article in *People Management* about a Self-Managed Learning (SML) programme at professional services firm KPMG. The firm had faced similar HR issues to NOP, which had found that its talented researchers often struggled to be effective managers.

Also it was clear that the ability to work alone (which characterises many brilliant researchers), did not always sit well with the need for team working and collaboration across business areas. So NOP had been looking for a new approach to management development.

NOP has six businesses within the group, each aligned with the clients it serves. For example, the finance business works with banks and financial services companies. The strength of this is the market expertise that researchers build up. Its weakness is that people tend to work for just their own business area and miss the corporate perspective.

Consequently, Moore wanted a cost-effective management development programme that facilitated cross-functional support and networking, and also linked personal development to the needs of the business, whilst encouraging individual ownership. The aim was to encourage a culture of continuous learning and development.

So when Moore saw the feature, she and her Group Managing Director, Phyllis Macfarlane, contacted Ian Cunningham, Chairman of the Strategic Developments International consultancy, who had designed the KPMG programme.

Prior to this, the NOP group had gone through a whole year of trial and error in its efforts to find the right kind of programme, with seemingly endless meetings piloting, evaluating and rejecting proposals that didn't quite hit the spot.

Moore and Cunningham identified four problems with traditional management development.

Firstly, it did not always respond to the needs of the business and individual managers. 'People learn differently and market researchers value their individuality and resent the idea that they should be "clones" of the ideal manager,' Moore says. Too often she adds, managers go through "sheep dip" training, imposing the same content and learning methods on everyone. Alternatively, they face a random array of courses and workshops, or rely too heavily on on-the-job learning. NOP's programme created an overall strategy for senior managers, whilst allowing each one to focus on personal learning goals.

Secondly, Moore questions whether or not people always learn what they are taught and apply it. 'There is a bizarre assumption in many organisations that what is taught in the classroom is automatically learnt and applied in real-work contexts.' In fact, what is taught often does not equal what is learnt, and research shows that learning often does not transfer back to the work environment. Personal ownership is key to the transfer taking place.

Thirdly, evidence indicates that training contributes only 10 to 20 per cent of the variance in management performance. Most of what makes a manager effective comes from on-the-job learning experiences.

Lastly, self-diagnosing development needs is a difficult and emotional problem. Most people do not realise that their management style is poor. The NOP programme tackles this through 360-degree feedback, psychometric tests, and through a learning environment where people open up more to their colleagues.

In each nine-month wave of the programme, 24 managers met in groups of six every five weeks. Each group was supported by a "learning group adviser" to help it function as an efficient learning environment. Most were senior, experienced NOP directors, but two of them were from outside the company.

The groups started with a half-day briefing session, putting the programme into its business context and introducing the concept of self-managed learning. Each manager then drafted a learning contract (a deal negotiated between the individual, their line manager and their learning group), in which they specified their own objectives and how to achieve and measure them. NOP developed a variety of evaluation measures including:

- Self-completed pre- and post-programme quantitative questionnaires, to measure attitudes to, and experiences of the programme, and to identify any shifts in manager's perceptions of their skills.
- A qualitative set of interviews with managers, before, during and after the programme.
- A questionnaire completed by line managers.
- End of programme presentations by learning groups to the NOP board.

Cunningham says, 'NOP was not interested in "happy sheets". By reviewing the process over 12 months, they found they could examine real business results. They found that people with learning contracts were more thoughtful about their learning. These were also easier to work with than short-term development plans.'

The results showed that participants improved dramatically in areas important to senior managers, such as time management, communication, strategic thinking and leadership. The different business areas also developed the habit of sharing knowledge.

'NOP hasn't implemented a training plan, it's engaged in strategic learning,' Cunningham says. Training was just part of a wider programme. There was no syllabus, no curriculum or imposed objectives – except business ones. Creating new cross-functional relationships and social capital was another aspect.

The main obstacle was time. Between them, participants put in more than 1,360 days during the year, much of which was by senior executives.

Is there anything we would do differently next time? Moore says, 'With hindsight, I would have got a better mix of communication. We had all the documentation (such as best practice guides) right, but we only had one all-staff presentation at the start. Next time I'd do more presentations at local business level. And I would slot in more early morning training sessions to ease people into SML.'

'No single approach is going to suit everyone and we did encourage those for whom learning groups were not congenial to opt out and implement their own personal development programme with the help of their line manager.'

'I would also have put more "blue water" between sessions for reflection, leaving managers more breathing space.'

Because of the time investment, Macfarlane was originally concerned that profits might be hit in the short term. Instead they increased by a record 30.5 per cent in a year.

The principles behind SML are simple, but the devil is in the implementation. Macfarlane admits 'The use of SML was initially greeted with scepticism. But once participants realised they had a chance both to manage the development of their careers and to contribute to organisational performance, they responded with enthusiasm.'

What is Self-Managed Learning (SML)?

The term was coined by Ian Cunningham to describe a new approach he developed at the Anglian Regional Management Centre in the 1970s.

It was influenced by action learning, introduced by Reg Revans (*People Management*, 28th December, 2000) in the 1940s, in which participants learn as members of a small group or set. Cunningham's version puts less emphasis on the action and more on the learning.

The other main influence on self-managed learning has been independent study. With this method of study each individual agrees their learning goals and how they will achieve them. The information is written up in a contract. In self-managed learning, the contract is negotiated with the learning group and the organisation.

Training and development

Source: The Sharper Focus Group by Carol Glover, which first appeared in *People Management*, 7th March, 2002, and is reproduced with kind permission.

Questions
1. What were the main benefits of a learning contract to individual learners?
2. How effective was the evaluation of the programme?
3. What were the additional benefits to the organisation, apart from individual development?

SUMMARY OF KEY POINTS
- Training and development begins at induction – the time the individual enters the organisation.
- Effective induction programmes are based on the needs of the individual and include job requirements, contribution to organisation business objectives, and information to help the individual feel welcome in their new work place.
- Effective training and development is planned following a Training Needs Analysis (TNA) to identify performance gaps that can be filled by training and development.
- Identify SMART aims and objectives to aid post-course evaluation.
- Consider different means of meeting training and development objectives, including the use of both formal and informal intervention.
- Delivery should meet the needs of the trainees and can include lectures, on-the-job training and group activities.
- Evaluation should measure the impact of the training on the trainee, their work and the organisation – the latter is very difficult to isolate.
- Training may produce long-term and short-term results that are not easy to measure quantitatively.

Improving and developing own learning
The following projects are designed to help you develop your knowledge and skills

further, by carrying out some research yourself. Feedback is not provided for this type of learning because there are no "answers" to be found, but you may wish to discuss your findings with colleagues and fellow students.

Project A

Plan to carry out a TNA for your team. What information do you need? How can you obtain this? Who needs to be involved?

What priorities for training have you discovered?

Project B

Following the TNA you have just completed, produce a training plan to meet the training needs identified in Project A.

Project C

Gather post-course evaluation forms from courses you have previously attended and from other courses used by your organisation. How well do they evaluate the effectiveness of the training taking place? What other means of evaluating the impact of training and development are used in your organisation? What improvements can you suggest?

Feedback to activities

Activity 10.1 Induction

One approach would be to explain the organisation from the position of a third party, and have slides covering its:

- History.
- Mission and goals.
- Values.
- Structure.
- Products and services.

Another approach might be to cover the same material, but from the perspective of a mythical employee, a customer, and a shareholder. If done well, this can have more immediate impact on the listener and hold their interest.

Whichever approach you used, how well did you identify the listener's needs? Did you do some research into them in advance, or did you mainly work from your own knowledge and perspective?

Activity 10.2 Training Needs Analysis (TNA)

A full TNA for an organisation can be a very time consuming exercise. You may have discovered:

- TNA on specific organisational issues such as project management.
- TNA activities being carried out at departmental and team levels, but not at a higher level.
- TNA activities being covered, but under different names and guises. The aggregation of personal development plans and subsequent implementation planning is one method used to conduct a TNA.
- TNA being facilitated by specific organisational forms and procedures, or alternatively designed on a case-by-case basis.

Activity 10.3 Planning development of skills

The first step is to prepare a SMART objective, preferably in discussion with the employee. It could be along the lines of 'In six months I will be able to explain my ideas to other people, taking into account their language and concerns, and answer any questions in a way which meets other's needs and builds support for my proposals, as assessed by the other people in my team.'

Depending on the options you came up with, you will have different answers. The table below shows some of the things you might have considered for three of the potential options:

- One-to-one work with the manager.
- A training course.
- Self study.

Evaluation criteria	One-to-one work	Training course	Self study
How well will it achieve the outcome?	Would probably achieve it. There is evidence that feedback and appraisal have had some impact to date, and employee now accepts that there is an issue. However, skills coaching will also be required.	There are many courses that address this specific issue, but there are some concerns about how well individuals bring the learning back into the work place. Likely to require additional work place support.	Does not allow skills practise outside the work environment. It also requires much self-diagnosis. It will not achieve the outcome on its own, as it would require feedback and one-to-one work as well.
How long will it take?	May take longer than we have on its own.	Initial 3 day course, plus skills practise and development over following months.	On its own, could take a very long time.
How much will it cost?	Additional managerial time required. Is this feasible?	Course cost, employee time, plus work place support (feedback rather than skills development).	Cost of books/tapes. Employee may do study in spare time. May require almost as much work place support as one to one on its own.
What value will it bring? Over what period?	Gradual impact over several months. May not bring results straight away.	Expect some immediate improvement, then gradual increase as new skills are practised.	Gradual impact, may be slightly faster than one-to-one support alone.

Evaluation criteria	One-to-one work	Training course	Self study
Is it appropriate for this individual or group?	Yes, although the individual often responds well to external influence.	Yes, individual responds well to outside influence. Will get feedback from other course attendees and trainer, so highly appropriate if we use an open course.	Up to a point. A lack of external feedback and coaching on using the skills could inhibit the value to this employee.

Activity 10.4 Evaluating training effectiveness

In carrying out this activity, you may have had to make many assumptions in assessing the value achieved.

- How does improved influencing skills feed through to bottom-line profit? Via a % increase in productivity?
- How might a specific marketing skill result in increased product sales?
- How can we assess leadership skills training in this way, given that the benefit is expected to reach fruition in the long term?

It is often more realistic and useful to assess any behavioural changes in the trainees than it is to assess (or predict) the link between it and the organisation's short and long-term profitability. Hence this is why it is the route that is usually followed.

However, it remains important to think through the issues and to regularly review the assumptions behind the links between learning and improved performance. Drawing a diagram showing the links may be sufficient, but there is a danger that in attempting to turn everything into numbers only short-term development will ever be pursued. For example, what is the impact of someone learning how to learn effectively?

The point is not necessarily to establish these links precisely. Managers aim to ensure that there is a case for a link, and that the cost is reasonable when contrasted against the potential impact on the organisation (and against other uses for the investment). In some cases the link may be transparent and assessable e.g. sales training, leading to observable differences in behaviour, leading to increased sales. In others you may be able to find relevant research supporting an approach.

Activity 10.5 Planning training

Your notes may contain all or some of the following points.

Training is used to develop new skills, impart knowledge, change attitudes and behaviours, and motivate teams and individuals. Adults have different preferred learning styles so learn in different ways. Therefore, the training should include a variety of activities and contain an appropriate balance between tutor-led and student-led activities.

Team building is a subject that most managers will have some experience of. Hopefully they will have worked in both successful teams and teams that failed to achieve their goals. However, most will not have explored the theory relating to this, even though they will have lots of ideas to share.

Before designing training it is important to understand the needs and characteristics of the trainees, to ensure that the training aims and objectives are designed to meet their needs. The criteria for evaluating the success or failure of the training also needs to be identified. Most training produces long-term benefits that are difficult to isolate and measure, so an evaluation sheet at the end of a short course is not sufficient. Other means of evaluation include reports, observation, and surveys, to ascertain how behaviour has changed – see later note.

Team effectiveness is difficult to measure. It is a combination of:

- Teams meeting objectives/producing results and exceeding expectations.
- Members working together in a cohesive and supportive way.
- Individual members experiencing personal development as a result of working as part of the team.

Team building training needs to help develop the skills that lead to personal development and positive working relationships, and also raise awareness of how teams develop and the factors affecting effectiveness.

The content of the training programme should include:

- Definition of a team – a small number of people with complementary skills, who are committed to a common purpose, performance goals and approach, for which they hold themselves mutually accountable. (Katzenbach & Smith, 1993).

- Why use teams – benefits such as the ability to solve complex problems, higher levels of creativity, teams being less risk averse.
- Different types of team – formal/informal, permanent/temporary.
- Team development – Forming, Storming, Norming, Performing and Adjourning.
- Activities that explore factors influencing effectiveness – size, common understanding of objectives, decision making, conflict resolution, leadership, etc.
- Activities that raise awareness of the skills required to develop good interpersonal relationships, such as communication.
- Activities that raise awareness of personal skills such as time management.
- A Personal Development Plan for individuals to raise their skills level.
- A Team Development Plan.

Delivery should take a practical approach, with short inputs from the trainer interspersed with activities such as team "games" and brainstorming sessions.

The achievement of the objectives depends on assessing the trainees understanding during the training at regular intervals, via feedback from activities, and then modifying content accordingly. The main learning points should be reinforced via regular summaries and activity debriefs.

The number of trainees on each course should be low (around 10-12) for each trainer. Trainees should be trained with the teams they are working in, but also need to experience ideas from outside this environment. Attending training with people from other parts of the organisation might facilitate lateral, vertical and horizontal communication within the small company units and across the units.

The evaluation of effectiveness can be measured by:

- Pre- and post-course team effectiveness questionnaires, and interviews with individual members of the team.
- Immediate post-course questionnaires completed by delegates, with a report from the trainer.

- Observations by the team leader pre-course and at relevant intervals, such as three months, six months and one year following the training.

Follow-up can be planned with the team once the training has taken place – the programme includes action and development plans.

Session 11

Managing client relationships and customer care

Introduction

This Session demonstrates the importance of developing good client relationships and the positive impact it can have on business. Marketing oriented companies gather information from internal and external sources to monitor and improve the services they provide for their customers and the way they look after their customers (customer care).

The last section in this Session reviews client negotiation skills, so you may want to refer back to Session 5, which discussed negotiation skills and how to achieve the outcome you want from negotiations.

LEARNING OUTCOMES
At the end of this Session you will be able to:

- Evaluate client relationships and their impact on business.
- Recognise the importance of effective customer care and "moments of truth".
- Monitor and improve levels of customer care.
- Explain the importance of customer focus.
- Plan and prepare effective client negotiations.

Understanding client relationships

The lines between organisations and their customers and suppliers have recently become more blurred than they were previously. For example:

- Supply chains have been more and more integrated. A supplier might use their clients' organisation's stock control and purchasing systems.
- Delivery to the customer, and most customer contact, can be carried out by a different organisation than the one with the customer sales relationship:
  - The distribution and delivery of products may be the responsibility of a different organisation than the one running the Internet site through which orders are taken.

- Any queries may be dealt with at a call centre run by yet another organisation.

Assessing and improving end-user customer relationships can therefore be an activity that requires co-operation and negotiation between several organisations. For example, consider the following scenario for the delivery of a product to the customer.

Figure 11.1 End-to-end product delivery

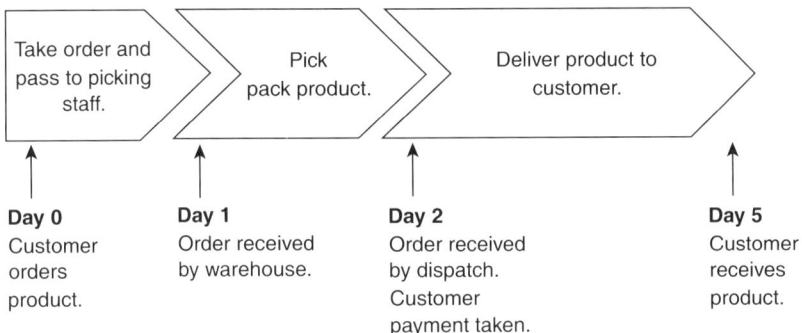

Day 0	Day 1	Day 2	Day 5
Customer orders product.	Order received by warehouse.	Order received by dispatch. Customer payment taken.	Customer receives product.

The first two stages can be carried out by the organisation that owns the main customer relationship. However, the last stage may be carried out by another supplier.

If the customer sees speed of delivery as extremely important, then a common error is to concentrate only on the process inside the organisation. Reducing this by 50% gives a 20% improvement in the end-to-end delivery time of 5 days. Reducing the dispatch-delivery time by one third gives the same improvement, and using next-day delivery reduces the end-to-end time by 40%. If this is of sufficient value to the customer, they may even be prepared to pay more for it than the actual costs incurred. Some of this additional benefit could then be passed to the distributor, resulting in a "win-win-win" situation.

Organisations need to assess the importance of their relationships with all their external contacts. They need to understand the contribution external contacts make to their overall relationships with their customers, and hence their own short and long-term profitability. Client relationship management and marketing is an area that extends across both customers and suppliers.

Evaluating client relationships

To evaluate relationships and identify areas for improvement, organisations need to consider the relationship from several perspectives:

- Their own. How successful is this relationship? What return am I receiving, given the resources and effort I contribute?
- The client's. How well are their needs being met? How do we compare with competitor offerings?
- Any other parties affected by the relationship.

The needs from the relationship will be affected by the stage the relationship is at.

Client selection and recruitment

Organisations, particularly in the finance industry, have been criticised for spending most of their time and effort on recruiting new customers to the detriment of other customer stages.

Client retention and maintenance

Needs change as a relationship develops, and if an organisation wants long-term relationships with its customers and suppliers then it needs to take account of this.

- Suppliers may be looking to develop added-value services that can benefit customers, albeit at a slightly higher cost.
- Customers may be looking for continuous improvement, and for an organisation that takes the time to identify new needs and find ways to satisfy them.
- Organisations may be looking for opportunities to cross-sell other products and services, and may require supplier co-operation to assist in this process.

Client retirement

When a relationship is no longer beneficial to both parties, then organisations may want to recognise this and walk away. Maximising profitability does not mean meeting the needs of every potential client. This could be for a number of reasons:

- A customer is no longer in the target market, perhaps because they now require a fully customised service that is simply unprofitable for an organisation established on off-the-shelf, quality, repeatable products to meet.

Managing client relationships and customer care

- A supplier can no longer meet an organisation's needs profitably.

Client retirement is not always a bad thing, so long as it is the result of a conscious decision and not a result of poor client maintenance.

Improving client relationships

Having assessed client relationships against the needs of all parties, the next question to ask is 'What changes will add the greatest value at least cost?', again for all parties.

- Think in different time frames, both short and long term.
- For one-on-one relationships, explore this actively with the other party.
- Be aware that the answers will differ between different client segments.
- Remember that you are looking for win-win-win improvements, which assist your organisation in meeting client needs effectively and efficiently, and thereby maximising profitability. This is in the context of your competitors, who will be looking to do the same.

Activity 11.1 Customer profitability?

Analyse the following salesperson's current customer base using a spreadsheet. Which areas require further investigation?

Customer	Time spent per week (hrs)	Annualised income (£)	Annualised costs (£)
1	0.5	20,000	5,000
2	0.25	80,000	6,000
3	1	10,000	4,000
4	2	5,000	3,000
5	3	30,000	15,000
6	1	4,000	2,000
7	2	3,000	2,000
8	2	10,000	4,000
9	1	25,000	10,000
10	4	60,000	10,000

Customer	Time spent per week (hrs)	Annualised income (£)	Annualised costs (£)
11	0.5	30,000	3,000
12	5	20,000	9,000
13	2	6,000	1,000
14	4	7,000	3,000
15	1	30,000	5,000
16	4	6,000	3,000
17	2	3,000	1,000
18	1	4,000	1,000
19	0.5	5,000	1,500
20	0.25	2,000	500

What is "customer care"?

Customer care refers to the entire experience that the customer has in dealing with an organisation. For example, an experience with an electricity or gas supplier may include:

- Requesting information about your account or about pricing levels.
- Meeting the meter reader when they call.
- Quality of supply e.g. planned cuts, unexpected breaks in supply.
- Responsiveness to problems e.g. supply connection, getting power back on after a cut, engineer visits to correct faults.
- Receiving promotional material.
- Seeing advertisements.
- Being inconvenienced by a supplier's vans – dangerous overtaking, bad parking.

Earlier in this Session the stages of a client relationship with an organisation were explored. Customer care issues may occur at any time during these stages, and can be affected by issues unrelated to the purpose of their relationship with the organisation, such as the bad driving by company representatives referred to above. Every point of contact between a customer and the organisation, both planned and unplanned, creates an impression of the organisation in the customer's mind.

Impact of effective customer care

If you ask someone about what they want from a product or service, they will often start by telling you about the qualities they are looking for, and the hard service standards (such as delivery time and desired features) they expect. If you ask someone to tell you about a good or bad customer experience they have had recently, the response tends to be quite different – they will tend to talk about the quality of care they received, such as:

- The friendliness of the staff.

- The response to complaints – whether staff wanted to put things right, or whether they were not interested.

- Any additions to the service which exceeded expectations, like providing a freephone helpline to answer queries about a software package; flowers or wine left in a hotel room; or a follow up phone call to check satisfaction with the product or service.

Customer care is focused on the whole experience of being a customer, rather than on basic product standards. These are of course important, but they are no longer enough (refer back to Session 8, Herzberg's Two-Factor theory).

Competitive advantage and customer care

In most industries, the basis for competition has changed dramatically. While organisations used to compete on the consistency and reliability of their offering, successful companies are effective and efficient enough now to provide this by default.

- Quality, consistency and reliability are still very important. If you can't even deliver these, you are not even in the game. Organisations need to continue to innovate and pay special attention to this area.

- Product features are easier to copy than the experience of being a customer of a company.

- Customer care is a major source of competitor advantage in many industries, not just the service sector.

Defining good customer care

The definition of what constitutes good customer care is in the hands of the recipient. Customer-focused organisations recognise this, and one of the jobs of the marketing function is to discover what customers value. Consider:

- Adding experiences that are highly valued by the customer, yet are not costly from the perspective of the organisation – again, looking for a "win-win" situation.

- Spending less on costly activities that customers do not actually value. It doesn't matter how proud the organisation is of, for example, being the only retailer to offer tea and biscuits free of charge in all its branches, if the customer does not value that aspect of the experience then it is probably not worth doing.

Activity 11.2 The customer experience

Interview several colleagues about one recent example of excellent customer service and one very bad example. Ask them what their perceptions are of the organisation(s) involved following the experience. What meaning have they made of the experience? Will they deal with them again?

Also do this exercise for yourself.

What factors were similar for you and your colleagues?

Identifying customer care points – "moments of truth"

As previously discussed, each time the customer interacts with the organisation it has an impact on their perception of customer care. Organisations therefore need to:

- Map the interaction between customer and organisation from the customer's point of view.

- Determine the factors that add or detract value for the customer.

- Understand how the organisation can influence these factors, in order to understand and assess their standards of customer care.

A very simple customer transaction might be analysed like this:

Figure 11.2 Simple customer contact flowchart

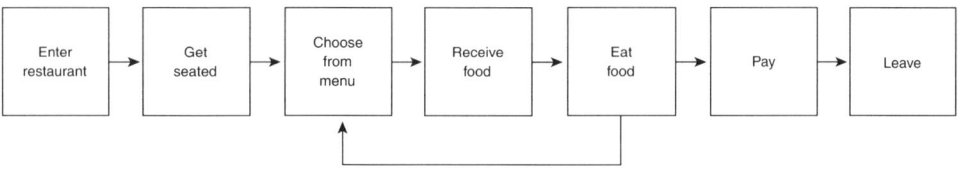

Figure 11.3 "Moments of truth"

Stage	Customer criteria	Care points
Enter restaurant.	■ Friendliness of staff. ■ Length of wait. ■ Cleanliness of surroundings. ■ Appearance of staff and surroundings.	■ Greetings staff. ■ Restaurant lobby/waiting area.
Get seated.	■ Position of table. ■ Cleanliness of table. ■ Length of wait.	■ Table and furnishings. ■ Restaurant surroundings. ■ Greetings staff.
Choose from menu.	■ Availability of food. ■ Extent of choice. ■ Ease of selection e.g. Are items clearly explained? ■ Appearance of menu. ■ Timeliness of menu being offered. ■ Range of prices.	■ Menu. ■ Waiting staff.

Effective Management for Marketing

Stage	Customer criteria	Care points
Receive food.	■ Length of wait. ■ Appearance. ■ Size of portions. ■ Accuracy. ■ Friendliness of staff.	■ Food. ■ Cutlery and crockery. ■ Waiting staff.
Eat food.	■ Taste. ■ Consistency. ■ Quality. ■ Ease of eating e.g. cutlery. ■ Availability of staff if required.	■ Food. ■ Cutlery and crockery. ■ Staff.
Pay.	■ Timeliness of bill. ■ Price. ■ Service charge arrangements.	■ Bill. ■ Waiting staff.
Leave.	■ Friendliness of staff. ■ Assistance given e.g. helping you with your coat.	■ Greetings staff. ■ Sweets. ■ Business cards.

At each stage of the customer's experience, the organisation has an opportunity to influence the nature of the customer care they receive. For the above, you would also want to map out other possible experiences the customer might have such as:

- Using the cloakroom facilities.
- Making a complaint.
- Asking to move tables.

- Requesting special requirements such as vegan food, gluten-free food, or a meal not on the menu.
- What happens before the customer walks into the restaurant and after they leave.

Organisations need to include the total end-to-end experience of potential and actual customers when assessing moments of truth and standards of customer care. For example, if a potential restaurant customer cannot find the details in a telephone directory, or they cannot get through to book, then they may give up and go elsewhere. To summarise:

- The end-to-end experience is from the point of view of the customer – from first thinking of dealing with an organisation, through to finishing using the product or service, and includes the other parties who were involved in the chain.
- Casual interaction with an organisation (such as a badly driven van or a disgruntled employee) can be just as significant in forming a customer's opinion of it as an intended interaction.

This is applicable to all organisations in every industry sector.

Monitoring customer care

Having identified the customer care points, the organisation needs to understand:

- What is of value from the customers' point of view?
- How can this be assessed and monitored?

Initially, this may be researched through the use of customer focus groups, marketing research, and piloting different approaches in different areas (the usual caveats on the use and abuse of such techniques applies). Once the key criteria have been identified, organisations may monitor the effectiveness of their customer care through the use of:

- Customer questionnaires. These could be used at point of sale, follow-up after an event, or in the case of relationship managed customers, via regular customer surveys.
- Mystery shoppers. These are people trained in assessing the customer experience on a number of pre-determined factors. These can range from "Was the name badge visible?", to an assessment of staff friendliness, or even an assessment of correct answers to queries.

- Measuring service levels to ensure that they meet or exceed promises, such as a supermarket's 'only one customer in front' policy, or delivery within three days. Automated measurement is usually the most accurate and appropriate method.

Identifying areas for improvement

Monitoring customer care levels enables organisations to prioritise possible areas for improvement. This may be because:

- Standards are dropping below those required by the organisation.
- Competitors are moving ahead (this can be identified by benchmarking).
- The organisation sees competitive advantage in an area.

Depending on the issues identified, the options for interventions can cover a wide range of areas and involve a number of people in the supply chain, from both inside and outside the organisation.

Activity 11.3 The end-to-end experience

Think of an organisation that you deal with a lot. Choose an end-to-end interaction you have had with them and, using a word processing and/or presentation package, map out your criteria and the way the organisation had an opportunity to influence you with each one of these.

Add in an assessment of the value each of your criteria had for you (use high/medium/low or a 1-4 scale as appropriate). Where could the organisation have influenced you positively to provide high value at minimal cost?

Now do the same exercise, this time thinking from the perspective of a customer of your own organisation. If appropriate, you may want to write up your findings and ideas to present within your organisation.

Barriers to effective customer care

"Walking the customer journey", as in Activity 11.3, enables the customer care manager to identify areas for improvements – barriers that are preventing consistent high standards of customer care. Common barriers include:

- A lack of understanding of customer needs.
- Raising customer expectations beyond that which can be delivered.

- A lack of responsiveness by organisations and managers in changing policies, procedures and systems to deliver what the customer wants.
- A lack of measurement, thus preventing effective control and improvement.
- Poorly trained staff – both management and front line.
- Poorly treated staff – staff who are not valued will not be motivated to provide excellence in customer service.
- Poor measurement systems – complacency may follow success. Organisations that assume they understand the customer, may become slow to realise that their customers' needs have changed, and even slower to make the changes to meet the new needs.
- A lack of benchmarking – letting the competition get ahead in understanding and meeting customer needs.
- A lack of action – being slow to respond to change even though it has been identified.
- A lack of priority – 'customers don't care how they are treated so long as they get the product or service they want'.

Negotiating with clients

Session 5 covered the processes and attitudes involved in negotiations (you may want to review it before reading on). This section looks at the information you might need when negotiating with clients; either customers or suppliers. A good negotiator will consider both before entering a negotiation, with the outcome of establishing, maintaining and/or improving a mutually profitable and effective relationship.

In addition, it can be valuable to consider the negotiation from another perspective, that of a "fly on the wall" or observer. What advice or additional information would they give you?

Supplier perspective

As a supplier you will need to know:

What interactions has this customer had with your organisation since you saw them last? What is their history with you? What is the pattern of their interaction? Is it problematic? Positive? What key concerns/praise have they had? You might look at:

- Letters. What are the topics? Who initiated the correspondence? How did you deal with them?
- Meetings. Who did they meet? What happened as a result? Was there any follow up?
- Phone calls. What was the purpose? Who did they speak to? What happened subsequently?
- Are there any outstanding issues?

What business have they done with you?

- Profitability? (Cost, which resources, income.)
- Regularity?
- What products and services have they taken?
- What contribution do they make compared to other customers?

What else do you know about their circumstances which is relevant to their interaction with you?

- Key events, such as life events, recent or planned changes in their organisation.
- Interest expressed in other products or services.
- Use of competitor products?

What opportunities are there for an even more mutually profitable relationship?

- Additional products and services.
- Additional value you can offer.
- Things which are costing the organisation a disproportionate amount, and which you would like to change. You may want to persuade them to take off-the-shelf products instead of customised ones.

How does what you offer compare with the competition? Where is your real advantage?

Under what circumstances would you want to walk away from this relationship, or supply of a particular product? What would be the consequences of this?

Customer perspective

As a customer you will need to know:

What products and services you have been taking, and how these contribute to your personal life or business:

- If part of a customer supply chain, what would add additional value to your customers?
- What are their competitors offering?
- What costs have you incurred, and what value have you received? Are there any areas of particular note, either of value or of concern? Do you have any outstanding queries or complaints?
- How has the organisation been dealing with you? Do you have concerns? Are there good things you want to continue?

What else might they be able to do for you for mutual benefit?

- Competitor offerings, can they better them?
- New products or services you are interested in.
- Changes to existing products or services, like a reduction in service failures, added value features you want, changes in ordering or delivery arrangements.
- Are you happy with the relationship, or are there changes you want to make, like invoicing arrangements, delivery times?
- Your estimated demand for their products and services over say the next twelve months.

Under what circumstances would you want to walk away from this relationship, or purchase of a particular product? What would be the consequences of this?

Activity 11.4 Dealing with complaints

Identify either:

- A recent purchase of a product or service with which you were dissatisfied.
- A recent problem a customer has had with your organisation.

> Think through the issue from the perspective of the customer. Write a complaint letter, setting out the nature of your complaint and your proposed solution.
>
> Now move to the perspective of the organisation. From their point of view, read and respond to the complaint letter.

Case Study – The railway business and relationship marketing

The railway industry in the United Kingdom was privatised in 1996, 50 years after it was nationalised. It had a long tradition of restrictive practices and adversarial industrial relations. The perceived attitude of British Rail to the paying customer was in the past seen as dismal.

The rail network has been broken up into numerous businesses, which includes Railtrack (who are responsible for the track and land), rolling-stock companies, and more than twenty operating companies (franchises). There are now some 60 companies that constitute the new privately owned United Kingdom railway system. Among the new owners are Virgin, Stagecoach, National Express and CGE of France. Since the first franchisees took over as new train operating companies their management has been adjusting to operating in the private sector.

All the new owners have had to implement large-scale restructuring of employment terms and conditions, which would be daunting for any well-organised business. The new owners have had to undertake this new challenge faced with a diversity of job grades and categories, restrictive work practices and in-built inflexibility and inefficiency.

Adding to the train companies' problems is the knowledge that their franchises will run out in 7 to 15 years, so there is no time to lose in establishing an efficient and effective operating company. Their ability to win further contracts depends on their success in operating the current franchises.

Poor customer service was synonymous with the old British Rail, with people being treated like passengers to process rather than customers to serve. Offering customer service was a little-known concept to British Rail, the original company. The newly formed companies have inherited this problem. A key feature of the changes taking place is that customer complaints are being monitored and recorded publicly, with serious penalties for companies who fail to achieve set standards of performance.

Another key feature is the need to work in partnership with other businesses within the national railway system. Each business is dependent on other privatised railway businesses to ensure a consistent and reliable national railway service.

A recent report condemned many of the train operating companies for a fall in customer service. The marketing manager of one such company has decided it is time to tackle the problem of improving customer service performance and has started a review of working relationships. She has recently carried out an initial audit that highlighted the following:

- Contact between the companies within the national railway system is ad hoc and tactical, and usually only initiated when something goes wrong.

- There is a lack of structure and guidelines for contacting companies, often resulting in actions not being taken, problems being left unresolved, and no one being prepared to take responsibility for customer complaints.

- Variation in working practices between the companies, particularly in gathering and tracking customer complaints.

Source: *Effective Management for Marketing* examination paper, June, 1999.

Questions

The marketing manager wishes to find ways in which the business might tackle the problem of improving the working relationships with the other companies within the national railway system, with a view to improving customer service. What advice could you give her on:

1. How the company might tackle the problem of improving relationships with other companies across the railway network.

2. The implications for marketing management of implementing this strategy (for example, implications for teamwork, communications, consistency of standards, processes).

3. Controls for ensuring success.

SUMMARY OF KEY POINTS

- Customers come into contact with suppliers in many different ways, both planned and unplanned. At each point of contact a favourable impression must be made.

- Customer care must be everyone's responsibility – seeking to identify and satisfy customer needs must be the norm.

- It is important to measure standards in order to control and improve processes.

- People are an essential part of the delivery of high standards of customer care – staff must be well looked after if they are to look after customers well.

- Successful negotiation with customers, clients and suppliers, requires that the negotiator views the situation from each party's perspective, and takes these needs into account – but still is assertive in achieving their essential outcomes.

Improving and developing own learning

The following projects are designed to help you develop your knowledge and skills further, by carrying out some research yourself. Feedback is not provided for this type of learning because there are no "answers" to be found, but you may wish to discuss your findings with colleagues and fellow students.

Project A

Think about the companies that you regularly do business with. How much is your loyalty influenced by the "customer care" you receive? If you have recommended your preferred organisations to others, what was the basis for your recommendation? Did you mention how well they look after their customers?

What suggestions for improvement could you make for your preferred companies that would further improve their standards of customer care?

> **Project B**
>
> For your organisation, or one you know well, find out how standards in customer care are measured. Are a combination of methods used, such as surveys, postal questionnaires, focus groups, mystery shoppers, interviews? What suggestions for improvements can you make?

> **Project C**
>
> Organisations that gain a competitive advantage through the high standards of customer care they deliver achieve this because it is part of their company culture. What evidence of this is there in your organisation or other companies that you do business with on a regular basis?

Feedback to activities

Activity 11.1 Customer profitability?

There are several analyses you may have carried out. One possibility is shown below:

Customer	Profit	Accumulative % share of profit	Accumulative % share of costs	Accumulative % time spent
2	74,000	27.3%	6.7%	0.7%
10	50,000	45.8%	18.0%	11.5%
11	27,000	55.7%	21.3%	12.8%
15	25,000	64.9%	27.0%	15.5%
1	15,000	70.5%	32.6%	16.9%
5	15,000	76.0%	49.4%	25.0%
9	15,000	81.5%	60.7%	27.7%
12	11,000	85.6%	70.8%	41.2%
3	6,000	87.8%	75.3%	43.9%
8	6,000	90.0%	79.8%	49.3%
13	5,000	91.9%	80.9%	54.7%
14	4,000	93.4%	84.3%	65.5%

Customer	Profit	Accumulative % share of profit	Accumulative % share of costs	Accumulative % time spent
19	3,500	94.6%	86.0%	66.9%
16	3,000	95.8%	89.3%	77.7%
18	3,000	96.9%	90.4%	80.4%
4	2,000	97.6%	93.8%	85.8%
6	2,000	98.3%	96.1%	88.5%
17	2,000	99.1%	97.2%	93.9%
20	1,500	99.6%	97.8%	94.6%
7	1,000	100.0%	100.0%	100.0%

The rationale for the way the salesperson spends their time is not known, however looking at the figures:

- Seven customers account for over 80% of the profit, yet less than 30% of time is spent on them.
- About 50% of costs are spent on customers who contribute about 25% of the profit.
- One customer accounts for over a quarter of profits, yet has the least amount of time spent with them. If this results in poor understanding of their needs, this customer could leave the organisation.

This pattern of profitability is not unusual. The situation may be different if looked at over a customer life cycle, yet organisations often spend the most time and effort on customers which end up bringing them the least return.

Activity 11.2 The customer experience

People do tend to base their opinion of what an organisation is "like" on just one or two significant experiences with what they see as a representative of the organisation. These opinions (for example, 'They don't care about customers', 'They are stand off-ish', 'They know almost nothing about their products') will then have an impact on their future dealings – particularly whether they want to have any future dealings at all!

Although this exercise was aimed as the consumer market, it would be useful to do the same check for business to business and not-for-profit organisations.

Activity 11.3 The end-to-end experience

Did you:

- Consider and map out the full end-to-end process? This is often easier to do for an organisation of which you are a customer than for your own (this is why the activity is structured in this way).

- Identify the factors and the organisational influences easily? Did any come as a surprise? Were you surprised to see how easy it is to influence a customer by relatively small actions, for good or for ill?

Activity 11.4 Dealing with complaints

Good communication and negotiation involves being able to see a situation from several different points of view. Some of you may have made more changes in your approach than others, depending on how used you are to thinking in this way.

Session 12

Managing change

Introduction

Organisations do not always manage change effectively, resulting in resistance to change and low morale. This Session explains how to plan and prepare for change, and shows the importance of communicating with the people involved.

> **LEARNING OUTCOMES**
>
> At the end of this Session you will be able to:
>
> - Plan change effectively in marketing oriented organisations.
> - Discuss the impact of change on people.
> - Explain how to develop effective implementation plans.
> - Discuss how to manage change.

Triggers for change

From a marketing perspective, an organisation may be required to respond to changes in many different areas:

- Customer requirements of products and services.
- Competitor advances.
- Legal and regulatory requirements – quality, customer communications, salespeople's qualifications, advertising, etc.
- Marketing skills, knowledge and development standards such as Investors in People, changes to CIM qualifications.
- Brand changes.

Some of these changes are imposed from the outside, such as legislation requiring product compliance, whilst others are planned from the inside, like brand changes. There are also changes that are planned and managed from within a team, such as the reorganisation of jobs and activities within the marketing department.

Understanding the scope of the change

The first step for any manager involved in planning change is to understand:

- The outcome of the change – what is it intended to achieve? By when? This needs to be expressed in terms of SMART objectives and include:
  - Costs.
  - Value to the organisation.
  - Perspectives of all those affected, such as customers, staff, shareholders and legislators.
- How the outcome differs from where the organisation is today (gap analysis). What specifically needs to change to achieve the outcome? There may be different options for achieving this:
  - Who will be impacted? How? For example, will customers need to fill in a new application form? Will salespeople need to be trained?
  - What systems and processes need changing? Do IT systems need to be changed? Processes redesigned? Jobs need reorganising? Training need to take place? New literature need producing?
- What other changes are taking place which will impact the same areas. Consider:
  - People.
  - Systems.
  - Customers.
  - Processes.
- The wider consequences of the change. What knock-on effects might there be? If as a result of the change salespeople need to be trained to a higher standard, then their existing salaries might be out of line with the marketplace and they may leave if this is not recognised.
- The extent to which the change is aligned with the culture and goals of those affected both inside and outside the organisation:
  - Linking sales targets to pay may be in line with the development of a customer care culture.
  - Busy, professional customers, may be hostile to having to spend more time with sales staff.

- A service that is highly successful for customers in the US may not suit an Asian or UK market.
- The scale and availability of resources required to affect the change.

Many changes are embarked upon without understanding these areas in sufficient detail, and organisations can pay dearly for this later on. One manager is highly unlikely to understand all these areas, and a workshop involving the people with the relevant skills and experience in all these areas will be much more effective than one person attempting to cover everything. What seems like a small change to a non-specialist may have wide reaching consequences, and there may be different and cheaper ways of achieving the same outcome.

Figure 12.1 Who to involve in change

Change affecting:	Consider involving:
Customers	Market specialists e.g. product managers, customer relationship experts, competitor analysts.
Ways of doing things	Operations people. IT specialists.
Organisational groups or teams	HRM specialist. Representatives of the group or team, or someone with experience of working in that area.
Legal issues	Legal representative.
Other change initiatives	Representative of the initiative.

A diverse range of management skills (such as managing meetings, negotiations, conflict handling, internal marketing, problem solving and decision making) are required by change managers.

Identifying and marketing change

Once you have understood the scope of the change, it is important that you ensure there is buy-in from the people who can facilitate the change in each area:

- This can make the difference between effective and efficient change, and everything grinding to a halt.

- For a small scope change, this may just mean ensuring the whole of your team, or your line manager agrees to the change. For large-scale changes this may be a significant undertaking, involving several departments for instance.

Planning the change

Implementation planning will be covered in more detail later on in this Session. Plans need to encompass:

- Everyone affected inside and outside the organisation. Even where they may not play an active role in promoting the change, you may want to include them in internal or external marketing plans.

- All activities associated with the change.

- Links with other initiatives. Are they contingent on some of your other activities? Are you making your plans dependent on their potential outputs?

- Dates when the benefits will be realised, linked to specific milestones and SMART objectives.

When planning change, identify the forces for the change and the forces acting against the change (Force Field Analysis). The forces for are termed change drivers, whilst those that are barriers to the change are termed restraining forces. Some will be more important than others, so when weighing the balance for and against change add these in. Remember that there is always the option of doing nothing!

Activity 12.1 The extent of change

Many organisations have made the decision to sell online. This has resulted in far-reaching changes within organisations and for consumers. For your organisation or industry, choose an existing product or service that is, or could be, sold via the Internet.

As far as you can, scope the changes that this has entailed or would entail, according to the checklist in the section "Understanding the scope of the change".

Individual perspectives of change

In the context of the overall organisation, some changes may seem much smaller than others:

- The appointment of a marketing manager from outside the organisation may only have an immediate impact on her team.
- Changes in legislation in the UK financial services industry over the last decade have resulted in significant changes to sales staff skills requirements, sales processes, product design, supporting IT systems, and customer literature.

However, whatever the scale of the change, in each case the recipients of change are all individuals looking at it from their own perspective. Change needs to be understood from the point of view of the individual, and not just the organisation. From the perspective of someone in the marketing department, their new manager will cause more changes to their individual circumstances than other wider-reaching organisational changes. The more out of alignment the change is with the individual's experience, values and needs, the more likely they are to react adversely to the change.

Personal reactions to change

People sponsoring a change can sometimes come to believe that their proposals are so obviously right and beneficial that they will be welcomed. While this may be true from their perspective, they have probably spent a lot of time thinking about and committing themselves to the change. The people being impacted by the change will be facing the unknown, and may react in a number of negative ways, including:

- Fear of loss. People may feel that their current way of working is being disparaged and that they will lose out.
- Denial – particularly if they've seen previous change initiatives come and go.
- Open criticism, finding all the reasons not to make a change.

It is important to realise that change can be very emotionally challenging for the people who are affected by it. Many need considerable support to cope with it before they can even consider coping with more information about the change.

The emotions that people experience during change can be expressed as a graph as set out overleaf:

Figure 12.2 Examples of emotional responses to change

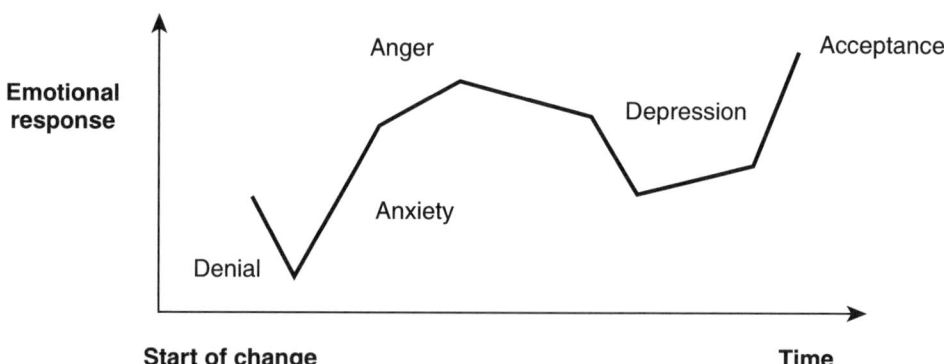

Overwhelmed by change

A worrying issue in many organisations is that there are too many changes taking place which impact on the same group of people. This may not even be recognised if different people are planning and implementing the changes.

Figure 12.3 Impact on one group of multiple sources of change

	Changes impacting on sales staff					
	January	February	March	April	May	June
Operations/ IT initiative	Training to use new IT system	IT system implemented	Implement new team roles design		Laptop sales system	
Marketing initiative	New product launch training	New product launched	Spring promotions		Rebranding exercise launch	
HR initiative	Investors in People assessment		Appraisal training and launch		Interim assessments	

The impact on the individual, and hence on their levels of stress and motivation, will feed through into organisational productivity. When planning change, managers need to take account of all the changes, not just those originating from their department. If many changes are planned, consideration should be given to stopping or delaying initiatives, and also to providing people with periods when little change takes place. This may result in faster and more effective change than attempting to do everything at once.

Marketing change

This issue has been covered to some extent in Session 5.

Marketing the change to individuals, and marketing the impact of the change, is crucial to its success:

- Providing people with the initial motivation to change. A rosy vision of the future, however compelling, is usually not enough to inspire your average worker. Most people require a "burning platform" (i.e. they need to be uncomfortable enough where they are to want to change).
- Making the change personal to them, and marketing to specific groups of individuals.
- Honouring and recognising an individual or teams previous contribution before expecting them to move on:
  - The idea that people are ready to "forget the past" immediately a change is proposed is more to do with the convenience of the change manager than it is to do with good people management.
  - Allow people to mourn (the "adjourning" stage in team development). In the long run they will move forward faster than if you deny them this experience.
  - There may be some new benefits to particular individuals, people you want to make sure you recognise and maintain (through for instance more varied and interesting jobs).
- Promoting the benefits of the change as they are realised, to help sustain motivation.
- Making sure there is effective, two-way communication. This means encouraging criticism as well as plaudits. If you do not acknowledge and welcome such feedback, it will simply go underground and undermine the initiative.

> **Activity 12.2 Change reactions**
>
> Collect some recent communications relating to a variety of changes impacting on you. These could be:
>
> - Government changes such as taxation.
> - Organisational changes, for example a reorganisation, job changes, procedural changes, etc.
> - Changes to you as a customer, such as the closure of a favourite shop, changes in products or services.
>
> What were your personal reactions to the changes? To what extent were these addressed in the communications you received? What else could have been done to assist you in adapting to the change?

Identifying implementation issues

If a change has been well planned and managed, then many implementation issues will have been identified and resolved.

However, once implementation has started, it may be too late to identify and plan how to tackle these issues. By involving stakeholders in the initial planning stage, managers can identify many of the issues in advance, and develop strategies to deal with them.

A common pitfall is that the "hard" aspects of implementation, such as activities, tasks and project resources, are planned before considering the marketing, communications and HR issues. As effective implementation may involve changing the plans to take account of these issues, experienced change managers build them into their approach from the start.

Remember that successful change depends on the willingness of people to carry it out.

> **Activity 12.3 The people issues**
>
> During times of change, organisations often find that morale is low and performance adversely affected. Prepare some notes for a brief presentation to a group of marketing students on this topic.

Options for implementation

Different approaches can be used for implementation (Figure 12.4).

Figure 12.4 Implementing change

Approach	Benefits	Issues
Pilot a change before rolling it out across the organisation.	■ Enables some issues to be ironed out prior to full implementation. ■ Clearly identifies benefits if these are unclear or open to doubt.	■ Requires statistical knowledge to set up and interpret. ■ May predict benefits that are not actually realised in the full rollout.
Implement change in one area at a time.	■ Enables the organisation to learn from each implementation. ■ Can enable the effective use of scarce implementation resources.	■ Care required in interpreting the results (as with the pilot approach). ■ May be a lengthy process, with the benefits not being realised as fast as required.
Rolling programme of benefits realisation.	■ Enables the benefits to be seen and celebrated early, helping to market the change. ■ Ensures the organisation sees an early return on its investment.	■ Need to ensure early benefits are realised as promised, or it will jeopardise the rest of the change programme. ■ Can stop at early wins if later benefits seem harder or more risky to achieve, but the changes would not achieve their full promise.

Approach	Benefits	Issues
Incremental approach.	■ Helps reduce the perceived impact of change on people.	■ People may get "change weary" and bored with the programme. ■ Benefits are only realised slowly, and may be easily reversed. ■ Change can peter out.
Big bang.	■ Benefits achieved quickly. ■ Pain is over quickly, and the organisation has time to heal.	■ High-risk strategy. ■ Resistance to step change may prevent it from being implemented effectively.

These approaches can be mixed and matched; for example by using a rolling programme of benefits realisation, combined with implementing the change in one area at a time.

Activity 12.4 Implementing change

Find someone who has recently been involved in implementing a change project (preferably a marketing-related project within your own organisation). Find out from them:

- The approach they took and the rationale for the change.
- The issues they came across.
- What they would do again in a future project?
- What they would do differently next time?
- Any learning they carried over from previous projects.

Managing change

Monitoring the progress of change projects

Professional project management tools enable managers to monitor the progress of any changes by tracking:

- Tasks.
- Milestones.
- Dependencies.
- Benefits management.
- Issues and risks.

Depending on the complexity of the project, managers may use such tools as:

- Gantt charts, showing the activities and tasks required to complete a project (as shown below).

Figure 12.5 Gantt chart

Task: Production of marketing leaflet

	Week1	Week 2	Week 3	Week 4	Week 5	Week 6
Brief designer	■					
Brief printers	■					
Brief contributors	■					
Compile copy	■	■	■			
Proof copy			■			
Proof final leaflet design				■		
Print leaflet					■	
Check and distribute						■

- Network analysis tools such as Critical Path Method (CPM) – see Activity 12.5. You may already be familiar with Gantt charts, but network diagrams may be less familiar to you. They show the start and finish of activities and also their dependency on each other. In network diagrams activities are shown as arrows and the start and finish indicated by a circle or node. Look at the example shown in Figure 12.6.

Figure 12.6 Network diagram

Task: Writing a sales report from secondary information

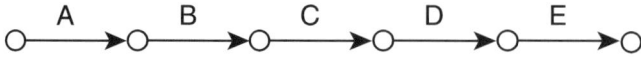

A = Determine report aims and objectives.
B = Identify sources of information.
C = Gather information.
D = Analyse information.
E = Write report.

In the above example, B is dependent upon A, C dependent upon B, and so on. However, if you also needed to interview the sales manager then the diagram would need to include this.

Figure 12.7 Network diagram

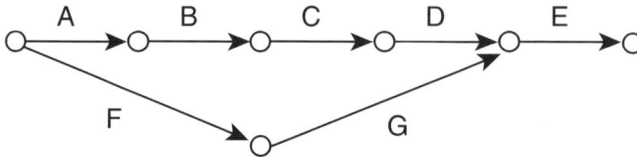

F = Interview sales manager.
G = Analyse results of interview.

Activity F is obviously dependent on A. Activity E is now dependent on D and G. If the time taken for each activity is identified, then the shortest or minimum time required to complete the task, in this case writing the sales report, can be calculated. This is known as the critical path.

The tools mentioned opposite allow the project manager to:

- Chart the interdependencies between tasks.
- Identify the minimum amount of time required to complete the project.
- Identify which tasks can be rescheduled without affecting the overall project time and resource requirements.

Other tools or activities that can help managers monitor the progress of change projects include:

- Issue and risk management databases, which can provide a means of recording issues, risks, and any plans to mitigate them.
- Benefits management databases, which ensure that the benefits of the project match those that were predicted by the SMART objectives (determined earlier during the scoping stage).
- Marketing and communications monitoring, which ensures that the people response is as planned.

While these will have been drafted in at the planning stage, these are live management tools, used throughout the monitoring stage, and therefore they need to be re-forecasted regularly as changes are identified.

Managing risks and issues

Risks and issues affecting the change programme will be both internal to the project team (such as the communications manager being taken ill), and external to the project team (for example the people affected by the change do not buy into the change). Potential risks to the project from both the team and those affected by the changes need to be raised and assessed:

- Risks can be prioritised based on the probability of them happening, their potential impact and their timing.
- The manager may be able to remove them, reduce them, or put a contingency plan in place.

Issues are risks that have been realised. For example, if the communications manager does become ill, then this needs active management to deal with the situation.

Monitoring and managing progress

Managers can use various indicators to identify whether or not the work is on track:

- Number of milestones met versus total number due. Missed milestones may be symptomatic of poor motivation, skills gaps, or overenthusiastic planning. Appropriately set milestones can help give early warning of problems before it is too late to get things back on track, either by rescheduling the work or by providing extra resources.

- Benefits realised versus benefits expected, based on the SMART objectives set in the scoping phase. Again, early warning mechanisms are useful in that plans can be reformulated if need be to ensure maximum benefit.

- Actual cost against budgeted cost.

- Regular project meetings. Interaction is an excellent way of identifying risks before they become problems.

- Regular communication with the recipients and sponsors of the change. Some of this may be formal, such as through roadshows or surveys of opinion. Sometimes it can be informal, for example by visiting people or picking up the phone to find out what is going on. The marketing and communications manager needs to build this activity into their plans.

Planning interventions

As a result of monitoring and identifying the causes of any symptoms, managers can now plan how to address the issues. Example interventions have already been covered in the earlier Sessions on managing conflict, negotiation, motivation and performance management.

By thinking in advance through the likely risks and issues for the planned change, change monitoring and management can be tailored to help identify problems early on. For example, if you believe that sales staff may well become poorly motivated as a result of implementing a new sales reporting system, then you need to plan support and monitoring systems into the project.

Activity 12.5 Critical path analysis

From the following information, carry out a critical path analysis using a simple network diagram. How long will the task take?

Task	Task to	Dependent on	Time
A	Identify main sponsors.		0.5
B	Design info sheet.		1
C	Determine numbers needed.		1
D	Estimate costs.	C	1
E	Agree design.	B	2
F	Find printer.	C	1
G	Write content.	E, D	2
H	Print.	G, F	1

Case Study – Innovation the only way out

Gary Hamel passionately believes that traditional businesses will disappear into insignificance unless they grasp the reality of a rapidly changing world.

'Change is increasingly non-linear and unexpected, and the pace of change has accelerated over the years. In the past, people lived in settled communities and new ideas took a long time to spread and take root. As time passed there was better communication between communities and new ideas sprang from interaction between people. Now we see an explosion of ideas, and the combination of completely different ideas together. In the past we thought we could be in the same business for ever. Today there is an underlying and disruptive pace of change. Companies need to reinvent themselves much quicker now.'

Hamel is convinced that the only way to win and gain competitive advantage now is to think differently and provide consumers with a different offer. This means creating radical new products, concepts and models.

Examples of companies embracing this shift already exist. 'There are some new satellite radio systems companies that are radically different,' notes Hamel. 'For $10 a month you have access to literally hundreds of radio stations from across the globe. DiaDexus is a post genomic company that carries out DNA testing looking at preventing diseases rather than just curing them. It's revolutionary stuff.'

Typically, points out Hamel, it is new commerce that is leading the way: the Internet companies. Most new wealth is coming from these new companies, the Microsoft, Dell and Cisco's of the world. But the challenge, says Hamel, is to do this more than once, to repeat the initial success. 'It will be interesting to see if the Bodyshop or Laura Ashley can reinvent themselves. Companies reach the end of the visionaries' headlights and then crash out and burn.'

In order for real innovation to take place however, it needs to become the remit of the entire business and move away from the preserve of R&D or marketing departments. 'Marketing people have historically been seen as responsible for innovation, but it needs to be everyone's responsibility, company wide. Otherwise you will be stuck with product-led, incremental changes.'

Some may question whether with an impending recession, traditional business is ready to adopt such radical innovation. Many have put their trust in the Internet but Hamel doubts that the benefits of e-commerce will last. 'Companies have invested a lot of hope in the Internet. I'm absolutely certain that the efficiency gains from IT will be given back to the customers in low prices. There are a lot of companies out there being serviced by the same IT companies, using the same business models, the same consultants. All gains made will flow straight back to the customers because everyone else is doing the same. For this reason, I tell clients not to put too much faith in the Internet. Recession will force companies to innovate their way out.'

Hamel urges companies to test and refine new business models, on a small scale to begin with, before gradually committing more resources as they prove their worth. However, he cautions against change for change's sake. 'Don't go off in a thousand directions. You need to experiment but there must be an underlying coherence to it all. You must have a dominant strategy that everything fits into. Take Virgin, for example. Their underlying strategy is brand. In all the markets that they enter it is their brand with its values that is central. Disney succeeded in business by exploiting a hitherto underdeveloped market. What drove the company and unified it was the vision of its founder. You can carry out lots of innovation, but there must be a unifying force, be it common roots, a competence or a brand.

Source: *Marketing Business*, April 2001.

Questions

Considering the information contained in the article, compile three or more slides to emphasise the importance of innovation and how companies should approach innovating.

SUMMARY OF KEY POINTS

- In marketing-oriented organisations change is a constant, as organisations continually adapt to meet changing customer requirements.
- Planning and preparing for change enables organisations to be in control of the process of managing change.
- When managing change it is essential to consider strategic, operations and HR issues.
- Change impacts significantly on people, so they need to be supported through the change.
- Regular and open communication is essential if change is to be managed efficiently and effectively.
- Effective implementation depends on using an appropriate plan, from piloting and phasing-in to overnight change.

Improving and developing own learning

The following projects are designed to help you develop your knowledge and skills further, by carrying out some research yourself. Feedback is not provided for this type of learning because there are no "answers" to be found, but you may wish to discuss your findings with colleagues and fellow students.

Project A

What changes have you been involved in recently? How effectively was each change managed? How good was the communication strategy? Were people kept informed or did they learn about what was to happen through rumour and informal contacts within the organisation? What improvements can you suggest?

Project B

As a marketing manager, you have decided that the customer service department will be run on a teleworking system. How would you prepare the staff involved for this change? Draw up a plan to include communications, operational activities and implementation.

Project C

If change has been handled badly in the past and people are now negative and resistant to change, how should the situation be managed to restore confidence and performance? If this has happened to you, think back to how you felt and what you wanted to happen. Talk to colleagues and friends about their poor experiences and how the consequences were managed.

Feedback to activities

Activity 12.1 The extent of change

You may have considered issues such as:

- Need to redesign the distribution chain. For example, set up a door-to-door distribution capability, where previously customers collected products in-store.
- IT developments.
- Staff changes, such as a reduction in face-to-face sales staff, and the development of telephone and web-based customer services.
- Customer concerns regarding the use of an Internet facility, such as security fears and the ease of use of the web site.

- Marketing changes, such as channel strategy, positioning.
- Pricing strategy and impact on profitability. For example, many Internet-based companies have sold on the basis of low prices, which has led to heavy losses.
- Alignment with brand.

Activity 12.2 Change reactions

You may have identified some strong emotions in your change responses, perhaps denial followed by anger. It is also possible that while at first you welcomed the change, when it was implemented the impact on you differed from your expectations, either because you did not appreciate the implications or because they were poorly explained and played down or over-sold. The latter is an extremely poor marketing strategy. It leads to buyer's remorse and is seen as being very unfair and hence demotivating.

Another poor strategy, often seen, is that of launching the change well but not following it up with information about progress. When the change then finally does impact, people have largely denied its existence and find it even harder to accept.

Activity 12.3 The people issues

It would be a good idea to involve the students in the presentation by asking them about what good and bad experiences of change they have had, and how these changes might have been managed more effectively.

Your notes might contain some or all of the following points.

Change is an unsettling process for many people within organisations, particularly if they do not understand why it is happening. In organisations where information is not shared or is communicated poorly there can be an "Us and Them" culture and a lack of trust in senior management.

Many people fear change because they are afraid that they will not be able to cope in the "new" organisation. If the benefits will only be realised in the long-term then people may perceive the change as unnecessary and not be committed to it.

Informal communication channels usually transmit messages faster then formal channels, so rumour and misinformation often precede accurate information about any changes. Consequently, it is not always believed.

Some of the person's energy for work will be taken up with coping with the change, so performance will also be affected. If people feel that they may not have a job

Effective Management for Marketing

as a result of the change then they may respond by working harder to ensure they survive, or less hard if they feel it is inevitable that they will be made redundant.

When morale is low associated problems often compound the situation. Small grievances are exaggerated and latent conflicts can surface. A higher level of absenteeism and greater turnover of staff may lead to a lack of availability of skills and experience, resulting in jobs not being completed on time. All of this will lead to a further downturn in productivity.

However, if there is a prevailing culture in the company that encourages the sharing of information, so that everyone understands what the organisation wishes to achieve through its strategic business plan, then people will respect and trust senior managers more, and change will be perceived as less of a threat. If people are consulted about the changes and kept informed about progress, then it is less likely that rumours will affect morale significantly.

If job losses cannot be avoided then the organisation must be fair and consistent and help prepare people to make the necessary changes in their lives.

It is important that people understand the purpose of change and why it has to happen. If there are no clear objectives then they may feel confused about the future. Clarity of direction, accompanied by clear and concise communication and appropriate support, will ease people through change and encourage loyalty. A culture that encourages trust, openness, respect and fosters a can-do attitude, should help prepare people to undergo change.

Activity 12.4 Implementing change

This will depend on the nature of the project, and the position the person held within the project. How many of the issues discussed so far have been relevant?

Activity 12.5 Critical path analysis

The task will take a minimum of 6 days.

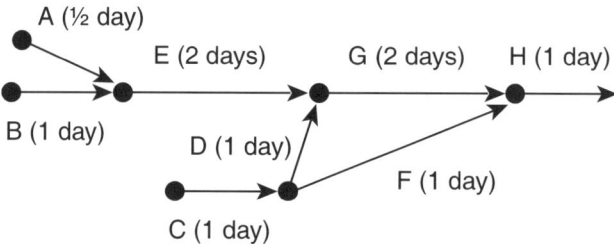

Session 13

Managing knowledge

Introduction

Learning organisations continuously gather and use information to make changes that result in better ways of servicing customers. This Session explores how organisations can identify the knowledge that they have and use it effectively. The final section is a reminder that information must be used effectively by organisations if they are to learn and transform themselves to remain competitive and continue to provide the products and services customers demand.

> **LEARNING OUTCOMES**
>
> At the end of this Session you will be able to:
>
> - Describe what is meant by knowledge management.
> - Discuss the barriers to effective knowledge management.
> - Explain why organisations and managers need good information systems.
> - Describe how to develop a culture of learning and development.

What is knowledge management?

Knowledge management refers to the way organisations develop, keep, and use their intellectual capital. Intellectual capital can be drawn from a number of sources, for example:

- Their people.
- Their customers.
- Their information systems.

Articles and books on knowledge management often tend to focus on one particular aspect of knowledge management, such as developing customer information systems or a learning culture.

Just as with our own memories, if we are to use knowledge effectively we need to have a way of:

- Capturing and developing knowledge that is valuable.

- Being able to store knowledge effectively.
- Being able to retrieve and use knowledge effectively.

Barriers to developing intellectual capital

Most organisations have lots of opportunities to develop their human and information systems capital, which are often either passed by or deemed too expensive to exploit. Some examples are given in Figure 13.1.

Figure 13.1 Examples of barriers to developing intellectual capital

Barrier	Example	Consequence
Time and cost.	Training courses are cancelled at the last minute because workloads are deemed too great and there is no short-term impact on the business.	<ul><li>Development is regarded as a luxury not a necessity.</li><li>Workforce skills become more and more outdated.</li></ul>
Lack of knowledge of what is available.	The customer data collected at point of sale is not analysed or used.	<ul><li>Customer needs are not understood or satisfied.</li><li>Competitors are able to gain competitive advantage by using their own data.</li></ul>
Undervaluing internal knowledge.	Marketing strategy is developed in head office without consulting customer contact staff.	<ul><li>Valuable organisation-specific knowledge is ignored in favour of generally available market analysis.</li><li>Organisation loses its competitive advantage.</li></ul>

Barriers to keeping intellectual capital

Even where intellectual capital is identified and developed, much of it can be lost or become useless if it is not actively used and kept up to date.

Figure 13.2 Examples of barriers to keeping intellectual capital

Barrier	Example	Consequence
Loss of people outside the organisation or department.	Staff are retired early as part of a cost-cutting plan.	■ Important files of information are shredded as no one understands their contents. ■ The intellectual capital of a generation of staff is lost to the organisation for good.
Lack of effective storage.	Useful information from a product launch is captured by individual team members, but is not stored for wider and future use.	■ The organisation does not improve its skills at as fast a rate as it could do.
Outdated systems.	Key customer knowledge is captured on a database, but when the software is updated the database is not moved over to the new system.	■ Valuable marketing information is squandered. ■ The organisation loses out to a competitor who is able to spot an emerging trend that was only visible in the data that was lost.

Barriers to using intellectual capital

Having and storing knowledge is insufficient if it cannot be either brought to the attention of, or accessed by, those that need it, when they need it. This can be one of the most challenging areas for an organisation to overcome.

Figure 13.3 Examples of barriers to using intellectual capital

Barrier	Example	Consequence
Overwhelmed.	Key information needs to be extracted from pages and pages of data and management information reports.	■ Information is never used, so the organisation gains no value from it. ■ Eventually the information stops being stored altogether.
Poor marketing.	Detailed product costing information is not seen by salespeople, as they do not know of its existence.	■ Sales do not understand some of the consequences of their customer negotiations. ■ Organisational profitability is reduced.
Limited access.	Customer database can only be interrogated by IT specialists after a one month delay.	■ Decisions are taken on dated information, as the information is not available in a timely fashion.
Secrecy.	Competitor information is kept by the PR department, as they believe this increases their perceived value to the organisation.	■ Product managers do not gain access to key information that would help them increase profitability.

Activity 13.1 Breaking down barriers

Consider the barriers to effective knowledge management in your organisation, specifically those that relate to effective marketing.

- What are the consequences of such barriers?
- What are all the factors keeping the barriers in place?
- What would happen if the barriers were removed?

> - What change would make the biggest difference to your organisation's ability to manage knowledge effectively? What would have to happen for this change to occur?
>
> You may wish to write notes on this or meet with someone in your organisation to discuss your findings.

Importance of information

Information is required by everyone in an organisation. It supports them in taking the relevant decisions and actions that enable and enhance organisational effectiveness. Look at your desk to discover all the different types of information you use on a daily basis. How do you access that information?

Organisational information systems can be both informal and formal. Examples include the "grapevine", meeting in a coffee area, formal reporting mechanisms, training courses, decision support systems, and the use of technology for automating and enhancing processes.

Organisations that can deliver the right information to the right person at the right time efficiently and effectively have a source of potential competitive advantage.

It may be helpful to review Session 5 at this point, as the discussion of barriers to effective communication apply here as well. A particular problem can be being overwhelmed. If relevant information is hidden in a blizzard of irrelevant emails and memos then it may as well not be there.

Collecting and processing information is expensive. Therefore organisations and individuals need to consider such issues as:

- What information is essential/nice to have/inessential to collect? What would happen if we don't have it?
- What are the options for ensuring timely collection in a useful format?
- What are the costs and organisational value associated with each option? Over different timescales?

Information systems flexibility

As well as information providing a trigger for change, the need and value of different types of information changes over time. One useful and favourite cost saving measure is to audit the current data and information provision. Almost invariably this finds reports which are no longer required, are in the wrong format, or are being delivered to the wrong part of the organisation. Equally important, it also tends to discover that some information that would be extremely useful is not actually being produced.

In response to this issue, some organisations have chosen to introduce databases that can be interrogated by users all over the organisation, to produce information relevant to their specific needs. This can be very effective and exciting for marketers who have access to customer data, but can catch inexperienced users out.

- It may be tempting to ask questions of data just for the sake of asking questions, which wastes time providing data that is not useful for supporting decisions. Sometimes natural curiosity and play can lead to significant breakthroughs, so it does have some value, but this needs to be balanced against producing known high-value information.

- Data integrity can be a major issue. It is important to appreciate the data source and any consequent integrity issues. If a field is not directly relevant for operational or audit use, then people may use it for something else, or the data may not be particularly accurate.

- Interpretation of the data needs to be undertaken with great care. It can be easy to inadvertently make inaccurate or unwarranted assumptions. The pattern you think you detect may be due to the way data was sampled, or the date it was produced, or any number of reasons. The only way to be absolutely sure is to involve the people who understand and are closest to the processes that produced the data.

Activity 13.2 Avoiding information overload

What information do you use in your work role? What information do you need? Try and identify the following:

- What information do you receive at the moment?
- What information do you provide at the moment?
- Which information would help you perform your role more effectively?
- What information could you provide to help others perform their roles more effectively?

> - What is the estimated cost and value of each type of information to your organisation?
>
> What actions can you take to make your contribution to organisational information systems more effective?
>
> Now consider a customer of your organisation, and carry out the same exercise from their perspective. How could your organisation provide more valuable information to them?

The learning culture

This has already been described in Session 10. When seeking to develop a learning culture it is important to understand:

- In what ways the current organisational culture differs from a learning culture.
- How significant these differences are according to:
  - The prevailing identity, beliefs and values of the organisation (and different parts of the organisation).
  - The processes and activities performed by the organisation (what it does, how it rewards people).
  - The beliefs, values, skills and actions of leadership teams throughout the organisation.
- The value that will be achieved by changing.
- The cost of not changing.

Developing a culture of learning and development needs to be treated as any other change programme (see Session 12). It is insufficient to just make cosmetic changes, such as increasing training budgets and introducing an appraisal system (although these may help), and just hope that people will do the rest.

Leading by example

Unless managers at the top of the organisation actively demonstrate that they fully value and embrace a learning culture, they are highly unlikely to persuade anyone else around them. Actions often speak louder than words. You will not get very far by:

- Claiming that self-managed development is critically important, whilst you:
  - Cancel your own training course or coaching session, quoting pressure of work.
  - Dictate which development activities your people should undertake, and what their career goals and actions should be.
- Saying that everyone has to be open to constructive feedback, then:
  - Refuse to accept negative feedback, when there is a lot of evidence that a change would be of value.
  - Say 'Well, that's just me isn't it?' and refuse to consider development activity.
- Telling people that any challenge of accepted norms and beliefs is expected and welcomed, then:
  - Talk over people who ask questions or challenge you in meetings.
  - Ignore ideas that have come from people you don't like or who earn less.
- Talking about the importance of considering change systemically whilst you:
  - Only consider your own or your department's interests and never anyone else's perspective, thus harming the organisation overall.
  - Refuse to indulge in joint problem solving with a supplier or customer when your decisions will obviously affect them.

To change the culture people have to change their behaviour – to live the change required.

Activity 13.3 Learning and learning organisations

You may wish to refer back to Session 10 before you complete this activity.

Knowing that you are studying for a marketing qualification, your Marketing Manager has asked you to research the characteristics of a learning organisation.

Produce a list that captures the essential characteristics of a learning organisation.

Case Study – An ideal solution

An interview with Mel Usher of IDEA.

The Improvement and Development Agency (IDEA) is well named. It is a stylish, not-for-profit organisation, full of enthusiastic, switched-on people, radiating energy and ideas out to local government.

Headed by Mel Usher, former Chief Executive of South Somerset District Council, the IDEA has taken over the performance improvement role and central London headquarters of the old Local Government Management Board. It was set up three years ago after Usher found himself sitting next to the then Local Government Minister, Hilary Armstrong, at a dinner. He suggested that local authorities could improve themselves if they had their own agency spreading information and good practice. A few months later IDEA was born, with Usher as Executive Director.

It meshes with UK government policy to promote quality in local authorities, which has seen Best Value replace compulsory competitive tendering, beacon status for high-performing councils, and in December (2001), a white paper on local government (Strong local leadership – quality public services). This promised more freedom to high-performing councils and less to those deemed failures.

Consultants from the IDEA have now carried out peer reviews with more than 100 local authorities, supporting modernisation and good practice. Last year Usher took on Martin Horton, former Global HR Director for Deloitte and Touche's Management Solutions business in New York, to lead the agency's critical knowledge and learning function. This supports the IDEA's consultancy arm with knowledge and e-learning databases, and runs what used to be called training but is now referred to as learning or, more grandly, "capacity building" – although to be fair, this fad phrase embraces a wider set of ideas than just training.

Horton, whose background was in local authority training and the North West Employers' Organisation before he went into private sector consultancy, says: 'The white paper talks about capacity building for change and modernisation. The challenge for IDEA is to support this process. We believe that sustainable improvement comes from within. The key is how to take the knowledge already in our organisations and the day-to-day experience of delivering services, and improve them by learning from that knowledge. It's about empowering people to make great changes themselves. It's not something you can do externally.'

Armed with this wisdom, he and his colleagues have searched out the good ideas from local authorities and installed them on a web site, IDEA Knowledge. Here, like a series of rags-to-riches fairy tales, are displayed the legends of modern local government. Replete with the public sector's latest concepts and buzzwords ("partnership", "one-stop-shop", "new leadership"), are accounts of councils such as Sheffield, which was "doing badly in 1997" and is now one of the best in the country. Or Newcastle and Gateshead, which were "doing great things separately", but are now contenders for the European Capital of Culture after deciding to do things together (in partnership of course).

Buzzwords aside, the site contains many genuine stories of hard work to counter crime, deprivation and despair, not to mention attacking the sheer muddle that has dogged local government for so many years.

So switched onto technology is Horton that he conducts half the interview seated at his computer, clicking away at sites for us to look at and discuss. Eager to elaborate, he brings in Chris Naylor who has been working with Ipswich Council in a pioneering organisation development and learning programme involving both councillors and officers. After only a few months, they have found maintenance engineers who are experts at project management and could teach the rest of the council a thing or two. Under the IDEA system that is exactly what the engineers will do; learning being seen as a matter of exchanging knowledge within authorities, as well as between them and the outside world.

The technology doesn't stop at IDEA Knowledge. In November (2001) the agency launched the Learning Pool, a system to enable local authorities and their employees to create, pool and swap e-learning materials. Set up in partnership with Epic, it uses "peer-to-peer file-sharing technology", which can create a virtual private network allowing information to cross firewalls whilst maintaining security.

'It's about communication, building a shared view of the issues, but also about acknowledging that there aren't necessarily any right answers, and saying "It's okay to copy," ' says Horton.

So, you might ask, where does good old personnel and training fit into this brave new world? Horton's answer echoes the debates in the private sector about extending the influence of HR into strategy creation. 'Historically, HR has dealt with the processes and procedures,' he says. 'But when it comes to the key questions (what sort of local authority do we want, what kind of people do we want working for it, how do we reward them and how do they learn), all too often HR is not involved in these discussions – it is just administering the decision.'

'People ought to be a critical item for debate. Local authority HR professionals should be asking: "Why are my people different to those people in that authority over there, or in that company?" Just take something simple like absence rates. Why do these vary between your local authority and the company next door which is taking people from the same area, drinking the same water, travelling on the same transport? HR ought to be a key part of the discussion about moving local authorities forward. I would like HR to contribute to how people learn and grow in their authority, rather than just controlling the training budgets.'

There is much scope for councils to learn from the private sector, but Horton believes that there is also room for knowledge gathered by the IDEA to flow in the other direction. 'The public sector ethos is important, as is the relationship between the service user and provider. And the last I heard', he adds, 'Enron wasn't a local authority.'

Source: 'An Ideal Solution', article by Jane Pickard, *People Management*, 21st March, 2002, and reproduced with kind permission.

Questions

1. Which aspects of IDEA's approach to working with clients do you think have been most successful in enabling them to harness knowledge?

2. How has this contributed to the success of learning within local authorities?

SUMMARY OF KEY POINTS

- Knowledge management is the way organisations maintain, develop and use their intellectual capital.

- Barriers to effective knowledge management include lack of awareness of knowledge resources, poor storage and retrieval, and lack of development of people and a learning culture.

- Many organisations are unable to respond effectively to change because they do not have the right information at the right time.

- Good information systems enable people to access information easily and quickly in the format required, so that they can respond to changing situations and make sound decisions.

- A culture of learning and development can be built if people are curious about why they do things, they way they do things, and what alternatives there are for improvement.

- An effective learning culture enables people to use the knowledge they have and the information they gather to make sound decisions about what to do in the future.

Improving and developing own learning

The following projects are designed to help you develop your knowledge and skills further, by carrying out some research yourself. Feedback is not provided for this type of learning because there are no "answers" to be found, but you may wish to discuss your findings with colleagues and fellow students.

Project A

Examine the information systems in your organisation, particularly the Marketing Information System. How effective is it? What suggestions for improvements can you make? Review how you store information. What improvements can you make?

Project B

What are the barriers to effective knowledge management in your organisation? How does this affect the ability of the organisation to respond to change?

Project C

Assess the gap between:

- Your own organisation and a culture of learning and development.
- Your own development needs in this area.

> Use the Internet to search for possible interventions and ideas to close the gap. Where appropriate put these into your personal development plan.

Feedback to activities

Activity 13.1 Breaking down barriers

While you should have considered all the areas discussed, your answers will be specific to your organisation. Did you also consider the contents of Session 12 in your approach to changing the organisation?

Activity 13.2 Avoiding information overload

Most people who do this activity will find several changes they can make for their own roles. For example:

- Stop providing it.
- Change it. For example, the channel it is delivered by, how often it is sent, the way the information is provided.
- Start it up. For example, you may have identified that you have very little contact with one area, and that you both have information that could help each other perform your roles better.

As far as customers are concerned, effective information provision is an important part of customer care. You may want to review Session 11 from this perspective.

Activity 13.3 Learning and learning organisations

Your list will probably contain some or all of the following:

- Organisational strategy is developed through a continuous process of review, activity and feedback, to prevent stagnation and encourage innovation.
- Organisational structures are flexible and adaptable.
- Business plans and policies are developed collaboratively so employees participate appropriately.
- Information about company performance is freely available to everyone.
- Effective team working extends beyond the traditional boundaries of the organisation; it includes customers, suppliers and other stakeholders.

- There is a prevailing culture of openness, trust and mutual respect.
- People are supported in their risk taking.
- Communication is open and constructive – people say what needs to be said not what they think people want to hear!
- Supervision and control are exercised appropriately not rigidly.
- Front-line staff are regarded as key sources of information about customers, competitors and company products and services. Their feedback is regarded as essential to strategic decision making.
- The learning culture ensures that people take responsibility for their learning and, where appropriate, the development of others.
- Everyone acknowledges (from "top to bottom") the importance of learning and development.

Session 14

Managing in a global context

Introduction

The final two Sessions explore the international influences on management, as businesses plan and organise themselves in a global world. Cultural influences are described and discussed to identify how management styles differ, and the impact of national culture on organisations and their managers is also considered.

> ### LEARNING OUTCOMES
> At the end of this Session you will be able to:
>
> - Discuss the relevant cultural issues when dealing with international clients and organisations.
> - Understand why cultural conflicts may develop in global markets.
> - Describe the impact of national culture on organisational culture.
> - Explain how management styles and perspectives may differ in global markets.

Management as a social construct

As previously discussed, every model of management, organisation and culture develops in a social context – people are influenced by what they experience around them. This includes the way they carry out their role and how others respond to this, the media, and other communication channels.

In the first two Sessions we discussed how management and marketing has developed historically. For example, the idea of a bureaucratic organisation grew from a time of environmental and organisational stability in the West. In the same way, theories of management need to be considered in their social context – the complete social and economic system in which they were developed, such as European, North American, Asian or Arabic.

The extent to which successful management is culturally embedded

Some of the practices described as you have worked through this Companion will have seemed very familiar and just common sense, whilst others will have seemed less so. This familiarity will be partly influenced by your own national culture. You will be more aware of some of your beliefs and values than others. The experience of having them surfaced and challenged contributes to the phenomenon known as "culture shock".

Considering the increasingly global nature of business today, it is possible that a universal model of successful management practice will eventually emerge, one that is likely to take far less account of cultural contexts. Historically, successful practices in one culture have been brought across to other cultures. American and Japanese approaches to quality management are used widely throughout the world, although it could be argued that these have been substantially transformed in the translation. Systems modelling is one potential route into creating this universal model – refer back to Session 2.

In the meantime, managers must still deal with the differences between national cultures. Management styles will differ in different countries due to the influence of national culture. In some cultures the leaders make the decisions and others are expected to follow, and this is regarded as good leadership. In British culture a more consultative style of leadership is expected.

Expectations of relationships, management processes, and communication protocols, all need to be taken into account by global organisations.

National stereotypes

One of the issues in dealing with international clients and organisations is that of stereotypes. A stereotype acts as an existing model of what to expect from, and how to relate to, someone from another culture with which you are unfamiliar. It also falls under the category of "a little knowledge is a dangerous thing".

- Stereotypes can be highly exaggerated, very generalised, and out of date.
- They are usually based on what you have read, seen and heard, probably in the media.
- They often get in the way of remembering that you are dealing with an individual, not just a blueprint idea of an Englishman, a Frenchman, an American, etc.
- They are no substitute for learning about and having some in-depth experience of another culture.

For example, anyone expecting all Americans to be brash and loud and dealing with them accordingly, will be in for a few surprises and could easily offend.

Making instinctive meaning of verbal and non-verbal signals

Another important area in cultural exchanges which people are often unaware of is their instinctive reaction to certain social signals. For example:

- Looking someone in the eye is an accepted signal for being honest, open, and interested in many Western cultures. However, it is considered very rude in Japanese and Chinese cultures.

- The Japanese say "no" by providing contextual cues, e.g. by what they don't say, and by the context in which they say things. Northern Europeans and Americans are more direct, and just say "no" in words. This is also true of other communication.

Being aware of the signals you are giving out and of your assumptions and (potentially inaccurate) conclusions of others is very important when dealing with people from another culture. It is important when developing working relationships with anyone, but the potential for misunderstanding is often that much greater with people from other nationalities because you may not be fully aware of the implications of the differences.

Activity 14.1 Researching cultural differences

What images of other nationalities do you have? Choose two nationalities other than your own, and if you can, choose nationalities with which your organisation deals (internally or externally). First of all, write down some of your assumptions about them, such as their likes and dislikes, and the characteristics you might expect to come across when dealing with them. Then collect newspaper reports, advertisements, and any other images and writings you can find. You may also want to include comments made by colleagues or friends in your research.

- What assumptions do you have?
- Are these assumptions portrayed in the images and writings you have collected?
- How do you think they see themselves?

If you can, find someone who comes from the particular country to discuss your findings with. What do they think about the way their nation is portrayed? What generalisations do they hold about you and your countrymen?

Sources of conflict

Cultural conflicts may arise for a number of reasons:

- False mental models we may hold of other people, and hence how we think they want to be responded to.
- Misinterpretations of the intention of actions or words.
- Clashes of strongly-held beliefs and values.
- Disagreements over what we believe to be true of business and society.
- Disagreements over what we think is important in business and society.
- Assumptions on the right way to go about things, based on our mental models of "the way we do things around here".

Notice that none of these factors are unique to dealing with other nationalities – they are just sometimes more noticeable in this context. Some of the most common areas of difference are listed below. Please note that this list is by no means exhaustive!

Attitudes to time

Suppose you are asked to meet up with a client from another culture to discuss a potential business deal. Two common differences in attitudes to time are:

- The extent to which business is governed by the clock, particularly with regard to the importance of deadlines, or being on time for meetings. Someone from a Northern European culture is likely to assume that if you are late it is because you have no regard for their importance, and therefore they might take offence at your late arrival.
- The anticipated timescale and process over which business relationships develop. What has to happen before a business deal can be struck? What meaning is attached to the first deal? Is it a trial? A firm commitment to a long-term relationship? Something else? What about the first meeting? Informal or formal? Social meeting or business meeting?

Personal space

People tend to have a personal space around them, which if invaded by someone else can make them feel very uncomfortable. This space tends to be different for different nationalities, as well as for different individuals.

If you meet with a client and then consistently stand too close to them, they are likely to feel threatened, or at least ill at ease. If you see someone backing off slightly, you must respect that. Unfortunately a common reaction is to continue to advance on the person, which just makes matters worse!

Individuals and society

The idea of the individual being all important is a Western one. Other nationalities emphasise an individual's place in society, and their relationships to others, rather than just the individual's perspective. Stressing values such as harmony and social responsibility with customers from these cultures is far more likely to win over clients than ideas of personal freedom and self-expression. If you are negotiating with someone from China you should reference your suggestions and actions to the relationship. If it is an American, you would do better to make reference to your own opinions and feelings.

This area also affects approaches to negotiation and conflict. The Japanese are used to a joint problem-solving approach, whereas Western negotiators are familiar with a more adversarial bid and counterbid approach.

Rituals

Simple actions such as shaking hands, having a meal together, or exchanging business cards can take on great importance – particularly if they are missed, misinterpreted or changed in some way.

In Japan it is important to spend some time reading a business card carefully before putting it away. Some societies are far more formal than others in their attitudes to ritual actions.

Attitudes to gender

This topic more than many others can raise very strong emotions, including the desire to change people's opinions. This is not usually practical. Managers need to deal with what they find rather than attempt to transform a whole culture. The way in which members of the opposite sex relate to each other and with society as a whole differs greatly between cultures. Some nationalities are extremely familiar with dealing with women in senior positions, whilst others are not.

> **Activity 14.2 Making sense of differences**
>
> Choose a nationality with which you are relatively unfamiliar, but with which you may be dealing in the future.

> Imagine that you have been asked to meet with a counterpart from that nationality to discuss a joint venture. Research:
>
> - What are the main differences between your culture and theirs?
> - Where might conflict arise?
> - What approach will you take to the meeting?
>
> Assuming that you agree the joint venture, what differences might there be in advertising campaigns in your country and theirs?

National forces shaping organisations

Organisations are inevitably shaped by the national environment in which they exist, particularly by the history and current state of:

- The economic environment.
- The political and legal climate.
- Social relationships.

All of these aspects also interact with one another. For example, social values will influence the legal and political structures put in place, which in turn will influence the economic environment. The UK's emphasis on individual responsibility has resulted in a labour market that is deregulated in comparison to many of the other countries in the European Union.

Whitley and Hofstede have both researched this area. Some of the differences in organisations they have found are outlined below. Again, the list is by no means exhaustive, but it is representative of some of the issues managers encounter. Once again it comes with a warning. Whilst it is possible to identify national tendencies and trends, each organisation and individual is different.

Organisational vision

The timescales being considered and the values that drive an organisation's mission and goals can vary greatly:

- Japanese management is famous for having a very long outlook when it comes to developing strategy, much in contrast to the UK or American perspective.

- Japanese organisations tend to co-operate with each other to expand their national interests, reflecting the value of harmony over individualism.

Decision making and organisational hierarchy

Italian organisations tend to emphasise the importance of the hierarchy and well-defined job roles when it comes to making decisions, which minimises any conflict during the decision-making process. In contrast, Swedish organisations tend to make decisions by consensus, getting any conflicts of interest into the open early and reducing them by negotiation.

People from the UK are far more likely to act on their own initiative and take risks than employees from Germany are.

Other values will also influence the outcome of a decision. An organisation that greatly values responsibility to family and the wider society is likely to produce a different decision to an organisation that places an emphasis on organisational goals above all else.

Employee motivation

People are motivated by what is important to them, by their values:

- Arabs are far more likely to be motivated by friendship and family connections than German or Japanese employees.
- UK employees are usually influenced more by their individual needs than Japanese employees, who tend to be driven more by organisational goals.

A Japanese manager who attempts to motivate their UK employees to greater efforts by reference only to organisational goals is likely to be unsuccessful. The idea of a "Company Song" is unpalatable and only good for a laugh to the average British worker.

Activity 14.3 Gaining awareness

1. Consider the team in which you work. With colleagues from that team, consider how your national culture has shaped your team norms and processes. How might these change if you were based in a different country? Where possible, choose nationalities with which your organisation has or might have dealings.

> What have you taken for granted? What would happen if you took on some of the beliefs and values of another culture? How would it affect your team's working?
>
> 2. Using the Internet, search for examples of adverts and sales sites aimed at different nationalities. Amazon has sites aimed at different countries and is a useful company to visit. What differences can you identify which may reflect different nationalities?

> **Activity 14.4 Cultural briefing**
>
> As a marketing manager, you have noticed that your team are inexperienced at working internationally and with people from different cultures. You have organised a briefing to give them some practical advice. Write some notes in preparation for the briefing.

Case Study – Worldly Wise

There isn't a glass ceiling in India, at least that's one of the impressions that Rory Fisher took from his involvement in BAE System's Strategic Leadership Programme (SLP), a 15-month scheme in which participants spend a week in each of five countries.

Fisher, a Group Commercial Director (Customer solutions and support), attended a range of unusual workshops and business conferences in Castle Abbey (Northamptonshire, UK), Bangalore, Washington, New York, Shanghai, Beijing and Slovenia. In each country the group spent roughly half the week looking at the local political and economic situations and the other half working on leadership techniques.

In India the group of 16 visited Wipro, one of the world's leading software companies. During the interviews with managers to try and discover what made the business so successful, a female manager was asked whether she felt that the organisation had a glass ceiling. Looking slightly puzzled she replied, 'How far I go up the tree is up to me'.

Her response demolished an assumption Fisher had held about the status of women in Indian companies. Western prejudices and expectations fell like ninepins throughout the course, he believes.

BAE System's investment in the programme is huge. It spends more than £25,000 on each delegate, taken from its top management cadre (see box at the close of the Case Study). 'It is fairly rare for a company to invest such time and thought into a leadership programme of this nature', Fisher says. 'In a way, it is quite altruistic, because there is no deliverable result in strict business terms. It is a personal journey that allows you to confront things that you would never usually confront,' he says.

'Ultimately, we learnt that companies around the world have the same business issues as in the UK. The recipe is a global one, albeit tailored to local conditions.'

Course participants were struck by the level of technological sophistication of ordinary Indians and the contrast with their surroundings. Some toured hospitals, schools and places of worship, while Fisher visited a family in their own home. 'They had basic amenities. The kitchen was small with simple stainless steel pots and plates. Three generations lived there, including granny and grown-up kids. They didn't leave home; it was very traditional.' But, he says, the family has a PC with full Internet connection, and outside, where there was barely a pavement, the authorities were digging to lay fibre-optic cables. 'In India they have jumped a technology generation and gone straightaway to digital,' Fisher says.

China was another revelation. The week the group arrived was the week China surpassed the USA in mobile phone ownership, becoming the biggest mobile using nation on the globe. 'Beijing felt very safe,' Fisher says. 'I felt safer walking round there than I do in most of London. They weren't a belligerent people.'

Fisher found China full of contradictions. 'It's ironic that you go to Red China and see the people are more capitalist than you are. Business is flourishing in China, and Shanghai looks like a cross between Hong Kong and Paris, yet you have one billion people living below the poverty line.'

'China is pursuing economic reform followed by political reform, which contrasts with post-Communist Russia and former Iron Curtain countries. They pursued political then economic reform and found it really didn't work.'

It might sound like a glorified round-the-world tour but the locations were chosen for specific business purposes and to demonstrate different facets of leadership. In the UK delegates started with "The repetitive mindset", examining their own management behaviour in the workshops run by clinical psychologists, and discussing the company's corporate strategy.

Part Two was "The reflective mindset – India", which encouraged delegates to slow down and to appreciate that they need time to enrich themselves, culturally and through learning, and also to reflect.

'We learnt to appreciate that we can be drowning in information but gasping for knowledge. We have so many emails and faxes and telephone conversations all the time, but you have to question how valuable they all are.'

'We did yoga and meditation each day, which was about controlling your breathing and making sense of yourself and understanding where you sit in society. I met a very learned gentleman, a yoga expert, who was 85 but didn't look a day over 40, who takes time to read and learn.' Fisher believes that this is contrary to Western organisational culture.

The third module was "The competitive mindset – USA", where delegates looked at energy, drive and risk-taking, and visited Wall Street and the Pentagon. The highlight for Fisher was a session with the Centre for Strategic International Studies think-tank, where two speakers, a pessimist and an optimist, predicted what the world would be like in 25 years time.

'The optimist would say, "We've cured cancer," but the pessimist would say, "A third of Africans have Aids, a third of people are over 60 years of age and terrorism is an active threat," ' Fisher says. 'It was very thought provoking and gave the message that the future state of the world depends on good decision making.'

Fisher says the fourth module, "The collaborative mindset – China", transformed his views of the country.

The group met the prime ministers of Bosnia and Slovenia during the fifth leg of the programme, "The catalytic mindset – Slovenia", which examined the type of leadership required to convert chaos into renewal. They took part in a music workshop in Bled, involving a percussion session that turned chaotic noise into music.

'The violinist taking the session was a cross between Rolf Harris and a top musician,' Fisher says. 'He played while we hummed and scribbled down what mood each part of the music conveyed.' The idea was to make a comparison between the composition of the music and what leadership and transformation is all about.

'We had to use more of our faculties and really had to listen to the music. The lesson was not to prejudge but to get below the surface,' he explains. 'Too often in business people think there is only one answer, but this programme taught me that this is not true.' Fisher believes he is a more effective manager because the programme allowed him to reassess his attitude.

'One aspect of leadership is pushing the boundaries of your own thoughts,' he explains. 'I used to be too quick to reach a conclusion and to leap before I looked. Until I came on this course, I had not been able to resolve that fault.'

While it is difficult to pin down tangibles in everyday work, Fisher believes that the long-term benefits of the programme will be profound. 'It is about making links between different approaches and finding solutions by looking at familiar things in an unfamiliar way. The point is to be non-judgemental and listen to everyone's views. I'm more aware of humanity and world events. It was an enlightening experience.'

High-flyers go global

Every year, BAE Systems selects around 16 managers and sends them around the world, where they discuss politics and business management and learn yoga and t'ai chi. It might sound like an odd way to groom future leaders of the company, but BAE claims that its Strategic Leadership Programme (SLP) is a success.

The idea behind SLP is that successful leaders need to apply different styles and philosophies to meet changing situations. The programme, which has been running for four years and which BAE Systems claim is unique, was developed by Tony McCarthy, Group HR Director, and Jonathan Gosling, a professor at Lancaster University. 'We looked at the specific needs of BAE Systems, which was predominantly a British company with British managers,' McCarthy says. 'We knew that the industry was consolidating and that we needed to become more global, so we wanted our managers to know how the world operates. Instead of being analytical, as engineers tend to be, we wanted to see how other companies around the world do things.'

Delegates are chosen on the basis of their performance and potential from a core group of about 650 people who form the company's "senior leadership population".

Source: From an article in *People Management*, 8th November 2001. *Worldly Wise* by Elizabeth Davidson and reproduced with kind permission.

Questions

1. The Case Study highlights the size of the investment made by BAE Systems in the cross-cultural leadership programme. List the benefits for the individual and the organisation.

2. How useful would this approach be for marketing managers working and managing across borders if the programme was adapted for the needs of marketers?

SUMMARY OF KEY POINTS

- Relevant cultural issues when dealing with international clients and organisations are related to national culture, which affects management and leadership style and the "way the people behave".

- Organisational culture is shaped by national culture, and environmental influences such as social and economic factors.

- Cultural conflicts can develop in global markets due to prejudice and bias, false assumptions about behaviour, or a lack of awareness of how to deal with differences.

- Management styles and perspectives differ from country to country. Important elements include personal space, attitudes to gender, and the relationship between leaders and followers.

Improving and developing own learning

The following projects are designed to help you develop your knowledge and skills further, by carrying out some research yourself. Feedback is not provided for this type of learning because there are no "answers" to be found, but you may wish to discuss your findings with colleagues and fellow students.

Project A

If your organisation works in a global market, research how differences are explored and managed when communicating with suppliers and customers.

Project B

Imagine that you are preparing to work with a project team in a country of your choice (other than your own). What differences in management and leadership styles do you anticipate? How will this affect your ability to work together and make decisions? How can the differences be managed?

Project C

How has your national culture impacted on your organisational culture? What influences can you identify?

Feedback to activities

Activity 14.1 Researching cultural differences

This activity should have led you to question some of your own assumptions and those of the media. From a marketing perspective you may have identified how national stereotypes are used in advertising.

Activity 14.2 Making sense of differences

In carrying out this activity did you refer to sections of Session 5 as well as to the material in this Session? The same disciplines should apply to this as to any other interaction.

You may also have considered the use of an interpreter and/or a cultural advisor from the country in question.

Activity 14.3 Gaining awareness

1. Attempts to transplant management models and ideas between cultures have more or less proved successful. You may have some direct experience of this. In practice, ideas such as Japanese quality management have often been "localised" by the people responsible for implementing them.

2. You may have noticed more similarities than differences! However, it is difficult for someone with little or no knowledge of a culture to identify which differences are significant and which are not (as "significant" can only be

defined from inside the culture). For example, there is no significance to the eating of either pork or beef for someone from a Christian background.

Activity 14.4 Cultural briefing

Your notes may contain some or all of the following points.

When working on long-term projects, teams should meet initially to explore any differences and construct a cross-cultural strategy. This involves determining how group processes will be developed to try and ensure that they work for the best for both the team and the project. What should be avoided is one culture taking on the cultural values of another long term. Rather it should be a "meeting of minds", with customer or sponsor needs determining how people and work are organised.

In practical terms when working internationally, you will find that people:

- Speak different languages – although many countries use English as a business language.
- Have different communication styles.
- Express their emotions in different ways.
- Have different social customs.
- Have different eating habits.
- Can be more or less tactile than you are accustomed to.
- Can be more or less aware of national stereotypes.

Other factors to consider are:

- Time differences. Office and working hours will be different, so consider the appropriate use of communication by email, fax, telephone and internal mail, and the time and place of meetings.
- Global teams may take longer to develop because members will not meet each other face to face on a regular basis, and because of differences in time and language.
- Decision making may take longer because of the diversity represented in the workforces of the different countries and the differences in management styles. Some countries will have cultures where employee involvement at every level in the organisation is encouraged, whilst others will have larger "gaps" between managers and subordinates.

- National cultures have different management styles. Role clarification is important to managers in some countries, such as Britain. Equally, British managers may feel the need to pay more attention to the needs of individuals than managers in some other cultures do.

Session 15

Managing across borders

Introduction

The final Session looks at the way organisations need to be aware of cultural differences when managing across borders. In particular, the way they communicate, share information and organise activities. The potential for conflict is also considered.

> **LEARNING OUTCOMES**
>
> At the end of this Session you will be able to:
>
> - Plan how to manage across borders.
> - Describe how to support others when managing across borders.
> - Discuss the role of communications and training in preventing cultural conflicts.

The role of planning

As discussed in Session 14, differences between national cultures can heavily influence people's attitudes and behaviour. In addition, differences in the business environment, for example in the social customs and political and legal systems, can make a difference not only to the form of an organisation, but also to the viability of a global business venture.

A full appreciation of the management issues involved in respect of a particular country is essential before any business venture goes ahead. As ever, it can be the hidden assumptions that managers make (because of their prejudice or adherence to their own national culture), which are the most important to uncover and challenge. Nothing can be taken for granted about customers, staff, competitors, or the environment in an international business environment. Session 14 has already outlined some of the major cultural issues that need to be researched. This Session explores the management issues in the business environment.

Factors in the business environment

How does business operate in another country?

Some of the issues that may arise are outlined below. These need to be adapted and expanded depending on the nature of the product or service to be delivered. Understanding these factors is essential, whether it is a new venture or an expansion of existing business that is being considered. Also look back at Session 14 for additional factors.

Political

How stable is the country politically? How might this affect doing business as a foreign organisation?

- What is the current political climate? What conditions would the proposed business be operating under?
- What are the policies of the different political parties? How would they affect the organisation's plans if implemented? When is the next election?
- What historical lessons are there? Does the country have a history of seizing foreign-owned assets?
- What risks are there for foreign nationals? To what extent are these unacceptable?
- What ethical issues are there? Is it usual for unofficial payments to be offered to government officials to do business? Is this acceptable to the parent organisation and its legal and ethical framework?

Legal and fiscal

What is the legal and fiscal environment? What would the organisation have to adapt to, or do differently?

- What are the barriers to entry and exit?
- What are the relevant regulations concerning employment?
- How are multinational organisations taxed?
- What about the products and services offered? What regulations might affect these?

Competitive

What is the shape and nature of the competition?

- What is the size and shape of the market? Who is the competition?
- How easy is it to enter the market?

- How have foreign organisations fared? What lessons can be learnt? Do local people do business with foreign organisations?
- What profits are available in the chosen market?

Consumer

How would consumers need to be approached?

- What cultural issues affect the marketing of this product or service? (You would need to look at advertising, branding, the buying process, attitudes to consumer care and consumer power.)
- What is the attitude of consumers to foreign organisations?
- What needs do consumers have? How would we be able to satisfy them better than the competition?

Options for management

There are several ways to enter an international market, for example:

- Operate a joint venture.
- Distribute products and services through a local intermediary.
- Buy a local organisation and manage it either with local management or with expatriate staff.
- Open a local business or office of the parent organisation:
  - Staffed with either local or expatriate staff.
  - Branded either locally or via the parent organisation.

All of these will have different management implications, and the advantages and disadvantages will depend on many factors. Whichever option is chosen, managers must consider all of the areas covered in this Companion, from employment, through performance management and reporting, through to motivation and teamwork. All of these need to be adapted according to the local environment.

Information sources

There are many information sources available to support managers who manage across borders. For example:

- Trade organisations (e.g. government sponsored groups), both in the organisation's own country and in the prospective trading country. Most countries are keen to attract inward investment.

- Consultants' marketing and trading reports. Many are available off the shelf from consultants who are considered specialists in an industry or in a specific country. Some may be held by business libraries and trade organisations.

- Professional services organisations that specialise in assisting organisations to set up in specific countries.

- Freely available information on the Internet.

> **Activity 15.1 Internet info**
>
> Choose a country with which your organisation, or one you know well, has dealings with (or may have dealings with in the future). Search the Internet for information that would be useful to you in managing a business in that country, following the framework set out above.

People issues

There are a number of different situations a manager may face in managing people across borders. For example, they may have to manage:

- Staff local to another country.
- Staff on business visits to another country.
- Multinational teams.

Some examples of the types of issues that may arise in these situations are outlined in the following sections. One issue common to all of these is effective communication.

- See Session 5 for a discussion of barriers to effective communication.
- See Session 13 for a discussion of management information systems. Effective management from a distance is highly dependent on a mutually agreed, accurate reporting and control system. Different local standards, such as in accounting, make it essential to specify information needs precisely.

Supporting local managers and employees

Managers who are involved in offering support to managers and other employees from another culture will not be effective unless they:

- Research and gain a knowledge of the other culture and business environment, preferably by getting some on-site experience, or at least a detailed briefing from someone experienced in that culture.
- Realise that just because something works in a certain way in one country, it doesn't mean it works that way everywhere.

Session 14 looked at some of the ways employees' attitudes and motivation can differ between cultures. All of these issues need to be taken into account when coaching or mentoring staff across borders. Induction programmes for local staff and managers can be useful in identifying and dealing with potential issues before they arise.

Supporting staff on business visits to other countries

Session 14 discussed how client and supplier attitudes can differ between national cultures. It is not always possible to send a member of staff who is experienced in a certain culture, so other support options need to be considered:

- Training and briefing the staff member fully (this is the bare minimum of support which should be given).
- Providing a local advisor whose job it is to support the staff member before, during, and after the business interaction, e.g. by advising on expected formalities, negotiation approach etc.
- Providing a translator.

Supporting multinational teams

Multinational teams present some particularly interesting issues:

- The impact of several nationalities coming together, not just two, needs to be considered. This needs sensitive and careful facilitation through team stages. For example in agreeing norms and taking explicit account of each person's values and beliefs.
- The practicalities of working together. For example, different time zones, any language issues, where and when face-to-face meetings should take place, how to build an effective team.

Technology has had a great impact on team working across borders. Teams can meet without the need to come together physically. The technology for virtual meetings is now well advanced, but does have drawbacks in that people are still operating in different time zones and it can be expensive.

Face-to-face meetings are still important. Some international teams choose to rotate the host country for their meetings, so that no one country is seen as dominating. It is also important to meet at milestones in the progress of a project – at the start, to celebrate major successes, and at the close.

Activity 15.2 Working across borders

Find several people in your organisation, or one you know well, who have experience of working across borders. Interview them about their experiences:

- What support were they given?
- What did they find the easiest part of the experience? What was the hardest?
- What came as a surprise (good or bad!)?
- What support would they like to have had? How would this have made a difference? To them? To the organisation?

Potential sources of conflict

As discussed in Session 14, cultural conflict can arise from any number of sources.

As with any management risk, it is possible to anticipate and prevent most conflicts by careful identification and planning. Some of the main strategies used to prevent conflict arising are:

- Good information gathering and business planning – examples are given throughout this Companion.
- Effective cross-cultural training.
- Having a written code of conduct (or team charter) that sets out the appropriate norms of behaviour for the project, rather than relating to just a single culture.
- Using local advisors, in particular before planning and implementing major change.

Behind all of these strategies is an unwritten assumption – that of respect for other people and their attitudes, values and beliefs, even where they are very different from your own.

The role of training

When managing across borders, language training is essential. Knowing the correct usage, pronunciation, and inflection of even a few phrases can be extremely useful. Other considerations include:

Culture
- Knowing what is acceptable and unacceptable behaviour, and its meaning.
- Understanding the beliefs and values of the culture, and where they originate, for example religion based or social norm.

Business life
- Pay.
- Staff motivation.
- Attitude to organisational authority.
- Expectation of management roles and perspectives.
- Organisational forms.
- Legal, political, economic, competitive issues.

Everyday life
- Characteristics of consumers.
- How people live and work.
- Safety issues and risks.

How to behave in an unfamiliar culture
- "Watch points" e.g. attitude towards time, body language.
- How to recover from giving offence.
- Correct forms of greetings.

As with all training, there is no substitute for the opportunity to use the skills learnt immediately in an appropriate context.

The role of local advisors

Once managers are dealing with people from different nationalities, they will continue to come across situations that demand a different level of knowledge and skills. Having a local expert who is on hand to advise can be a valuable asset. For example, organisations often employ the services of a translator because:

- A skilled translator will be able to put across some of the subtleties of a point which may have been lost otherwise – words from one language to another cannot always be directly translated to give the same meaning.
- The communications issues caused by encoding and decoding a message can be ameliorated.

It is extremely important that a skilled translator is used, and that every attempt is made to represent what is being said accurately. Otherwise the impression given may be a lack of openness and honesty. Remember that people may have a rudimentary grasp of your language even if it is insufficient to use in business discussions.

Having a written code of conduct

Practices that seem reasonable within one culture can be viewed as unacceptable in others, particularly in areas such as off-the-record payments to government officials, dress codes and child labour. Putting into writing "the way we do things around here" can be very valuable in preventing conflict, and forces organisations to make explicit choices. Considerations include:

- To what extent does the code need to reflect local practice?
- To what extent does the code need to reflect the parent organisation's practice?
- What are the implications for the organisation of each part of the code?

Decisions made locally reflect on an organisation's global operations, values and brand, not just its local presence. A code of conduct can prevent adverse publicity or even legal action in case of potential misunderstandings. For example, US-based organisations are restricted from making questionable payments in any country.

Activity 15.3 Communicating across borders

Review the complexities of effective communication that were discussed in Session 5. Considering this in the context of international management, what barriers might exist that prevent effective communication?

How can these be ameliorated or removed?

Case Study – Convenient, safe and face to face

The terrorist attacks on New York and Washington (September 11th, 2001) undoubtedly boosted the sales and usage of videoconferencing systems, as companies grounded top executives and looked for alternative ways of conducting meetings.

The conferencing company Genesys Conferencing reports that in the period following the attacks, daily levels of activity increased by 45% over the weeks leading up to September 11th. But it would be wrong to assume that an inability or unwillingness to fly is the only factor behind the increasing use of videoconferencing technology.

According to Martin Hill, Managing Director of videoconferencing solutions provider Call2View, there are other factors too. 'Economic conditions have been very positive for the past few years and this has almost provided a reason for using videoconferencing,' says Hill. 'But when you hit an economic slowdown, and companies look to cut costs, including travel costs, it does tend to be one of the industries that does well.'

There is also a more positive side to the industry's advancement. Companies involved in producing videoconferencing hardware have mostly adhered to agreed standards, which enables buyers to mix and match between brands with reasonable assurance of interoperability. Added to this, improvements in technology, from the codec (coder/decoder) which determines the quality of sound and pictures, to the networks over which they run, means that, according to Hill, 'People who last experienced videoconferencing five years ago are pleasantly surprised when they come back to it now.'

For marketers the technology has obvious applications, from agencies presenting creative concepts to clients in distant offices, to marketing directors in one country remotely attending meetings with their peers in another.

New media agency Euro RSCG Circle uses videoconferencing to communicate with colleagues, clients and suppliers in offices in the UK and across the world. Circle Head of IT Robert Clayton uses it instead of picking up the telephone. 'Videoconferencing gives it more of a meeting-like feel and it's easier to get people to stick to the agenda.'

However, Clayton's feedback is not all positive. 'It's not as easy as picking up the phone. If you're IT literate it's fine, bit if you're not you could struggle,' he says.

Circle Business Group Director, Alistair Daly, says he finds videoconferencing invaluable when long distance clients need a project turned around quickly. 'I wouldn't use it for new clients, but where there's already a good relationship and they need us to get on with something, it's a good solution.'

ISDN is the most common delivery mechanism for videoconference calls, and with national ISDN rates at 20 pence per minute, and transatlantic rates of between £1 and £3 per minute, it doesn't take too long for a videoconferencing system that's used regularly to start delivering a return on the investment made in it. Satellite links are also used occasionally, but these tend to be reserved for situations where it is too difficult, or too expensive to hook up an ISDN connection.

In the future IP (Internet Protocol) is expected to dominate the videoconferencing market. Many companies already make use of web casts to hold virtual meetings, or at least to make presentations to the public via the web, or employees and/or shareholders via a corporate Intranet.

As more businesses opt for broadband Internet access, this type of activity is set to increase in the future. Frost and Sullivan predict that by 2005 it will account for 57% of the virtual meeting market. Analysts Wainhouse estimate that IP's share will rise and ISDN's fall to 50% each during 2003, and by 2006 80% of the videoconferencing traffic will run over IP networks. The challenge for the videoconferencing industry is to deliver on the promise of the technology.

Source: *Marketing Business*, December/January 2002.

Questions

1. What factors have contributed to the rise in videoconferencing? In the future, what will impact on the use of this facility?

2. What are the advantages of this system over other forms of communication (such as email, telephone and fax) for virtual teams (those separated by distance, time and possibly organisation)?

SUMMARY OF KEY POINTS

- When planning to manage across borders it is important to understand the differences that might exist in business and organisational environments in order to understand how to manage people and projects.

- People working in countries other than their own need support and training to help them work effectively with people from other cultures – including awareness of social and business structures and customs.
- Potential conflicts when managing across borders can be minimised by effective training and the drawing up of a code of conduct.

Improving and developing own learning

The following projects are designed to help you develop your knowledge and skills further, by carrying out some research yourself. Feedback is not provided for this type of learning because there are no "answers" to be found, but you may wish to discuss your findings with colleagues and fellow students.

Project A

As a manager, if you were to transfer to an office in a country of your choice, how might you adapt your normal management style? Why would these changes be necessary?

Project B

Imagine that you are the project manager for a team launching a product of your choice in a country other than your own. Draw up a code of conduct or team charter to cover general operating practices for a team that includes members from at least three countries (of your choice).

Project C

Select some marketing material produced for consumers in your country, then choose a country that your organisation already operates in, or may do so in the future. How would you plan to market the products and services to people in that country? What are the main differences?

Feedback to activities

Activity 15.1 Internet info

Hopefully you have identified a lot of relevant information. For example, searching www.google.com for expatriate sites can provide a lot of information on local culture (http://www.expatriate-online.com has information for expatriates working in Belgium for instance). Searching for information on doing business in a country can also provide unexpected learning for managers involved in international business. Visit the site of the Japan External Trade Organisation http://www.jetro.go.jp and http://www.eurotechnology.com/doing-business-in-japan . Government organisations are also excellent sources of information.

In addition, searching for the sites of competitor organisations can also yield information, not only on the organisation itself, but also on its approach to consumers in the country of interest.

Other relevant web sites include:

http://www.dfat.gov.au Australian Department of Foreign Affairs and Trade.

http://www.infoexport.gc.ca/menu-e.asp Canadian Department of Foreign Affairs and International Trade.

http://www.fco.gov.uk/trade UK Trading information.

Activity 15.2 Working across borders

You may well have come across some issues that have not been covered. Cultures are very diverse and can throw up many cultural problems. However, most of these can be mitigated by understanding that people are different, and by identifying and working with those differences rather than expecting everyone to be the same.

Activity 15.3 Communicating across borders

You will have considered barriers in:

- The message's purpose. For example, communicating how a product or service emphasises your individuality is unlikely to appeal to most people in Japan.
- Encoding. There have been several well-publicised examples of product names meaning something inappropriate in the consumer's language; poor translations may affect product descriptions and ultimately sales.

- Message channel. There may be differences in the acceptability and use of mail shots in different countries for instance.
- Decoding. The receiver may infer something that was not intended to be encoded in the message, such as an attack on their religious beliefs.

Training and the use of local knowledge will go a long way in preventing these sorts of errors. Other methods of prevention include drawing up a code of conduct on communications strategy and regular meetings with the relevant people.

Glossary

Glossary

The following relevant terms have been taken from the CIM's online glossary. If you would like to see a full listing of marketing terms please visit www.cim.co.uk, and look under Services and then the Library and Information Service section of the site.

Above-the-line – advertising for which a payment is made and for which a commission is paid to the advertising agency.

Account management – the process by which an agency or supplier manages the needs of a client.

ACORN – a classification of residential neighbourhoods: a database that divides up the entire population of the UK in terms of housing in which they live.

Added value – the increase in worth of a product or service as a result of a particular activity (in the context of marketing this might be packaging or branding).

Advertising – promotion of a product, service or message by an identified sponsor using paid for media.

AIDA (Attention, Interest, Desire, Action) – a model describing the process that advertising or promotion is intended to initiate in the mind of a prospective customer.

Ambush marketing – a deliberate attempt by an organisation to associate itself with an event in order to gain some of the benefits associated with being an official sponsor without incurring the cost of sponsorship.

Assessment centre – used for the evaluation of individuals, commonly for promotion and recruitment, via activities and exercises designed to test set competences.

Balanced scorecard – a technique allowing a company to monitor and manage performance against defined objectives. Measurements typically cover financial performance, customer value, internal business process, innovation performance and employee performance.

Brand – the set of physical attributes of a product or service, together with the beliefs and expectations surrounding it.

Bureaucracy – a system that sets out rules and procedures for people to follow, allowing little or no room for personal judgement.

Business plan – a strategic document showing cash flow, forecasts and direction of a company.

Business process view – putting the customers' needs at the centre of processes that must be designed to eliminate waste to facilitate speed of response and two-way communication.

Business strategy – the means by which a business works towards achieving its stated aims.

Business-to-business (b2b) – relating to the sale of a product for any use other than personal consumption.

Business-to-consumer (b2c) – relating to the sale of a product for personal consumption.

Buying behaviour – the process that buyers go through when deciding whether or not to purchase goods or services.

Centralisation – the majority of decisions are taken by top management.

Channels – the methods used by a company to communicate and interact with its customers.

Comparative advertising – advertising which compares a company's product with that of competing brands.

Competitive advantage – the product, proposition or benefit that puts a company ahead of its competitors.

Confusion marketing – controversial strategy of deliberately confusing the customer.

Consumer – individual who buys and uses a product or service.

Consumer behaviour – the buying habits and patterns of consumers in the acquisition and usage of products and services.

Corporate identity – the character a company seeks to establish for itself in the mind of the public.

Corporate reputation – a complex mix of characteristics such as ethos, identity and image that go to make up a company's public personality.

Corporate strategy – the policies of a company with regard to its choice of businesses and customer groups.

Critical success factors – those aspects of the business or process which must result in order for objectives to be achieved, i.e. factors that are critical to success.

Culture – a shared set of values, beliefs and traditions that influence prevailing behaviour within a country or organisation.

Customer – a person or company who purchases goods or services.

Customer loyalty – feelings or attitudes that incline a customer to return to a company, shop or outlet to purchase there again.

Customer Relationship Management (CRM) – the coherent management of contacts and interactions with customers.

Customer satisfaction – the provision of goods or services that fulfil the customer's expectations in terms of quality and service, in relation to price paid.

Customer service programme – strategy for assuring customers a positive buying experience, in order to improve customer loyalty, increase cross-selling and promote advertising by word-of-mouth.

Data processing – the obtaining, recording and holding of information which can then be retrieved, used, disseminated or erased.

Database marketing – whereby customer information stored in an electronic database is utilised for targeting marketing activities.

Decision Making Unit (DMU) – the team of people in an organisation or family group who make the final buying decision.

Demand and supply – demand is the desire for a product at the market price, supply is the quantity available at that price.

Demographic data – information describing and segmenting a population in terms of age, sex, income and so on which can be used to target marketing campaigns.

Differentiation – ensuring that products and services have a unique element to allow them to stand out from the rest.

Direct mail – delivery of an advertising or promotional message to customers or potential customers by mail.

Direct marketing – all activities that make it possible to offer goods or services or to transmit other messages to a segment of the population by post, telephone, email or other direct means.

Direct Response Advertising (DRA) – advertising incorporating a contact method such as a phone number or enquiry form with the intention of encouraging the recipient to respond directly to the advertiser.

Distribution (Place) – the process of getting the goods from the manufacturer or supplier to the user.

Diversification – an increase in the variety of goods and services produced by an organisation.

E-commerce – business conducted electronically.

Effectiveness – a measure of the degree to which objectives are met.

Efficiency – a measure of output in relation to input.

E-marketing – marketing conducted electronically.

Electronic Point of Sale (EPOS) – a system whereby electronic tills are used to process customer transactions in a retail outlet.

Entrepreneur – someone who sees an opportunity and risks their own money to set up a business organisation in order to get it.

Ethical marketing – marketing that takes account of the moral aspects of decisions.

Export marketing – the marketing of goods or services to overseas customers.

External analysis – study of the external marketing environment.

Field marketing – extending an organisation's marketing in the field through merchandising, product launches, training of retail staff, etc.

FMCG (Fast Moving Consumer Goods) – such as food and toiletries.

Focus groups – a tool for marketing research where small groups of participants take part in guided discussions on the topic being researched.

Forecasting – calculation of future events and performance.

Franchising – the selling of a licence by the owner (franchiser) to a third party (franchisee) permitting the sale of a product or service for a specified period.

Group – two or more people who regard themselves as having a common purpose.

Human Resource Management (HRM) – management of the organisation's people in order to enhance achievement of corporate objectives.

Industrial marketing (or business-to-business marketing) – the marketing of industrial products.

Innovation – development of new products, services or ways of working.

Internal analysis – the study of a company's internal marketing resources in order to assess strengths, weaknesses and opportunities.

Internal customers – employees within an organisation viewed as "consumers" of a product or service provided by another part of the organisation.

Internal marketing – the process of eliciting support for a company and its activities among its own employees in order to encourage them to promote its goals.

International marketing – the conduct and co-ordination of marketing activities in more than one country.

Job analysis – a process to identify the characteristics of an area of work so that a job description (roles and responsibilities) and person specification (personal attributes required to do the job) can be drawn up.

Joint venture – a business entity or partnership formed by two or more parties for a specific purpose.

Key Account Management (KAM) – account management as applied to a company's most valuable customers.

Knowledge management – the collection, organisation and distribution of information in a form that lends itself to practical application. Knowledge management often relies on information technology to facilitate the storage and retrieval of information.

Logo – a graphic usually consisting of a symbol and or group of letters that identifies a company or brand.

Macro environment – the external factors which affect companies' planning and performance, and are beyond its control (PEST or SLEPT factors).

Market development – the process of growing sales by offering existing products (or new versions of them) to new customer groups.

Market penetration – the attempt to grow ones business by obtaining a larger market share in an existing market.

Market research – the gathering and analysis of data relating to markets to inform decision making.

Marketing research – the gathering and analysis of data relating to marketing to inform decision making (includes product research, place research, pricing research, etc.).

Market segmentation – the division of the marketplace into distinct sub-groups or segments, each characterised by particular tastes and requiring a specific marketing mix.

Market share – a company's sales of a given product or set of products to a given set of customers, expressed as a percentage of total sales of all such products to such customers.

Marketing audit – scrutiny of an organisation's existing marketing system to ascertain its strengths and weaknesses.

Marketing communications (Promotion) – all methods used by a firm to communicate with its customers and stakeholders.

Marketing information – any information used or required to support marketing decisions.

Marketing mix – the combination of marketing inputs that affect customer motivation and behaviour (7 Ps – Product, Price, Promotion, Place, People, Process and Physical Evidence).

Marketing orientation – a business strategy whereby customers' needs and wants determine corporate direction.

Marketing planning – the selection and scheduling of activities to support the company's chosen marketing strategy or goals.

Marketing strategy – the broad methods chosen to achieve marketing objectives.

McKinsey Seven S's of management (7S Model) – a framework for considering business strategy with reference to seven interrelated aspects of the organisation: Systems, Structure, Strategy, Style, Staff, Skills and Shared values.

Merger/Acquisition – Merger: the formation of one company from two existing companies. Acquisition: one company acquiring control of another by purchase of a majority shareholding.

Micro environment – the immediate context of a company's operations, including such elements as suppliers, customers and competitors.

Mission statement – a company's summary of its business philosophy, purpose and direction.

Model – simplified representation of a process, designed to aid understanding.

New Product Development (NPD) – the creation of new products, from evaluation of proposals through to launch.

Niche marketing – the marketing of a product to a small and well-defined segment of the marketplace.

Norms – commonly understood rules that provide guidelines for personal behaviour. Rules are usually informal.

Objectives – a company's defined and measurable aims or goals for a given period.

Packaging – material used to protect and promote goods.

Participative models of change – those that use change agents to encourage the involvement of those who are informed about the change and affected by the change.

Performance appraisal – formal review of a person's performance against objectives over a set period of time. Often used to set objectives for the future and to identify development needs.

Personal selling – one-to-one communication between seller and prospective purchaser.

Profit Impact of Marketing Strategies (PIMS) – a US database supplying data such as environment, strategy, competition and internal data.

Porter's Five Forces – an analytic model developed by Michael E. Porter that analyses the competitive environment and industry structure.

Portfolio (and portfolio analysis) – the set of products or services that a company decides to develop and market. Portfolio analysis is the process of comparing the contents of the portfolio to see which products and services are the most promising and deserving of further investment, and those that should be discontinued.

Positioning – the creation of an image for a product or service in the minds of customers, both specifically to that item and in relation to competitive offerings.

Product Life Cycle (PLC) – a model describing the progress of a product from the inception of the idea, through its growth and maturity to its eventual decline.

Promotional mix – the components of an individual campaign which are likely to include advertising, personal selling, public relations, direct marketing, packaging and sales promotion.

Public Relations (PR) – the planned and sustained communication to promote mutual understanding between an organisation and its stakeholders.

Pull promotion – addresses the customer directly with a view to getting them to demand the product and hence "pull" it down through the distribution chain.

Push promotion – relies on the next link in the distribution chain, e.g. the wholesaler, to "push" out products to the customer.

Qualitative research – information that cannot be measured or expressed in numeric terms. It is useful to the marketer as it often explores people's feelings and opinions.

Quantitative research – information that can be measured in numeric terms and analysed statistically.

Reference group – a group with which the customer identifies in some way and whose opinions and experiences influence the customer's behaviour.

Relationship marketing – the strategy of establishing a relationship with a customer which continues well beyond the first purchase.

Return on Investment (ROI) – the value that an organisation derives from investing in a project.

Sales promotion – a range of techniques used to increase sales in the short term.

Sampling – the use of a statistically representative subset as a proxy for an entire population, for example in order to facilitate quantitative market research.

Selection test – tests designed to assess a candidate's suitability for a job.

Skimming – setting the original price high in the early stages of the product life cycle to get as much profit as possible before prices are driven down by increasing competition.

SLEPT – a framework for viewing the macro environment – Socio-cultural, Legal, Economic, Political and Technical factors.

SMART – a mnemonic referring to the need for objectives to be Specific, Measurable, Achievable, Relevant and Time-bound.

Sponsorship – specialised form of promotion where a company will help fund an event or support a business venture in return for publicity.

Stakeholder – an individual or group that affects or is affected by the organisation and its operations.

Supplier – an organisation or individual that supplies goods or services to a company.

Structure – the way a group is organised, such as reporting lines, lines of authority, specification of roles (commonly shown on the organisational structure chart).

SWOT analysis – analysis to determine Strengths, Weaknesses, Opportunities and Threats.

Targeting – the use of market segmentation to select and address a key group of potential purchasers.

Team – two or more people, with complementary skills, who share a common purpose, approach and objectives, and hold themselves accountable as a group for results. Team results depend on effective interaction between members, unlike a group which may only interact socially or share information and best practice. Team results are greater than the sum of the individual parts, whereas group results are the sum of the individual efforts.

Unique Selling Proposition (USP) – that benefit that a product or service can deliver to customers that is not offered by any competitor.

Vision – the long-term aims and aspirations of the company for itself.

Virtual teams/organisations – teams or organisations that deliver products and services but which have few of the physical features associated with teams or organisations.

Word-of-mouth – the spreading of information through human interaction alone.

Appendix 1

Feedback to Case Studies

Session 1

1. **Suggest ways in which the structure of tomorrow's organisations might change.**
   - Years of downsizing will influence the number of people in the reporting structure. "Lean and mean" organisations tend to lead to managers having a larger span of control within a flatter structure.
   - Although there is still a requirement for specialists, the structure will need to accommodate and support more flexible generalists working on projects. Therefore the structure will be geared towards teamwork; a matrix type rather than a rigid hierarchy.
   - Structures must be flexible and adaptable, particularly so for some functions more than others. Marketing might become more project based, whilst Finance retains a more permanent hierarchical type structure.

2. **Suggest ways in which the prevailing culture of tomorrow's organisations might change.**
   - Teamworking should enhance a culture of sharing (information and ideas) and lead to more open communication.
   - Culture should support individuals and teams in a results-focused environment, leading to a greater understanding for each person of what he/she needs to do to ensure customer satisfaction – customer focus not cost focus (although profit is essential).
   - In a fast moving, competitive environment, people should feel able and supported to take risks, and want to take on more responsibility to solve the problems that prevent customer satisfaction as quickly as possible.
   - A culture of continuous improvement with people taking responsibility for their own development.
   - A culture that recognises and celebrates success in customer satisfaction rather than a ruthless drive towards efficiency.

Session 2

1. **What skills and experiences are needed by Multi-Unit Managers?**
   - Management and marketing skills, as Multi-Unit Managers (MUMs) need

Appendix 1

to be more customer focused and accountable for profitability.

- The management skills needed include problem solving and decision making, personal organisation (time and territory management), managing and motivating individuals and teams, planning, control, monitoring and reviewing the performance of people and operations, negotiating, and excellent communication skills and leadership.

- The marketing skills needed include developing and managing brand identity and integrity, internal marketing skills, customer service skills and general marketing and communication skills.

- MUMs require both general management experience of running teams and projects, brand management and communications experience, customer service experience, and an operational background, including negotiating with senior managers and external agencies.

- Relevant business or marketing degree.

2. **What special attributes would you include and why?**

    - The ability to manage teams and projects, as this is fundamental to the job.

    - The ability to think quickly and solve problems is essential in a fast moving environment where the MUM is working with a number of "complex units" which are like businesses in their own right.

    - The ability to interpret strategic plans and communicate objectives to others, as the MUM is often the interface between upper management and junior staff.

    - The ability to manage the brand, as this is key to the success of the role.

    - The ability to lead others through change, due to the pace of change currently being experienced.

Session 3

1. **What are the likely problems of these new work practices for managers and employees?**

    - Staff who work from home may feel isolated from their colleagues and manager. Therefore, the manager needs to understand how to motivate staff at a distance to maintain high and consistent levels of service to customers, even when they are feeling lonely and unappreciated.

- A lack of social contact may increase feelings of isolation, so the manager needs to find ways of increasing the level of team communication, so that teleworkers do feel part of a larger team and organisation.
- Domestic issues may intrude so managers need to be able to control work and supervise as necessary.
- The teleworkers are front-line staff and company representatives, so internal marketing practices must keep them in touch with corporate and brand identity so that they all communicate consistently.
- As staff have less direct supervision, they will need training to take more responsibility for problem solving and decision making themselves.

2. **What are the main implications for the business, such as the impact on business operations and the implications of setting up teleworking?**
   - The initial implication is the cost of setting up the teleworking system so that staff can communicate with customers and the office. In the long term less office space will be required for customer services, thus increasing profitability in this area.
   - The Health and Safety and insurance implications for home workers need to be resolved.
   - There may be tax benefits of purchasing new computers for teleworkers.
   - It may be easier to recruit new staff, as many workers see working from home as a significant advantage. However, they will need to be able to attend the office for occasional team meetings and training.
   - The reward system will need to be revised to recognise the need for incentives to overcome possible higher levels of demotivation.
   - The system will take time to set up, and may need to be phased in so that our customers do not notice any temporary decrease in service as we switch from one system to another.
   - The system should provide greater service flexibility, as staff are not wasting time in travelling to an office and may be able to work from home more flexibly.
   - All relevant current operating systems, such as gathering feedback from customers and service monitoring, need to be examined to identify how they can be accommodated once the teleworking system is fully operational.

- As customer services includes sales and technical support, teleworking staff need to be able to communicate with each other.

Session 4

During periods of change and uncertainty, people tend to be risk averse and consequently they do not seek out new ways of solving existing problems. Alternatively they might look for the "easy option", one that will incur the least upset. However, it is at times like these that staff need to be able to solve problems and make decisions that feel unfamiliar, otherwise progress will not be made. The following three slides could be used for a briefing designed to help staff feel able to take responsibility for their decisions.

Decision making

- Identify problem to be solved.
- Gather information from both primary and secondary sources.
- Generate options.
- Evaluate options against objective criteria.
- Select best option.
- Implement, monitor and review.

Supporting decision making

- Creating an enabling culture where people communicate and share information.
- Establishing a blame-free culture.
- Helping people to learn when things go wrong.
- Providing training and development opportunities.

Actions for marketing team

- Conduct individual skills audit to identify training needs.
- Set up coaching and mentoring support within team.

- Carry out training using internal and external support.
- Evaluate effectiveness of training at team meetings.
- Celebrate effective problem solving and decision making.

Session 5

1. **What does the Case Study suggest are the main barriers to effective communication with consumers at large sporting events such as the Olympic Games?**
   - The clutter of messages is so great that less prominent or well-known brand messages are lost to consumers in information overload.
   - The number of high-profile brands participating.
   - "Unofficial" messages sent out by companies using the event to sell their product.
   - Broadcast media that carry communications from companies not sponsoring the event.

2. **As a marketing consultant, what advice would you give to an organisation sponsoring a large sporting event, to help them ensure their communications are more effective than those suggested in the Case Study?**
   - Ensure the values of the event match corporate values.
   - Set specific objectives so that effectiveness can be measured for future information, as sponsoring such events is very costly. The minimum spend for the Sydney Olympics was $40 million.
   - Ensure that the sponsorship deal is part of an integrated campaign, so that consumers receive consistent messages from a number of sources.
   - Identify opportunities that will attract attention among target groups – research is vital to get optimum specific coverage, not just widespread blanket coverage.

Session 6

1. **What has led to the situation that UEA find themselves in now?**
   - Lack of Human Resource Management (HRM) planning.

Appendix 1

- No structured job role analysis.
- Ad hoc or piecemeal revisions to terms and conditions – possibly completed by different people in different ways.

2. **What are the potential problems facing recruiters?**
   - Identifying the specific vacancy.
   - Identifying a job description and person specification that "fits" with other members of the team or department.
   - Gathering information. There may be insufficient information on the current job holder and no other reliable sources to check how that job needs doing in the future.

3. **What are the potential problems of providing a succession of short-term contracts to the same person?**
   - Job holder may feel unsettled or insecure and undervalued.
   - Job holder may prefer to look for a longer-term contract.
   - It may become normal practice.
   - Job holder is not considered for longer-term training and development.

Session 7

Creating new marketing teams:
- Decide how teams should be structured and organised – by product, customer segment, or perhaps as one large team. Examine the marketing plan and objectives to identify an appropriate structure.
- Determine any major requirement for external specialists and agencies and how these need to communicate with internal teams.
- Create teams that contain relevant technical, managerial, intellectual and emotional skills – use Belbin to identify any potential lack of balance.
- Conduct a HR audit to identify existing knowledge, skills and experience and identify potential gaps.
- Identify a time scale for setting up the teams, including recruitment and training needs.

Building effective marketing teams:

- As people from both organisations will be coming together in new teams, ensure that people issues are dealt with during the merger and that communication is regular, open and honest.

- Communicate the new corporate vision, values and business plan to the teams and identify consistent marketing values.

- Apply Tuckman's Forming, Storming, Norming, Performing and Adjourning model of team development to the team, and identify their stage of development, the support they require, and what would be an effective leadership style for them (see description in Session 7).

- Identify individual training needs and implement training and development.

- Set up coaching and mentoring schemes to enable the more experienced team members to guide and support the less experienced members.

- Create a programme of team building events – both formal and informal (social) events, to help people learn together and find out more about each other's strengths and weaknesses.

Session 8

In answering Question 1 you may wish to adopt an approach that follows a planning tool, such as SOSTAC (Situation, Objectives, Strategy, Targets, Action, Control).

1. **How would you develop and implement an internal communications plan that improves the process of communications, motivation and team spirit?**

    - Conduct a communications audit to identify what is happening at present and how effective it is.

    - Set SMART objectives for the plan. The actors and managers need to understand the overall business objectives and how they can contribute towards these.

    - Identify a strategy for the development and implementation of the plan. Different methods can be used to convey this, such as internal newsletters and briefings. It is not feasible to use electronic forms of communication as the actors and managers in the theatre are not "networked" like office staff, and not everyone will have access to the Internet. In addition, actors may stay for only one production, perhaps for a maximum of 18 months.

Appendix 1

- Identify what the target audience needs to know and how it can be communicated to them. Also consider what do they already know. Poor communication in the past has led to an "us and them" culture of suspicion and mistrust.
- Actors need to be motivated to perform consistently during long and unsociable hours. Their successes need to be recognised and their talents celebrated. Positive external reviews need to be communicated to them, possibly through briefings, and poor reviews discussed openly. Actors should have clear goals and receive feedback on their performances.
- In addition to being managed as individuals, they need to be made to feel a valuable part of the whole organisation. Senior managers and theatre directors must be visible and seen to be concerned about the actors' problems to enhance team spirit. Corporate vision, values and objectives need to be shared.
- Experienced actors could be used as mentors for newer colleagues so that they can benefit from the experience within the team.
- Once the plan has been implemented, it should be monitored and reviewed by conducting the same staff survey, to see what progress has been made.

2. **Briefly explain how this would contribute towards the brand.**
   - It would help develop a better knowledge and understanding of each other and what each other is trying to achieve – breaks down the "us and them" barrier.
   - It would encourage commitment to the RSC and the brand.
   - It enhances staff loyalty and staff would help communicate brand identity.

Session 9

1. **Discuss the potential problems of linking an annual performance appraisal to the pay structure.**
   - Consistency – different managers, appraising different staff, will give different assessments of performance.
   - Staff may not feel able to talk openly about what prevents them from producing results, in case they are regarded as incompetent and given a lower pay award.

- It gives the appraiser a base for power.
- It is often regarded as unfair. Some individuals may not have achieved their objectives due to unforeseen circumstances that were beyond their control. How can that situation be dealt with fairly and consistently?

2. **What are the benefits that Siemens hopes to gain from employee dialogue?**
    - Open communication, where people feel able to say what needs to be said, rather than what people want to hear.
    - Everyone participates and feels involved, which is motivational and aids commitment.
    - This new and different approach to the giving of feedback and sharing of information should aid decision making as all views are sought.

3. **How is employee dialogue linked to performance review at Siemens?**
    - Through a 360-degree appraisal, so people receive feedback from those below them, on the same level and above, so as to gain a full perspective of how they conduct their role in the organisation.
    - There is more feedback, which should help enable the appraisee to identify where development is needed and prioritise those needs – the more people that give negative feedback the greater the need for development.

Session 10

1. **What were the main benefits of a learning contract to individual learners?**
    - The word "contract" implied it was binding, and therefore people were more committed to achievement.
    - The individual was an important part of the process of drawing up the contract – again leading to greater commitment.
    - Individuals were in control of their own learning.
    - The learning contract was developed with others who could then act as enablers and encourage completion.
    - It provided a record of learning that was relevant to both the individual and the organisation.

Appendix 1

2. **How effective was the evaluation of the programme?**
   - By measuring the results over a period of time the evaluation was able to assess the impact of the training on the business.
   - Participants were able to comprehend and measure their development by the use of pre- and post-questionnaire.
   - Line managers were involved so that learning could be validated, and it also provided the opportunity for further development if the line manager was able to help the learner identify new opportunities to use the knowledge and skills gained on the programme.
   - Both quantitative and qualitative measures were used to add greater objectivity.

3. **What were the additional benefits to the organisation, apart from individual development?**
   - Cross-area communication and sharing of knowledge that supported teamworking.
   - The development of group working skills (learning groups).
   - Cross-cultural relationships leading to the creation of social capital.
   - The development of a culture of learning and development that was aligned with business needs.
   - Individuals who were able to take responsibility for their own learning.

Session 11

What advice could you give her on:

1. **How the company might tackle the problem of improving relationships with other companies across the railway network.**
   - At present contact appears to be ad hoc, only initiated when things go wrong. This reactive approach should be replaced with a proactive one, where points of contact are identified and the nature and frequency of communication required is also identified. This should be ongoing so that changing needs are identified.
   - Teams should operate across company borders, with shared goals for performance standards and a commitment to solving the shared problems that prevent customer satisfaction or improvements in service standards.

- There should be shared values across companies, set jointly, of high-quality services and continuous improvement.
- Marketing should reflect this shared approach, so that customers feel valued across the network – it should not be a source of competitive advantage!

2. **The implications for marketing management of implementing this strategy (for example, implications for teamwork, communications, consistency of standards, processes).**
    - Relationship building across the network.
    - Joint understanding of relationship marketing and customer focus.
    - Customer feedback made available to all companies so that teams can work together to solve problems.
    - Development of an effective communications strategy, both formal and informal. Who, what, when, why, where and how?
    - Development of customer databases for marketing.
    - Monitor and review the changes made to operations, such as online booking, to evaluate customer response.

3. **Controls for ensuring success.**
    - Shared standards for customer service measured consistently across the network.
    - Information gathered from customers through surveys.
    - Nature and levels of complaints monitored and acted upon.
    - Response to complaints evaluated – successful resolution, time taken to deal with etc.
    - Customer service training for all staff.
    - Feedback on performance given to staff and support given to improve.
    - External measures, such as relevant consumer surveys and reports and media reporting.

Appendix 1

Session 12

The Need for Innovation

- Non-linear change demands companies rethink their business.
- Organisations need to respond to the increasing rate of change.
- Companies need to think differently to remain competitive.
- Consumers become bored fairly easily.
- Survival?

Innovating Effectively

- Identify and respond to appropriate product/process trends and developments.
- Ensure innovation is everyone's responsibility.
- Develop a workforce that is comfortable with change.
- Ensure curiosity is part of the prevailing culture.
- Know what the customer needs – now and in the future.

Barriers to Innovation

- Limiting innovation to Research & Development or Marketing functions.
- Continuing on previous track.
- Unwillingness to rethink vision or process.
- Previous poor experience.
- Change for change's sake.

Session 13

1. Which aspects of IDEA's approach to working with clients do you think have been most successful in enabling them to harness knowledge?
    - IDEA encourage and facilitate the "uncovering" of talents, skills and

knowledge within an organisation, and show them how to make best use of this.

- IDEA encourages the sharing of learning and developing a culture of continuous improvement.
- IDEA leads the way by creating learning and knowledge resources that clients can use.
- IDEA focus on what people can do and know, and how that can be used to best advantage by everyone within the organisation.
- IDEA encourages organisations to accept change as a way of life and people as a competitive advantage!

2. **How has this contributed to the success of learning within local authorities?**
   - Ability to learn is recognised as a valuable skill.
   - Learning becomes the norm.
   - Learning is relevant to the achievement of objectives.
   - The passing on of knowledge can be bottom up or top down, so no one is excluded. All talents are utilised according to their worth to others.
   - Knowledge is pooled so it is accessible to all.
   - People are encouraged to learn from each other.

Session 14

1. **The Case Study highlights the size of the investment made by BAE Systems in the cross-cultural leadership programme. List the benefits for the individual and the organisation.**

   For the individual this includes:
   - Working knowledge – not just information!
   - Greater cultural awareness and practical examples that represent a real live learning experience.
   - Opportunity to explore prejudices and their impact on communication and management styles – useful when working across borders.
   - Opportunities to experience cultural differences.

Appendix 1

For the organisation this includes:

- Developing a workforce that has learnt to communicate and work across cultures (appreciation of how advertising messages need to be adjusted etc.).
- Developing managers who can think globally.
- Gaining global competitive advantage through the skills of a global workforce.

2. **How useful would this approach be for marketing managers working and managing across borders if the programme was adapted for the needs of marketers?**

   In addition to the benefits outlined above for the individual, from a marketing perspective it enables managers to gain knowledge, skills and experience to help them:

   - Communicate advertising and other promotional messages accurately and appropriately, avoiding causing offence by using the "wrong" phrases, colours or style.
   - Develop a global perspective to help them facilitate cross-cultural and international marketing teams when carrying out tasks such as product launches internationally.
   - Develop a network of international business contacts.
   - Understand how marketing information is organised in different countries.

Session 15

1. **What factors have contributed to the rise in videoconferencing? In the future, what will impact on the use of this facility?**
   - Reluctance of companies to let their valuable assets, such as senior executives, travel in the aftermath of the terrorist attacks on September 11th in the USA – perception that travel is less safe than it used to be.
   - Cost (compared to transatlantic telephone calls for example) – realisation that if used regularly it is cost effective.
   - Ability to talk face to face – technology has improved.
   - Ability to hold a meeting not just a telephone call (Robert Clayton's feedback).

- Rise in the number of virtual teams and projects, which will continue to increase as more companies become confident in a global market.
- Time efficient way of holding a meeting – no travelling time to add on or jet lag to recover from!

2. **What are the advantages of this system over other forms of communication (such as email, telephone and fax) for virtual teams (those separated by distance, time and possibly organisation)?**
    - Can be a cost effective form of communication.
    - Is face to face.
    - Enables people separated by distance, time and possibly organisation, to "meet" each other – personal contact enhances commitment.
    - It is carried out in real time, so replies are current. If you are sending an email the situation may have changed by the time the receiver is ready to reply.
    - Can be used to develop a relationship (Alistair Daly's feedback).
    - It is versatile – as it is visual, documents, plans, creative work, etc. can be viewed and discussed by all parties.

Appendix 2

Syllabus

Effective management for marketing

Aims and objectives
- To examine organisational theory and its impact on marketing management practice.
- To introduce the concepts of management theory and examine their effectiveness in practice.
- To relate management theory and practice to the role of marketing and how marketing activities can be improved.
- To introduce the concepts and consequences of change management and marketing's role in managing change.
- To introduce international influences on current management practice.
- To develop and enhance personal effectiveness and the key skills required within a marketing management context.

Learning outcomes
By the end of this module, you should be able to:

- Understand international organisational cultures and their impact on marketing management.
- Explain the theory underpinning effective management of self, other people, resources and client relationships.
- Describe the principles of managing change that minimise resistance and maximise successful outcomes and the role of marketing in this change.
- Determine communications problems typically faced by managers and describe strategies for improving and solving these problems.
- Explain the principles and techniques of successful negotiation with internal colleagues and external customers, suppliers, distributors etc.
- Undertake a personal skills audit, using mechanisms introduced on the course, with the intention of identifying personal strengths and weaknesses and planning and implementing improvements.

Appendix 2

- Understand the role of human resource management planning and its contribution to ensuring effective levels of marketing staffing and skills.
- Devise training and development plans for marketing personnel to improve individual and team effectiveness and motivation.
- Devise methods for motivating marketing staff to improve individual and team effectiveness.
- Explain concepts of building and managing effective teams and the role of leadership.
- Describe international influences on management practice and their uses and abuses.

Indicative content and weighting

4.1 The nature of management and organisation issues (15%)

4.1.1 Changing nature of business.

4.1.2 Organisation cultures and their impact on marketing management practice.

4.1.3 The role and functions of the manager.

4.2 Personal effectiveness (30%)

4.2.1 The responsibilities and activities of the marketing manager and leadership styles.

4.2.2 Personal skills audits and improving management performance.

4.2.3 Improving time management, delegation, managing meetings, problem solving and decision-making.

4.2.4 Interpersonal communications effectiveness (verbal, non verbal, listening skills, negotiating, internal marketing, handling discipline and grievances).

4.2.5 HRM planning for marketing jobs, tasks and marketing personnel.

4.3 Managing people (40%)

4.3.1 Managing and improving effectiveness of individuals.

4.3.2 Managing and building effective teams.

4.3.3 Motivation and improving marketing job satisfaction.

4.3.4 The role of marketing personnel appraisals.

4.3.5 The role of marketing personnel performance – training and development.

4.3.6 Managing client relationships, customer service and conducting negotiations.

4.3.7 Managing change effectively through individuals and teams.

4.3.8 Knowledge management.

4.4 International management (15%)

4.4.1 Different management perspectives and their values.

4.4.2 Problems encountered by global organisations.

4.4.3 Managing across borders.

Appendix 3

Effective Management for Marketing

Examination paper (December 2001)

 The Chartered Institute of Marketing

Advanced Certificate in Marketing

Effective Management for Marketing

8.33: Effective Management for Marketing

Time: 09.30-12.30

Date: 5th December, 2001

3 Hours Duration

This examination is in two sections.

PART A – Is compulsory and worth 40% of total marks.

PART B – Has **SIX** questions; select **THREE**. Each answer will be worth 20% of the total marks.

DO NOT repeat the question in your answer, but show clearly the number of the question attempted on the appropriate pages of the answer book.

Rough workings should be included in the answer book and ruled through after use.

 © The Chartered Institute of Marketing

Appendix 3

Advanced Certificate in Marketing

8.33:   Effective Management for Marketing

PART A

Managing Mergers – The People Issues

Mergers, acquisitions, buy-ins or buy-outs continue with growing frequency. Research shows that many of their desired benefits do not materialise, while the costs of integration are usually underestimated.

The most frequently cited reasons for these poor results are people related. During the acquisition phase, most deals focus on financial, legal and, sometimes, technical or marketing factors, but rarely on the human issues.

In 1999 the total value of cross border mergers and acquisitions reached over 1.1 trillion dollars, a tenfold increase in 8 years (source: UN 2000). The OECD says that this often does not yield any benefits, owing to the costs of merging different organisation cultures. To address this, merging companies need to consider developing a process for post merger integration, which focuses on all human aspects of the organisation. The aim is to ensure that all facets of people's roles and contributions to the organisation are thoroughly investigated within the context of the emerging business strategy.

Before the merger, this includes culture, climate and communications, competence (the quality of skills, leadership and teamwork) and the management of core information and data.

After the merger, the new organisation needs to assess candidates to create new teams and set up team building events; carry out a cultural analysis; roll out a new vision, values, culture and strategy; and further develop competency profiles and appraisal processes.

Compensation and benefits will need to be integrated and new Human Resource (HR) strategies and policies put into place. Support for the HR function itself should be considered. And, lastly, there is likely to be an outplacement programme to manage. In everything that is done, internal communications are crucial.

Many companies have achieved significant improvements to mergers by adopting some of these ideas. But, as yet, no organisation has adopted an entirely integrated approach.

The number and value of mergers is growing rapidly, particularly in cross border acquisitions within the European Union. There were 195 deals completed in the UK in 2000. Yet a recent survey of 58 mergers in the UK found that only 14 had considered the cultural issues before the purchase decision was made.

Adapted from People Management 2001

PART A

Question 1.

You are the Marketing Manager for a car manufacturing company that is considering merging with another car manufacturer (within the same country). Your Chief Executive has read the above article and is concerned about how this merger can be managed successfully. Any recommendations will involve both companies so will require the co-operation of people from both companies. The Chief Executive has asked you to prepare a report making recommendations on how:

a. An audit can be conducted, before the merger, on organisation culture, communications and competence (quality of skills, leadership and teamwork). It is important you consider how you will encourage the co-operation of people from both companies and timescales.

(12 marks)

b. You will communicate, after the merger and implementation, a new vision and cultural values to staff.

(12 marks)

c. You will create new marketing teams across the new organisation and set up team building events.

(16 marks)
(40 marks in total)

PART B – Answer THREE Questions Only

Question 2.

You are the Customer Service Manager of a busy call centre for a Travel Operator. Your team has recently doubled to 20 and your time is increasingly spent responding to the demands of new recruits. You want to manage your time better. Prepare and explain a plan of action on:

a. How to improve your management of time.

(10 marks)

b. How to train new staff more effectively using existing resources to greater effect.

(10 marks)
(20 marks in total)

Question 3.

You are the newly recruited Marketing Manager (a new position) for a charity of your choice. Your first task is to help the charity improve its poor performance. Your preliminary review has identified that morale is low amongst both employed staff and volunteers and they feel demoralised. Write a report to the Chief Executive explaining how you will improve morale and motivation.

(20 marks)

Question 4.

As Marketing Manager for an engineering company, much of your time (and your team's) is taken up in meetings with Research and Development staff trying to solve customer problems or implement new ideas. These meetings could be more productive and result in more successful outcomes. Prepare guidelines to your colleagues that explain:

a. How meetings might be analysed to identify the problems.

(10 marks)

b. How meetings can be improved.

(10 marks)
(20 marks in total)

Question 5.

As Customer Liaison Manager for a telecommunications company you have been asked to write a report explaining:

a. What relationship marketing is.

(10 marks)

b. Why the effective management of people is important in building customer relationships.

(10 marks)
(20 marks in total)

Question 6.

You work for a software company and your Managing Director has announced plans to grow the business by 35% in the next two years. The product range will be extended to support this growth. Write a report to the Managing Director on the Human Resource planning issues involved and how you intend to identify and ensure appropriate marketing skills levels to support this growth.

(20 marks)

Question 7.

You are the Marketing Manager for a clothes wholesaler. Your Sales Manager has had an argument with a salesperson who has been verbally abusive to a customer. This person has also failed to follow through queries and problems on the customer's order. This is the second time there has been a problem with this person. Write a memo to the Sales Manager explaining how to conduct a discipline interview.

(20 marks)

Appendix 4

Specimen answers

The following do not represent full specimen answers to the specimen examination paper, but instead look at:

- The rationale for the question – what the examiner is looking for.
- The best way to structure your answer.
- The key points that you should have included and expanded upon.
- How marks for the question might have been allocated.
- The main syllabus area that is being assessed.

Please note that many of the key points are represented here in the form of bullet point lists. All of these points should be expanded in your answer, unless the examiner **specifically** asks for a bullet point list.

Remember to follow the instructions on the paper. When organising you time to answer an exam paper, allow a little time for reading the Case Study, planning your answers, and choosing which questions you will answer, before working out how much time to spend on each question. Look at the mark allocation for each part of each question to help you do this.

Part A

Question 1.

The Case Study for this paper is about managing mergers and in particular:

- The increasing number of mergers.
- The poor success rate due to the lack of consideration of the people issues.
- What should be done pre- and post-merger to facilitate the merging of two different cultures and workforces.
- The lack of importance/priority that many organisations give to people issues in a merger.

The important thing to remember about approaching the mini-case question is that you must apply the **concepts** that the examiner is looking for to the **context** and situation described in the Case. With every question that is broken up into sections, you also need to consider how marks are spread across the various parts of the question, as this should dictate how much time you allocate to each part.

The examiner in this case has asked you for a **report** for the Chief Executive of the car manufacturing company for which you work as Marketing Manager. Your company is considering merging with another car manufacturer within the same country. This not only tells you the format in which to answer, but the **audience** you are addressing in your report. The report needs to include:

a. What is to be audited (for both companies):
- Organisation culture.
- Communications.
- HR/Training and development.
- Management and leadership – skills and performance management.
- Organisation of teams and team working.

How to conduct the audit:
- Questionnaires.
- Interviews.
- Observations.

How to encourage people to participate and respond (always a problem during periods of uncertainty).

Timescale for conducting the audit.

b. How to communicate the new vision and values post-merger. It is important to consider how to segment the target audience (the staff of the newly formed car manufacturer), and what methods of communication are appropriate for each. For example, newsletters and an Intranet are a blanket approach, whereas a personal letter and team briefings are more specific. Remember also to include the planning of the communications – who needs to do what and by when.

c. Create and build new **marketing** teams (so consider the different marketing roles required). In creating the teams consider the range of skills required (Is that information available from the audit?) and how they need to be structured and organised across the company. Apply relevant theory, such as

Tuckman's forming, storming, norming and performing, to identify the stages of team development. Remember, the new marketing teams will consist of people who have not worked together before. Identify team building activities that will encourage people to learn more about each other, how to work together, and individual strengths and weaknesses etc. You might also suggest mentoring or buddy schemes, so that the less experienced team members have a more senior colleague to refer to and use as a sounding board to aid their development.

Syllabus reference – 4.1, 4.2 and 4.3.

Part B

Question 2.

The context for this question is a busy call centre for a travel operator, so your answer must reflect this.

a. In preparation for the plan to improve your time management identify how you spend your time at present and the main areas you need to improve – remembering that you have 10 new recruits to deal with as the Customer Service Manager. For your plan consider:

- Prioritising tasks – distinguishing between urgent and important.
- Better scheduling of work.
- Delegating tasks – identifying which tasks to delegate and to whom.
- Using techniques such as uninterrupted time, batching small tasks etc.

b. The training of new staff should begin with an induction and identifying the skills they need to have in order to do the job. Consider how to use the existing workforce in the plan, so methods might include work shadowing, on-the-job training and coaching. Consider also how to integrate the new recruits into the existing team.

For both plans identify the time scale for implementation and the resources required. For example, the plan to train new staff may require input from HR and/or the Training Department.

Syllabus reference – 4.2 and 4.3.

Appendix 4

Question 3.

The format for you answer is a report for the Chief Executive of the charity.

You are asked to consider how to improve moral and motivation for both employed staff and volunteers – each group has different needs (Maslow and Herzberg). Pay will not be an issue for volunteers but financial rewards certainly will be for employed staff!

Structure your report to identify:

- The problems for the organisation due to low morale and motivation.
- The possible reasons for low morale and motivation.
- The needs for each group. If the charity is performing poorly then self-esteem will be low for both groups. Remember that motivators can be intrinsic and extrinsic.
- How to meet these needs. Re-establishing vision and common values, effective performance review and feedback, training and development (so people have the skills to do the job), team building to improve support and co-operation within teams and between teams, employed staff and volunteers.
- How the people of the organisation can be involved in identifying how to improve performance and implement changes.

Syllabus reference – 4.3.

Question 4.

Avoid throwing everything you know about meetings at the examiners. The context for your answer is set out in the question – the meetings are between the Marketing and R&D departments, and their purpose is to solve customer problems and implement new ideas.

The format for your answer is guidelines for colleagues, and this could be set out as a memo on the effectiveness of meetings. It could include:

a. How to analyse meetings to identify problem areas:

- Is there a clear purpose and agenda communicated to everyone in time for them to prepare for the meeting?
- Is the information they will need for the meeting circulated in time (for

example information on customer problems if the meeting is debating these and looking for solutions)?
- Are appropriate people invited?
- Are meetings effectively chaired and controlled so that they start and finish on time?
- Do meetings achieve their objectives?
- Is the date, time and place convenient for everyone?
- Are minutes circulated quickly following the meeting?
- Is everyone committed to completing actions agreed at meetings?

Consider how to involve colleagues in the above analysis.

b. This follows on from the problems identified above. For example, if you have identified that the group are no good at problem solving and decision making then look at the balance of roles (technical and managerial [Belbin]), and include techniques to improve idea generation (such as brainstorming) and training on problem solving and decision making.

Syllabus reference – 4.2.

Question 5.

The format for your answer is a report. Set out clearly who the report is for, perhaps the Chief Executive of the telecommunications company.

The report needs to identify:

a. What relationship marketing is, explaining:

- The key concepts behind CRM – retaining customers, focusing on the long term, use of customer knowledge to improve the ability to meet customer wants and needs, role of quality and customer service and making it everyone's responsibility in the organisation.
- The importance to the telecommunications company of building long-term customer relationships – customer loyalty, differentiation, competitive advantage.

b. The importance of effective people management in building customer relationships:

Appendix 4

- Looking after staff so that they look after customers.
- Involving staff in identifying how to improve the company's ability to meet customers needs.
- People as an important and unique asset – rivals can copy products and processes but not people.
- Developing a culture where staff are willing to take responsibility to solve customer problems (empowered staff).

Syllabus reference – 4.1 and 4.3.

Question 6.

The format for your answer is a report to the Managing Director of the software company you work for.

This question is about HR planning (identifying what people will be required and with what skills) in the context of business growth, supported by the extension of the product range.

The report should identify:

- How to analyse current marketing skills – job analysis, information from appraisals and job descriptions.
- What skills will be required to support the corporate objectives.
- How to meet the skills gap identified – internal and external recruitment, training and development etc.
- Potential barriers to meeting the skills gap – skills shortage etc.
- Time scale – bearing in mind that the plans to grow the business are to achieve a 35% growth in just two years.

Syllabus reference – 4.2.

Question 7.

The context for this answer is the disciplinary interview for the salesperson who has behaved inappropriately. The format is a memo to the Sales Manager on how to conduct a disciplinary interview.

There are a number of important points that must be included in the memo:

- Preparing for the interview; establishing the facts and obtaining evidence.
- Setting up the interview – convenient time and place, informing the salesperson of the purpose of the interview, ensuring that they know how to prepare their case, and their right to have an appropriate representative with them.
- Liaising with HR to ensure correct procedures are followed at each stage.
- The importance of planning the interview – what to say, anticipating responses etc.
- How to conduct the interview – detail how the interview should be opened, how the facts should be presented to the salesperson, and how he/she should be allowed to state their case.
- Advice on communication skills such as questioning, listening, appropriate body language, etc.
- Explain what behaviour needs to change and how.
- Detail the support that the salesperson will receive to help them change their behaviour.
- Detail the consequences of the interview – verbal warning/written warning etc.
- Gain agreement from the salesperson.
- Explain what happens next – review, consequences of not carrying out the actions agreed.
- How to record the interview and follow-up.

Syllabus reference – 4.2.

Appendix 5

Assessment guidance

There are two methods used for assessment of candidates – Examination or Continuous Assessment via projects.

The Chartered Institute of Marketing has traditionally used professional, externally set examinations as the means of assessment for the Certificate, Advanced Certificate and Postgraduate Diploma in Marketing. In 1995, at the request of industry, students and tutors, it introduced a continuously assessed route to two modules, one at Certificate level, and one at Advanced Certificate.

The information in this appendix will:

- Help you prepare for continuous assessment.
- Provide hints and tips to help you prepare for the examination.
- Manage your time effectively in preparing for assessment.

NB: Your tutor will inform you which method of assessment applies to your programme.

Preparing for continuous assessment

If you are being assessed by project you will be given a full brief for the assignment. This will include what you have to do, how it is to be presented, and the weighting of marks for each section. **YOU MUST READ THIS BEFORE YOU START, AND CHECK YOUR UNDERSTANDING OF WHAT IS BEING ASKED OF YOU WITH YOUR TUTOR**.

The assignment will consist of a number of tasks, each with their own weighting, so make sure you take account of this in your final presentation of the project.

The size of the project will be identified by a recommended word count. Check your final word count carefully, but remember quality is more important than quantity.

The assignment tasks will include a reflective statement. This requires you to identify what you have learned from the experience of undertaking the module, and how you have applied that learning to your job.

Questions you might want to consider in helping you write this reflective statement include: What was the most difficult part? How did you feel at the start of the exercise and how do you feel at the end? Did you achieve your objectives? If not, why not? What have you learned about yourself as you have worked through the module? How much of your learning have you been able to apply at work? Have you been able to solve any real work problems through the work you have done in your assignments?

This statement will be personal to you, and it should look forward to the points you have identified as needing work in the future. We should never stop learning. You should keep up this process of Continuous Professional Development as you go through your studies and your career, and hopefully you will have acquired the habit by the time you need to employ it to achieve Chartered Marketer status!

Examinations

Each subject differs slightly from the others, and the style of question will differ between module examinations. All are closed book examinations apart from **Analysis and Decision** (see below).

For all examinations, apart from **Marketing in Practice** (see below), the examination paper consists of two sections:

Part A – Mini-case, scenario or article

This section has a mini-case, scenario or article with compulsory questions. You are required to make marketing or sales decisions based on the information provided. You will gain credit for the decisions and recommendations you make on the basis of the analysis itself. This is a compulsory section of the paper designed to evaluate your practical marketing skills.

Part B – Examination questions

You will have a choice from a number of questions, and when answering those you select, ensure you understand the context of the question. Rough plans for each answer are strongly recommended.

The examination for **Marketing in Practice** differs in that the compulsory questions and examination questions are all linked to the mini-case and additional relevant information given, such as memos and reports.

The examination for **Analysis and Decision** is an open book examination and takes the form of a Case Study. This is mailed out 4 weeks before the examination and posted on the CIM student web site (www.cimvirtualinstitute.com) at the same time. Analysis and preparation should be completed during these four weeks. The questions asked in the examination will require strategic marketing decisions and actions. The question paper will also include additional unseen information about the Case Study.

CIM code of conduct for examinations

If being assessed by examination you will receive examination entry details, which will include a leaflet entitled "Rules for Examinations". You should read these carefully, as you will be penalised by CIM if you are in breach of any of these rules.

Most of the rules are common sense. For example, for closed book examinations you are not allowed to take notes or scrap paper into the examination room, and you must use the examination paper supplied to make rough notes and plans for your answer.

If you are taking the **Analysis and Decision** examination ensure that you do take your notes in with you, together with a copy of the Case Study.

Hints and tips

There are a number of places you can access information to help you prepare for your examination, if you are being assessed by this method. Your tutor will give you good advice, and exam hints and tips can also be found on the CIM student web site (www.cimvirtualinstitute.com).

Some fundamental points are listed below.

- Read the question carefully, and think about what is being asked before tackling the answer. The examiners are looking for knowledge, application and context. Refer back to the question to help you put your answer in the appropriate context. Do not just regurgitate theory.

- Consider the presentation style of your answer. For example, if you are asked to write a report, then use a report format with numbered headings and not an essay style.

- Structure – plan your answer to make it easy for the examiner to see the main points you are making.

- Timing – spread your time in proportion to the marks allocated, and ensure that all required questions are answered.

- Relevant examples – the examiners expect relevant theory to be illustrated by practical examples. These can be drawn from your own experience, reading of current journals and newspapers, or just your own observations. You could also visit "Hot Topics" on the CIM student web site to see discussions of topical marketing issues and practice.

Managing your time

What is effective time management? It is using wisely one of your most precious resources, **TIME**, to achieve your key goals. You need to be aware of how you spend your time each day. Set priorities, so you know what's important to you and what isn't. You need to establish goals for your study, work and family life, and plan how to meet those goals. Through developing these habits you will be better able to achieve the things that are important to you.

When study becomes one of your key goals you may find that, temporarily, something has to be sacrificed to find the time needed for reading, writing notes, writing up assignments, preparing for group assessment, etc. It helps to "get people on your side". Tell people that you are studying and ask for their support – this includes direct family, close friends and colleagues at work.

Time can just slip through your fingers if you don't manage it, and that's wasteful! When you are trying to balance the needs of family, social life, working life and study, there is a temptation to leave assignments until the deadline is nearly upon you. Don't give in to this temptation! Many students complain about the heavy workload towards the end of the course, when, in fact, they have had several months to work on assignments, and they have created this heavy workload themselves.

Knowing how to manage your time wisely can help you:

- Reduce pressure when you're faced with deadlines or a heavy schedule.
- Be more in control of your life by making better decisions about how to use your time.
- Feel better about yourself because you're using your full potential to achieve.
- Have more energy for the things you want or need to accomplish.
- Succeed more easily because you know what you want to do and what you need to do to achieve it.

Finally...

Remember to continue to apply your new skills within your job. Study and learning that is not applied just wastes your time, effort and money! Good luck with your studies!

Index

See also the Glossary on page 324.

You may find referring back to the Learning Outcomes and the Summary of Key Points at the beginning and end of each Session will aid effective use of the Index.

Only where subjects are relevantly discussed or defined are they indexed.

7S framework 29

ABC model of culture 16, 23
Adidas 118
advertising 48
ambiguity, management of 38
analysis
- Critical Path Method/ Analysis 270-271, 272-273, 278
- environmental 18
- job analysis 129-131
- market 47
- skills 58-60

Andersen Consulting (Accenture) 63
appraisals 197-208
- agreeing development actions 202-203
- benefits of 197-198
- follow-up role 205-206
- forms of 198
- giving feedback 202
- informal feedback 207-208
- information requirements 199-200
- planning interview 200-201
- purpose of 197
- self-appraisal 200
- structure of interview 201

background reading 7-9

BAE systems 302-305
Beblin's team roles 156-157
British Airways 63
British Rail 252-253
business change
- impact on marketing management 23

business environment, factors in 311-313
- competitive 312-313
- consumer 312-313
- legal and fiscal 312
- political 312

Business Process Improvement 20
Business Process Re-engineering 20-21

Call2View 319
centralisation 15
Centre for Tomorrow's Company, The 26-27
chain of control 14-15
change
- extent 262, 276-277
- forces for, responding to 53
- identifying 261-262
- implementation issues 266-268, 278
- individual perspectives of 263
- initiatives 20-21, 28

- management of 38
- marketing of 261-262, 265-266
- monitoring progress 269-271, 72
- multiple sources of 264-265
- organisational 17-18, 22
- personal reactions to 263-264, 266, 277
- planning 262
  - intervention 272
- risks and issues 271
- triggers 259
- understanding scope of 260-261
- who to involve 261

change, management of 38
Chartered Institute of Professional Development (CIPD) 208
China 302-305
clients
- negotiating with 249
- relationships
  - evaluating 240
  - improving 241-242
  - understanding 238-239
- retention and maintenance 240
- retirement 240-241
- selection and recruitment 240

code of conduct 318
communication
- across borders 318-322
- barriers to 97-99
- channel 96
- effective 97-100, 121
  - barriers to 97-99
    - physical 99
    - physiological 99
    - semantics 99
- in marketing 94-95
- internal 115-117
  - planning 115-117
- interpersonal 94
- non-verbal 104-105
- oral presentations 105-106
- process of 95
- questioning and listening 101

communications systems 19
complexity, management of 39
conflict 158-164
- importance of in group decision making 162
- in teams 158-164
- inter-group 162, 163
- intra-group 162, 163-164
- relating to groups 161-162
- with customers 164, 171

Consignia 88
consumer legislation 17, 18
consumer power 18
Critical Path Method/Analysis 270-271, 272-273, 278
cultural differences 297
- sources of conflict 298-300, 316

customer care 242-249
- barriers to 248-249
- competitive advantage 243
- defining 244
- identifying areas for Improvement 248
- impact of 243
- "moments of truth" 244-247
- monitoring 247-248

customer interface management 53
customer perspective 251-252
Customer Relationship Marketing

(CRM) 16
decentralisation 15
decision making 83-86
- process 83-84
decoding information 95
delegation 77-79
development 220-233
- different methods 220
- formal and informal activities 221
- opportunities in the work place 221-222
- planning 222, 231-233
DiaDexus 274
direct marketing 48
disciplinary interviewing 112-114
- conducting 113
- follow up 114
- preparation 112-113
Disney 274-275
diversity, management of 39

employer/employee loyalty 16
employee motivation 301
employee performance, management of 196-212
employment legislation 18
encoding information 95
environmental analysis 18
European Commission 63
European Union 63
external forces 18

Follett 34
Fayol 34
Fifth Discipline, The 23
forces for change, responding to 53
Forte Posthouse Hotels 40-41
France Telecom 63

Gantt chart 269
gender, attitudes to 299

Genesys Conferencing 319-320
globalisation 18
group polarisation 162-163
groupthink 162

Hall's ABC model of culture 16, 23
Handy, Charles 21, 23
Herzberg 177
hidden messages 99-100
hospitality industry 40
Human Resource Management 125-142
- involvement in recruitment and selection 128-134
- role of 125-126
- support of marketing 126-128

IBM 16
Improvement and Development Agency (IDEA)
India 302-305
induction 140-142, 214-216, 230-231
- reviewing effectiveness of 216
- planning 215-216
- purpose of 214-215
- what to include in 141-142
information systems 19
innovation 273-275
intellectual capital and capabilities 19
- barriers to developing 281
- barriers to keeping 281-282
- barriers to using 282-283
internal communications 115-117
- planning 115-117
internal forces 19

internal marketing 114-115, 117, 122-123
interpersonal communication 94
interviewing 103, 121
- disciplinary 112-113
- grievance 114

job analysis 129-131
job characteristics model 178
job description 131, 135-138, 147
- interpretation of 135-136
- purpose and contents of 135
- writing of 136-138
job specialisation 15

knowledge management 280-281
KPMG 225-228

learning culture 286
- leadership of 286-287
learning organisation 22, 23-26, 287, 292-293
- customer focus in 25-26
listening, effective 101-102
logos 13

management
- across borders 211-223
  - information sources 313-314
  - options 313
  - people issues 314
  - role of local advisers 317-318
  - role of training 317
  - sources of conflict 316-317
  - supporting staff 314-316
- activity of 36
- as a social construct 295
- as culturally embedded 295-296
- knowledge 36, 44
- in a global context 295-309
- of team conflict 161, 173
- perspectives 35, 42
- qualities 44
- role of 33
- skills 36, 50
- theorists 33

manager
- as natural scientist 34
- as social scientist 34
- multi-unit managers 40
- product manager 37
- project manager 37

managing
- ambiguity 38
- change 38-39
- complexity 39
- diversity 39
- mergers 164-165
market analysis 47
Marketing Manager 47-69
- key roles and tasks 47-49
- personal barriers to 50-51, 66
marketing models 10-11
marketing skills 49, 65
- activity 50
- planning 54, 67-68
marketing strategy 48
market research 49
Maslow's hierarchy of needs 177
mergers, management of 164-165
Mayo 34
McDonald's 16
McKinsey 7S framework 29
McClelland's achievement motivation theory 177

377

meetings
- effective 79-80
- follow-up 82-83
- planning 80-82

mental models 24-26

messages
- sending and receiving 96

models
- Hall's ABC model of culture 16, 23
- job characteristics 178
- leadership
  - transactional 55
  - transformational 55-56
- marketing 10-11
- mental 24-26
- negotiation 108

motivation 176-194
- applying theory 179
- satisfying needs 177
- behavioural consequences 178
- decision making 178-179
- designing jobs 179-180
- equity theory 178
- expectancy theory 179
- intervention to change 187-189
- job design 178
- McClelland's achievement motivation theory 177
- poor motivation
  - causes of 184-186
  - intervention 187-189
  - prevention of 186-188
  - symptoms of 183-184

motivational
- drivers 179, 192-193
- strategies

- job design 180
- job enlargement 180
- job enrichment 180
- job rotation 180
- individual needs 181-182
- management approach 182

multi-unit managers 40

national stereotypes 296
negotiation 107-111, 121-122
- managing the process of 110-111
- models of 108
- strategies 108-109

network analysis tools
- Critical Path Method/Analysis 270-271

New Product Development (NPD) 49

non-verbal
- communication 164-165
- signals 297

NOP 225-228

Olympic Games 117-119
oral presentations 105-106

organisational
- change 17-18, 22
- hierarchy 301
- vision 300-301

organisations
- characteristics of 13-14
- culture 16-17, 21-22, 28, 29
- design 126
- development 53
- models of 13
- performance 22
- shaped by national forces 300-302
- structure 14, 19, 29

- impact of trends on 14-15
outsourcing 20-21

pay issues 126
PDP (Personal Development Plan) 60-62, 69
People Management 27
performance management 126, 196-212
- role of performance objectives 203-208
performance objectives
- determining 203-204
- links between targets and remuneration 205
- setting 203-204
performance review meetings 206-207
personal development 56-57
- planning 60-62, 69
personal effectiveness 50-57, 71-92
personal mastery 24
personal space 298-299
person culture 22
person specification 132, 139-140
- contents of 139-140
- purpose of 139
Peters & Waterman 35
poor motivation
- causes of 184-186
- intervention 187-189
- prevention of 186-188
- symptoms of 183-184
pressure groups 18
priorities 72
problem solving 83-86
product management 48
project management 51
project planning 51

power culture 21
public relations 48

questioning and listening 101-103

railway industry 252-253
Reebok 118
recruitment
- of sales staff 134, 146-147
- selecting the candidate 133-134
relationship marketing 252-253
reward structures 19
rituals 299
Royal Mail 87-88
Royal Shakespeare Company 189-190

self-appraisal 200
self-assessment 57-58, 68
self-development 53
Self-Managed Learning (SML) Programme 225-228
Senge, Peter 23
shared vision 24
Siemans 208-209
skills analysis 58-60
skills
- analytical 86-87
- communications 86-87
  - use of in marketing 94-95
- creative and intuitive 86-87
- facilitation 86-87
- information gathering 86-87
SLEPT factors 18, 29
Small and Medium-sized Enterprise Statistics 39
SMART objectives 64, 152, 154-155, 182, 203, 204, 216, 29, 222, 231, 262
span of control 14

sponsorship 117-119
stakeholder value 26
statistics 39, 45
Strategic Leadership Programme (SLP) 302-305
structures
- reward-based 19
- team and project-based 15
supplier perspective 249-250
systems perspective 35
systems thinking 25

task culture 21
Taylor, Frederick 33-34
team conflict 158-164
- as trigger for change 158-159
- consequences of 159-160
- identifying 159
- management of 161, 173
- mediating or facilitating 160-161
- responses to 160
team learning 24
teams 149-174
- effectiveness 152-153, 170-172
  - benefits of 150-151
- leadership 153
- planning interventions 154-155
  - individual 155
  - task 155
  - team 154-155
- processes (forming, storming, norming, performing) 151-152
- role 156
  - Beblin's team roles 156-157
- implications 157-158
- scope for performance improvements 154
teleworking 63-64
time, attitudes to 298
time management
- controlling 75-76
- delegation 77-81
- mind mapping 76
- planning 72-74
- priorities 72
- support tools 76-77
- "To do" list 74-75
training and development 214-236
training effectiveness
- evaluation of 222-225, 233-234
Training Needs Analysis (TNA) 217-218, 219, 231
- development of 217-218
- purpose of 217
training plans, compiling of 218-219
training session, planning 219-220, 234-236
transactional leadership 55
transformational leadership 55-56

University of East Anglia 142-143

vacancies
- marketing of 132-133
verbal signals 297
Virgin 274
virtual teams 158, 172

web sites 4-6
Webster & Fayol 34
Wipro 302
working with teams 52-53